TIME, BEAUTY, *and* GRIEF

A HIKE THROUGH WISCONSIN'S 50 STATE PARKS

Written and Illustrated by
BETSY KORBINYR

LITTLE CREEK PRESS

MINERAL POINT, WISCONSIN

Little Creek Press.
5341 Sunny Ridge Road
Mineral Point, WI 53565

ORDERING INFORMATION
Quantity sales. Special discounts are available on quantity purchases
by corporations, associations, and others. For details, contact
info@littlecreekpress.com

Orders by US trade bookstores and wholesalers.
Please contact Little Creek Press or Ingram for details.

Printed in the United States of America

Cataloging-in-Publication Data
Names: Korbinyr, Betsy, author.
Title: Time, Beauty, and Grief: A Hike Through Wisconsin's 50 State Parks
Description: Mineral Point, WI: Little Creek Press, 2024.
Identifiers: LCCN: 2024912329 | ISBN: 978-1-955656-74-0
Subjects: TRAVEL / Special Interest / Hikes and Walks
NATURE / Regional
TRAVEL / United States / Midwest / East North Central (IL, IN, MI, OH, WI)
TRAVEL / Special Interest / Senior
SPORTS & RECREATION / Hiking
4.0.1.4.12.0.0 LEVEL_5 Wisconsin

Book design by Little Creek Press

For my beautiful bird

Flute on !! :)

Betsy Koberup

Table of Contents

The Basics
Safety and Etiquette

My musings aren't meant as a "be all, end all" trail guide. You are welcome to utilize them for what they contain. This book provides information and insight on various aging concerns. However, it should not be relied upon as recommending or promoting any specific method, and it is not intended as a substitute for treatment by a qualified provider. Readers with questions about a particular issue are encouraged to consult with their primary physician.

I use the following acronyms frequently throughout the book:

- IAT stands for the Ice Age Trail. It is an approximately 1,200-mile national scenic trail located entirely in Wisconsin. It follows the edge of the glacier that once covered the majority of the state.

- C2C stands for the Coast to Coast Walk across England. At roughly 192 miles, it is one of the most popular long-distance walks in the U.K. The path runs from the Irish Sea to the North Sea, traversing several national parks.

- CCC stands for the Civilian Conservation Corps, a New Deal program that provided jobs to millions of unemployed young men. It operated from 1933 to 1942, primarily focusing on infrastructure improvements to state and national parks.

- DNR or WI-DNR refers to the Wisconsin Department of Natural Resources. The department manages the state's wild areas and is a fount of knowledge.

This book is not affiliated with the Wisconsin Department of Natural Resources. The views are mine, not theirs. Be that as it may, they are a taxpayer-funded entity; therefore, I take advantage of the excellent resources available from this agency. The park websites are a wonderful location for maps, history, trail information, etc. Check their *Conditions* tab before you visit. It will alert you to current closures, storm damage, floods, fires, and more. At the end of each chapter, you will find "The Particulars" section, providing you with further details and other basics about my experience at the parks.

Hiking and trail etiquette is important to note. Some guidelines are known, and I throw in some as well:

- Hikers going downhill yield to hikers going uphill.

- Slow hikers yield to fast hikers. Younger hikers yield to older hikers. Polite passing is allowed, but not rude huffing and other passive-aggressive behaviors.

- Never come up from behind someone without making your presence known before you get too close. You might find yourself doused with bear spray if you do!

- Dogs are to be leashed in all state parks except in designated areas. Trails are *never* designated areas.

- Hikers with dogs yield to everyone. If passing, ensure you have complete control over your dog before you do.

- Horses have the right of way, always.

- There is an astonishing sense of entitlement accompanying playing music out loud when hiking. Don't bring that into the forest. Nobody else wants to hear it. Use your earbuds.

- Please have mercy on those of us with respiratory disabilities, and don't wear perfumes, colognes, and other scented products when you are out on a trail. The off-gassing miasma from many of them can extend 10 to 20 feet around you. Not only does it cause us to reach for our inhalers, but it also negatively affects birds and flying insects.

- Don't leave signs of human activity, like cairns, branch forts, etc.

- Try to purchase hiking clothes that are *not* anti-microbial. The chemicals making them that way harm your health and the environment as a whole. If you're worried about stink, try using my roller derby friend's advice: spray them with cheap vodka before washing.

- Keep a safe distance from the edge of cliffs, bluffs, and shorelines with drop-offs. They may be undercut and collapse beneath you. Do this in memory of Kelsey Musgrove, the young Wisconsin cardiothoracic surgery fellow who died in April 2022 as a result of such an undercut.

- Stay on the trails and treat the parks with reverence and respect. You will experience countless more wonders if you do.

Risk-taking is a good thing. It challenges us to grow outside our comfort zone. I like to say it is better to die on an adventure than falling down the stairs at your house. However, the risks of hiking can be mitigated with the proper preparation. Take the time to make an emergency kit to carry in your backpack. Hiking safety includes having adequate water and proper clothing, planning for ticks and poisonous plants, and not messing with wildlife. It also includes watching out for personal safety when it comes to accidents and other humans:

- Have a hiking safety buddy. Let someone you trust know where you are going and when you will return home.
- Take a photo of the posted emergency information with your phone as you enter the park. That way, you will have it with you, should you need it.
- If you listen to music or books while hiking, use only one earbud so you can keep tabs on your environment.
- Carry pepper and/or bear spray and stay alert to other hikers and their whereabouts.
- You don't have to be friendly or sweet or nice to anyone. Better to be called a "bitch" than not feel safe. On the flip side of that, don't be a jerk! Don't harass people on the trail. Keep your distance and be respectful.
- Always, always, always trust your gut! If a situation doesn't feel right, it isn't!

The majority of the state parks have volunteer groups raising money and making improvements. When you visit a park and love it, take the time to contribute to its "Friends of" organization. In fact, to set this example, I pledge to donate 20 percent of the proceeds from the sale of this book to these groups.

No book about Wisconsin is complete without sincere gratitude and acknowledgment that everywhere I walk—every place I hike—is Native land. I hope, in some small way, my discussions in this book remind us to be gentle and reverent as we visit the state parks never forgetting the history of this beautiful and sacred place.

I want to thank my dear friends who went hiking with me on my Quest. I changed your names, but you know who you are. I am profoundly honored to have you in my life. A heartfelt thank you to my child for their unwavering support of my creative self and the divine joy they bring to my life. And a hardy "Huzzah!" to all the friendly, hard-working rangers out there. Your guidance and support were invaluable.

The Introduction
Liminality and History

My new favorite word is *liminality*. It comes from the Latin word for *threshold*, meaning an in-between or transitional state of being. When someone is in a liminal space, they are moving from the old to the new, from the familiar to the unknown. Moving, but not quite there yet. Uncomfortable, unsure, excited, hopeful; it is a feeling of wanting time to move faster and slower at the exact same moment. It can touch all the parts of ourselves: emotional, physical, and philosophical. In my life, I have had numerous transitions such as these. Ones in which I truly believed, outside of my peripheral vision, Rod Serling was lingering, adorned in his skinny black tie and about to let anyone who would listen know I was in a "zone." They included the loss of a big love, moving to different states, a pregnant belly (hell, the entire motherhood experience), a divorce, an empty nest, and the loss of a job. Now, it is a significant milestone that again finds me on a threshold.

It was due to liminality my Quest was born. It evolved from the death of a steadfast companion and this impending birthday. Also, from the desire to begin an uplifting hike tempered by caution for travel due to the pandemic. I had as my gauge the hike I had completed when I turned 60—the Coast to Coast Walk across England. It was a life-changing hike, and I wanted to replicate those emotions for my sixty-fifth. I wanted to push my comfort level to celebrate this coming-of-age, but I needed it closer to home. The angst over the passage of time, the processing of loss, and the constant battle between integrity and despair profoundly affect this year of our lives. With all these aspects in mind, my Quest to hike at least five miles in each of Wisconsin's 50 state parks was conceived.

The companion lost to me was a 60-foot-tall noble fir tree that grew in my front yard. I bought my house because of that tree. All the gifts that came to me living here were wrapped up in his all-encompassing shade, the sublime grapefruit smell of his needles, and his rough, lichen-covered bark. I named the tree Baldar, after the Norse God of Divine Love, because I felt clarity, happiness, and safety when I stood near him. I openly wept the day I had to have arborists cut him down as a result of a canker in his trunk. The grief of losing such a spectacular and influential tree prompted me to seek out more of the forests of Wisconsin. I wanted to encounter the fantastic variety of outstanding trees remaining protected and those endangered by oak wilt, emerald ash borers, white pine blister rust, and beech bark disease. Besides, it was time for a Life Review, as I have done on my other milestone birthdays.

Life Reviews improve mental health and support successful aging. They are a way of coordinating our thinking as we look back, helping us to accept our lives as a whole. This reminiscence is an important and necessary task as we age. It enables us to find purpose and meaning, something we all need as the years roll on. To this end, I welcome you to discover your own Life Review as you read the book. You will find questions at the end of each chapter. Use them to contemplate your aging along with me.

My voice is intimate, honest, and slightly self-deprecating. With it, I tell a poignant and funny, perceptive and relatable coming-of-age story. If we are lucky enough, it is one we all get to face. I include the stories of the elders I knew as friends and as clients. Their accounts range from tales of WWII battles to minds lost to dementia to witnessing the Trinity bomb.

While researching and planning my Quest, I found it difficult to locate a complete list of the parks. Many state forest and recreation areas are colloquially known as "state parks." Some lists had more; some had less. Some had this one, but not that one. I finally decided to do the 45 listed on my 2022 *Rand McNally* map of Wisconsin. I especially liked the alliteration of the three fives in the name I gave my Quest: 45 x 5 = 65. My parameters included the ones requiring a state park sticker and not run by a city or a community organization. I hiked at least five miles in each of these 45 state parks from mid-April to mid-October. In the smaller parks, this meant hiking the trails several times. In the larger ones, the mileage was easy to reach, but all the hikes were interesting and beautiful in their own ways.

In this book, the parks are in the order I hiked them, not by region or features. Purposeful at times, but highly random for the most part, akin to being retired and lacking adult supervision. Reading the book from beginning to end results in a narrative of travel, memory, and evolution. It is filled with truths we all share in the universal human experience of aging.

I incorporate my social work knowledge throughout the book. I received my Bachelor of Social Work from Southwest Missouri State University in Springfield and my Master of Social Work from the University of Arkansas at Little Rock. I am, now, retired after 30-plus years, but I continue to maintain my Wisconsin licenses and to volunteer. I have a Certification in Thanatology from the Association for Death Education and Counseling (ADEC). Obtaining it required over 3,000 hours of professional practice in the fields of death and dying, and grief and bereavement. To sustain the certification since 2001, I have had an additional 300-plus hours of professional learning regarding a myriad of aspects of the subject. The ADEC is the premiere worldwide organization devoted to this topic and produces several scholarly journals. I was chosen to present at their annual conference in 2005 on the importance of rituals at the end of life. I was also a member of the Dane County Suicide Prevention Task Force from 2008 to 2012 and facilitated discussions at their annual conferences.

Over the course of my Quest, I decided I would do the remaining state parks I had not initially included. I thought they would be easy additions, but chaos has a way of intervening. I finally hiked in those parks months later. They became their own Quest, the Addendum Five.

As a final word, ageism and the negative stereotypes about how we are supposed to behave harm us as a society. It is valuable, as a result, to have stories available regarding older people challenging themselves and to celebrate the importance of those stories. Only about 17 percent of Americans are over sixty-five. We are allowed to be grateful for our aging and to embrace it wholeheartedly. Not accepting the conventional myths and staying positive really does make for a happier, healthier, and longer life.

Governor Nelson State Park
Waunakee

5.07 miles
Highest Point: 790 ft
Lowest Point: 677 ft

April 16, 2022
Preparation and Grief

L ast night, I opened a bottle of wine. I had been attracted to it
solely for the label, which had a drawing of the seven phases of
the moon, from waxing gibbous to waning crescent and every shape
in between. I pulled out the cork and was surprised to find a special
fortune written there. It read, "Open your eyes. It's time to make
your dream a reality." No more delays. It's time to begin my Quest!

There are countless studies out there about how, as we age, we
must continue to challenge ourselves and do difficult things, even if
they offer few extrinsic rewards. Though our efforts may have little
significance to others, they remind us they are about the journey, not

where we eventually end up. We can find purpose in our endeavors, and we are able to do more than we expect of ourselves. With all the negative societal expectations placed on older people, I am glad I am set to engage in a random and frivolous adventure starting tomorrow!

Getting my pack together for this first of 45 parks is somewhat of a challenge, considering I haven't hiked since last October. I want to make sure I have everything I could possibly need, even though I might not use it today. I want my backpack to be ready to go from now on into the future with the following: phone charging battery, matches, first aid kit, rain jacket, bug spray, tissues, zipper bags, pocketknife, ID, money, credit card, and my ubiquitous reading glasses. Even though it makes it slightly heavier, one never knows what might arise on the trail. I don't have any pepper spray. Sadly, I need to buy a new one.

I pull out my Asolo hiking boots. I smile remembering hiking in them across England, through many parts of Ireland, and on a mountain at the headwaters of the Ganges in India. They have been through the countless miles I put in training for those long walks, never giving me a blister—well, except the first time I wore them. The only issue I've ever had with them is that the strings broke after one year, and I needed to replace them.

These boots have seen significant mileage and have been constant companions on my solitary sojourns. Of course, you can hike with other people, but for the most part, it's done alone. One of the reasons I enjoy it is I can do it by myself. I can get up, realize the day is gorgeous, and simply head out to a trail. I don't have to rely on anyone else, and it's not intimidating to be out there by myself, except for the thought of needing pepper spray. I could stay home and not require it, but that's not the way to spend the year I turn sixty-five.

I recently read a meme about regret, anxiety, and gratitude. Each was correlated to a different time frame: past, future, and present. It elicited in me the wisdom of doing a Life Review this year as I come closer to my birthday. For this milestone, as I have on previous ones, I process how my life has been up to this point. I think about the regrets and try to find places for them, find healing, and find

Governor Nelson State Park

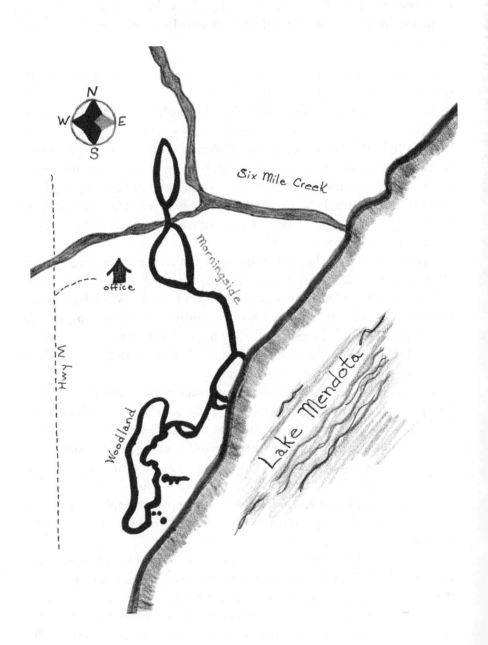

lessons. I actively attempt to fight off any anxiety about what may come, good or bad, splendid or tragic. We never know what the chaos of time will bring us, and worry only robs us of joy. Gratitude, on the other hand, is easy. I am 64 years old, still able to hike five miles, and incredibly thankful for that ability. Gratitude keeps me here, moving forward on this Quest, at this park today, and in my life.

Arriving at Governor Nelson, I find the office closed. I am glad I brought a park map downloaded from the Wisconsin Department of Natural Resources (DNR) website. I have been here many times before, but it is always wise to bring directions along. As I need proof of my Quest, I stop to take a selfie in front of the state park sign— something I plan to do at each one.

I start my hike on the Woodland Trail, eventually merging onto the Morningside Trail. My trusty GPS app will ensure I achieve my self-imposed requirement of five miles. The Woodland is graced with remarkable effigy mounds created by the original inhabitants of this land. They are truly fascinating, especially the panther! At this time of year, the emerging wildflowers are only identifiable by their leaves. Slender spotted trout lilies are carefully surfacing all across the forest floor. Everything is still too cold, but the anticipation of bursting into color in the coming weeks is palpable. Downy woodpeckers and robins flit among the branches of the burgeoning trees. It smells of white pine needles, swampy ground, and spring! The tiny sounds of newly emerged frogs and toads croak in the distance on the Morningside while pussy willows and deer tracks dot the edges. The trails take me through the windswept prairie areas and to the scenic and quiet shore of Lake Mendota.

I like to listen to audiobooks when I hike. The one I am listening to today has a touch of magic and time travel in it—two things I hope my Quest will allow me to find at each of the parks. It's about a woman and her relationship with her recently deceased mother. It is strikingly pertinent as to why I am making this 45 x 5 effort. I'm turning 65 and not just thinking about the loss of my mom but also about how I will be lost to my own child soon enough. This first of the 45 is, therefore, bittersweet.

The death of one's mother is a complex passage, no matter our age. It can happen when we're 15, and our mother is 35, when we're 70, and our mother is 101, or anywhere in between. Whenever it happens, it is a unique and specific kind of grief. It is the loss of our creator, our first home. Whether our relationship with them was indifferent, loving, or toxic, it remains a highly complicated loss. Every cell in our body was created by that person, and our bodies remember. As the old song by Blind Willie Johnson says: "Motherless children have a harder time when mother is dead." For many, acknowledging Mother loss is part of turning sixty-five. It includes finding meaning and processing regret in memories of her.

It feels good to make my muscles ache slightly and experience these first five miles of my Quest. Last week, I purchased some glorious, multi-colored butterfly stickers to use to mark the days on my calendar when I complete one of the parks. Today, I will use the first one! They will be small, visual, and extrinsic rewards to remind me on hard days of my accomplishments and of my efforts to challenge myself.

Governor Nelson State Park

The Questions

1. What about this chapter resonated with you?
2. How are you able to find gratitude in your daily life?
3. As you begin this journey with me, in what ways have you challenged yourself in the last year?

The Particulars

Sticker Required: Yes

Map on the State Park's Website: Yes, and nicely detailed

Bathrooms for Day Hikers: Yes, but in the office

Office or Kiosk: Office which is frequently closed depending on the day or season

Trail Markings: Infrequently marked

Seasonal Closures: None

Flooding Concerns: Trails may be wet, but no flooding issues

Five Miles: Easy to get with no circles

Big Foot Beach State Park
Lake Geneva

5.38 miles
Highest Point: 1,011 ft
Lowest Point: 876 ft

April 23, 2022
Music and Lost Love

I read an article yesterday morning about how the pandemic has taken away our sense of spontaneity. Therefore, I resolved to do spontaneous things on my daily neighborhood walk. I stopped to talk with an elder woman who was raking leaves in her front yard. She told me how she had just gotten out of the hospital after having COVID and was enjoying the sunshine. I chatted with a red-haired woman about the joys of spring while petting her Brittany Spaniel, a dog whose hair matched the colors of her person. It felt exceptionally wonderful to connect with random strangers.

There comes a time in your life when you have to give yourself permission to be spontaneous—to just be yourself, do what you want, and be free. Hopefully, sooner rather than later. With that in mind, I danced around my living room later in the evening, somewhat tipsy on a Friday night. I don't care what society or anyone else thinks of me. I am happy right now, and it is enough.

I have done many things and been through many changes in the last 10 years. I divorced the albatross around my neck. I changed my name to one I chose for myself. I got some tattoos and my first brand-new car. I had a breast cancer scare. I left my career, unable to cope with the retaliation directed at me for speaking out. I had wanted to do some of them, finally allowing myself. Others, I would not have wished on my worst enemy or would ever have imagined I would be dealing with at this point in my life. I guess these experiences have made me stronger, made me a warrior, but I don't know if I consider it a fair trade.

In preparation for my 45 x 5 = 65 Quest, I made a playlist of all the songs holding deep emotional resonance with me, hence the late-night dancing. Songs which, when I hear them come on the radio, in the background at a store, or even as Muzak in an elevator, I make a point to stop and listen to them. I thought it would be nice for the long drives to and from the state parks as my Quest expands. I listen to my new song list on the drive to Big Foot Beach as I contemplate my solitary life.

I am thinking about another time of aloneness. I was in my late 20s, alone out of choice, to heal from a lost love. How different the feeling was then from the aloneness I feel now. That late 20s alone was of heartbreak and hope for the future, of finding myself again and dreaming of new love. Aloneness, then, made me worry I was missing something out there in the world. At almost 65, the aloneness now is the true understanding I am not missing out, and that being alone is better than having the wrong relationships. Now, it is more of a resignation to the state of being, of attempting to find happiness and meaning in my one and only-ness.

Last night, it rained hard. It will be wet out at this park today, but I have my hiking boots, which walked across bogs in England's "green and pleasant land," and I am all set. It is the first time this year I can wear my nylon hiking pants and lightweight moisture-wicking shirt.

Big Foot Beach State Park

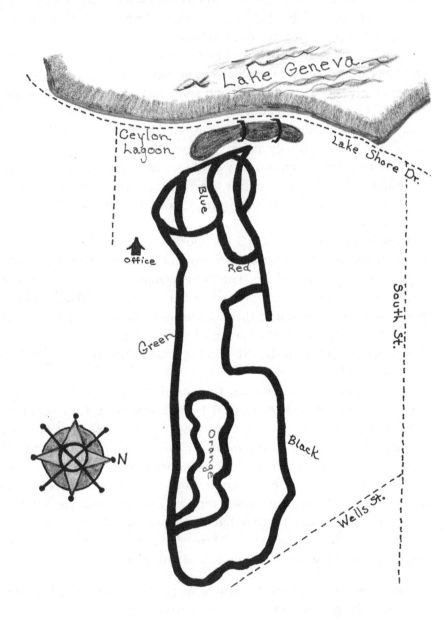

No winter clothes on me! It's in the high 70s today, with episodes of sun.

It wasn't easy to take my eyes off beautiful Lake Geneva to find the entrance to Big Foot Beach State Park. There is a small, shed-like office with a bit of merchandise (merch) and some maps. Two friendly rangers help me realize the park is not named for a crypto-creature but for a Potawatomi leader who was forcibly removed in 1836. The U.S. government relocated Big Foot and the Potawatomi first to Missouri and then to Kansas. They never saw their beloved Kishwauketoe ever again. The lake's original name meant "clear water," and it remains a stunning site.

The park primarily has short trails; therefore, it will take a combination of several to reach my goal. I hike the Red, the Blue, the Green, the Orange, and the Black to score my five miles. The trails are inviting in this unusual urban park. The Red and Blue Trails wander through rolling wooded areas, the tree trunks still dark and dripping from last night's deluge.

The Green Trail leads me through a pine forest, whispering gently on this breezy day. It proceeds past a baseball diamond and tennis courts. This is a posh neighborhood for a state park! Hiking on soft needles and smelling the pine fragrance on this strangely hot spring day gives me a sense of hope for the future. Hope is a gift; one we must continually give to ourselves as we age.

The Orange Trail winds through a delightful, tall grass prairie, golden brown at this time of year, but with sparks of green brightening the last visages of autumn's colors. Yellow dances among the dry grasses as goldfinches spread their showy wings.

At times, the Black Trail is inches under water, but my boots keep my feet dry and happy. This trail follows the curves of the Ceylon Lagoon and is graced by tremendous cottonwoods. The emotional and territorial trill of redwing blackbirds is everywhere around this lovely place. They remind me of the best halcyon days of summer. I cross the elegant arched bridge over the lagoon for the sake of the views provided at its apex.

As I drive home, listening to my song list again, I am aware of the influence music has on memory. It has the aspect and manner of a time machine, allowing me to revisit the past men in my life. There were those I liked and those I enjoyed for the time I was with them. Some left happy memories; some left trauma. Only one left a lasting memory as to be in my heart for my entire life. Today, on my first longer drive to a state park, I understand the reason why I chose the songs on my playlist. It was to be transported in time to those people I knew, including the times with my younger self and with my baby, now grown.

Pulling into my driveway, I step out of my car, and for a brief moment, I pretend I am akin to Ferdinand the Bull. The warrior in me is relaxed and peaceful as I inhale the incredible scent of the glorious Korean spicebush growing in my neighbor's yard. It is heady with the promise of spring, and I am as well.

Big Foot Beach State Park

The Questions

1. What about this chapter resonated with you?
2. In thinking about the music of your youth, what songs function as "time machines" for you?
3. Make a list of the ways in which your life has changed in the last 10 years. What stands out to you as something you finally gave yourself permission to do? What do you find caused you to become stronger as an individual?

The Particulars

Sticker Required: Yes

Map on the State Park's Website: Yes, and nicely detailed

Bathrooms for Day Hikers: Yes, but in a building which may be closed depending on the day or season

Office or Kiosk: Small office which may be closed depending on the day or season

Trail Markings: Infrequently marked

Seasonal Closures: None

Flooding Concerns: Trails may be wet and flooded at times of high water

Five Miles: Circles required

Lake Kegonsa State Park
Stoughton

5.15 miles
Highest Point: 902 ft
Lowest Point: 850 ft

April 26, 2022
Coming-of-Age and Downsizing

I made a checklist of what I need to have on these hikes: backpack, hiking poles, snacks, hiking boots and socks, audiobook, KN95 mask, water, and maps. I added to it the need to contact my hiking safety buddy (HSB). Having an HSB—someone you can let know when and where you are going, how long you plan to be gone, and when you arrive safely home—is vitally important. It must be someone who has your back because if something were to happen, you would need to be able to count on them to contact the appropriate authorities. It is also a good idea to leave in your car your name and phone number, your HSB contact, what time you left for the hike, where you plan to go, and your ETA back. It shouldn't be displayed in your car, but left for someone to find if needed. It adds another layer of protection for an aging hiker going out alone.

There is too much to remember every time I go. Having it written down will make it exponentially easier to run through before I leave my house for a hike. It is not because I am close to 65 and getting forgetful. It is because I am a Virgo with ADHD, and I like lists!

Lake Kegonsa State Park has a fantastic Visitor Center, but it is closed. Perhaps it's because it's before Memorial Day. They don't have any little blue information brochures or trail interpretation guides available to pick up from outside information slots. I do find the same map I had printed off the park's website. A great deal of public funds have been spent building this enormous entrance office. Not having a ranger here is sad. Don't get me started on all the tax cuts to state parks and how difficult it has been for those of us who love Wisconsin's green spaces.

I begin my hike on the White Oak Trail. There are 13 points of interpretive signage along the trail, but no information is available. I would've liked to have read about the Native effigy mounds. There's a spur cut-off trail to a Pine Plantation. I love walking under pines, the beautiful fragrance of the needles, and the gentle ancient energy of gymnosperms. Funky stick-built structures are circling a few trees on this side trail. They're very quizzical and ripe for exploration. Many animals probably sleep in them on cold winter nights. I am not sure why they are here or who made them, but they definitely go against the idea of "leave no trace."

As I continue to the Prairie Trail, an osprey flies low over my head, carrying a wriggling fish. How fabulous! When an osprey appears in your life, it reminds you to stay focused on your goals and believe you can obtain them. As my hike continues, I see the osprey's nest and have a calm sense of going in the right direction, not only here at this park but in my life. The nest is high up on one of the giant, almost cat-like electrical structures which, unfortunately, run through the park. A little farther along this winter-brown prairie, turkeys are running on the trail. What a day! Even though it's cold and cloudy, with occasional surprises of blue peeking through, this is a marvelous park, and I'm glad I made time to come here.

Lake Kegonsa State Park

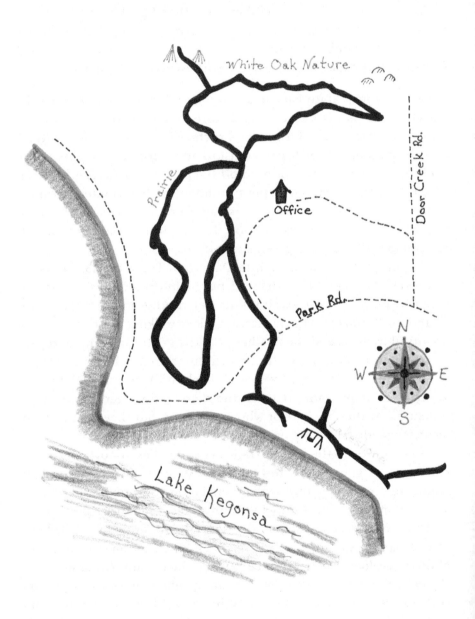

I find a delightful, metal park bench swing. It is a lovely and ideal place to relax after today's hike, here along the shores of the enchanting Lake Kegonsa. It is tranquil to swing and think, enjoying the sound of the waves and the birds and forgetting all the world's woes. I want to remove my hiking boots and socks to stick my feet in the crystal water, but I'll wait until warmer days before I do any wading.

This is my third park, and I feel positive about making this Quest for myself. It is helping me put some time into thinking about what I need to do at this point in my life.

Finding coming-of-age stories for those of us turning sixty-five is difficult. Most of them are about teenagers becoming young adults. They are great novels, don't get me wrong. I have read many of them, but the complexity of turning 65 makes them pale in comparison. Knowing you only have 10 to 15 years left of your life, if you're lucky, maybe 20—talk about existential angst! It is remarkably different than when you're 20 years old, and you think about how weird it will be to turn forty, fifty, or sixty. I remember the feeling. When I was partying like it was "1999" in 1982, I thought about the fact I would be 41 years old at the turn of the century. It felt incredibly crazy and unbelievable. Now, here I am, turning 65, grateful to be able to reach this age.

During my hike today, I am pondering a couple of the major dilemmas of aging; the first is purging. I have been actively getting rid of things around my house, eliminating more and more as the years go by. Some things are more difficult to let go of than others. They are the items infused with elaborate and complex memories, items functioning as time machines.

It is hard for me to throw out, to donate, to pass on the two bags of New Mexico "beach" glass I collected from the desert behind my house in Carrizozo. It is a unique type of glass repeatedly rolled in the sandy soil. It was left in the unrelenting sun for decades to turn exquisite shades of lavender and purple, its late 1800s manganese reacting to the ever-present UV rays. These bags also contain smooth pieces of green and brown glass as well as broken dishes of all hues decorated with multi-colored flowers and swirls of blue. My little adobe house was situated on the edge of town. I used to walk in the range behind it after I got home from work as a way to decompress, searching out forsaken things and watching the barnburner sunsets. I would wander back and forth looking, carrying home only what I could fit in my hands. It was a self-imposed time limit to my desert larking. It was peaceful, relaxing, and spiritual to walk there among the prickly pears and cholla, studying the ground for sparks of color, the remnants of long-ago homesteads.

When I touch them now, I can still feel the heat of the New Mexico sun and the dry warmth of the air scented with yucca flowers and sage. I am working toward saving only my favorites, the absolute best pieces. The diminutive ear of a porcelain doll, the four-inch bottle in the shape of a little girl in a fancy dress, and the Blue Willow china tree are exceedingly special. They are talismans of another time, of another me.

A second dilemma of aging is downsizing. I read an article the other day about how part of the issue with the lack of affordable homes is because boomers are not moving, instead deciding to age in place. There was nothing in the article about the fact that small, accessible houses have not been built for several decades. Apartments, condos, and mega houses are being built. Ranch houses like mine are the perfect size homes, which is why they were built in the first place in the late 1950s and early 1960s.

As a young boomer, this article made me think critically about my living situation. I live in a modest 1964 ranch in a treed neighborhood. I can walk to the grocery, the library, the post office, and a small shopping center. My house is approximately 1,000 square feet. I can see needing to downsize if you were in a 4,000- to 6,000-square-foot house. Those would be ridiculously big to rattle around in as a single person turning sixty-five. My little house with its tiny bedrooms and dine-in kitchen is big for me if I think about it. On the other hand, where could I find a well-appointed three-bedroom apartment, even a one-bedroom, with all utilities included, costing me about what I pay now with owning the house, taxes, and insurance? I'd be hard-pressed to find such a place, especially one accommodating any disabilities.

Downsizing requires me to think about yet another quandary: how long will I be able to stay in my house? Over 25 years ago, I knew an occupational therapist who shared some wise advice on this issue. She told me I would need extra handrails, grab bars, and ramps because if I didn't, it would mean I had died young and healthy. As I recall her astute counsel, I have to start thinking about what upgrades I need and how to make my house easier to maintain and maneuver.

The concepts of purging, downsizing, and preparing are ones we all must confront as part of the aging process. Many nonfiction books give tips on being older in your home, but I sincerely wish more fiction expressed the emotional turmoil of this liminal time in life, similar to teenage coming-of-age books. I will need to search harder for such stories.

April 27, 2022
The Day After

I got my new state park sticker in the mail today and am positively giddy! I took the dramatic step of scraping off all the old stickers on my car's windshield to make room for this new one. I am feeling genuinely delighted and happy about my 45 x 5 = 65 Quest. I purchased a new *Wisconsin Atlas & Gazetteer* in case I drive somewhere and lose my GPS. As I put them in my car, I find an old Wisconsin State Park brochure in the map pocket behind the passenger seat. Even my car needs to be purged. The brochure was adorned with a smiling Governor Jim Doyle. I wonder if the DNR still puts these fun little booklets out. They contain good information and would save me from much online searching. I will have to see if I can find one with Governor Tony Evers on the cover!

Lake Kegonsa State Park

The Questions

1. What about this chapter resonated with you?
2. When you are out hiking, or just out in the world, what things do you do to increase your sense of personal safety?
3. While purging your belongings as you get older, what objects do you find difficult to let go of? What memories do they hold for you?

The Particulars

Sticker Required: Yes

Map on the State Park's Website: Yes, and nicely detailed

Bathrooms for Day Hikers: Yes, but in the office

Office or Kiosk: Office which is frequently closed depending on the day or season

Trail Markings: Infrequently marked

Seasonal Closures: None

Flooding Concerns: Trails may be wet, but no flooding issues

Five Miles: Circles required

Tower Hill State Park
Spring Green

5.20 miles
Highest Point: 1,112 ft
Lowest Point: 891 ft

May 1, 2022
Circles and Cemeteries

I am tackling this park with my good friend Petra. I love hiking because of its solitary nature, which fits seamlessly with the solitary lifestyle thrust upon me. Nonetheless, it is a welcome privilege anytime a friend can join. There is a small office, but it is not open. All these closed offices must have something to do with the time of year and the day of the week. There is information available in outside slots, and I grab a state park newspaper. It will complement the map I brought along, downloaded from the DNR's website.

Beginning our sojourn through this park, we take time to explore the ruins of an old barn, stacks of tawny brown sandstone making up its remaining foundation. The area around Tower Hill was originally called Helena. It was where the laborers who worked at the Shot Tower lived, giving up their lives too early to the scourges of lead poisoning. We start the five miles on the Old Ox Trail, winding up to the Smelter House and the Shot Tower, which contains a small museum. Close to the Smelter House is a tall, misshapen dead tree. At its apex sits a bald eagle, scanning the surrounding forest, its fierce eyes concentrating on the river below.

We talk about everything under the sun while hiking on this fine morning—plans for the future and concerns from the past. At any age, it doesn't get much better than having someone you can share parts of yourself with, have conversation flowing in multiple directions, and who laughs at your jokes.

Rounding another loop of the Old Ox Trail, we overhear an amusing conversation as we take a break in the little gazebo slightly off the trail. We listen as two young women walk by, talking about not really understanding what "shot" is and why it would be made here. We start talking about all the archaic things, the specific knowledge we both possess from a rural Wisconsin upbringing. We know about shot because of growing up on farms. As older adults, we kind of expect everyone to know this stuff! Sadly, for some things and gladly for others, the old ways are slowly being forgotten.

In our continued loops, we venture close to the bottom of the Shot Tower, only to find one of the trails is closed for repairs. The still-open one also appears damaged. A tree had crashed down, breaking several fences that were subsequently haphazardly and hastily rebuilt. Many of the trails here need some loving care. Victims no doubt of the cuts in funding to our state parks.

Continuing along the bottom, on the remaining open trail, is a wonderful, almost circular-shaped indentation in the sandstone bluff. Big enough for me to stand in, it has a cozy feel. It is approximately five feet deep, six feet wide, and about six feet high. I tease Petra about what a great picnic place this would be. We could perch ourselves here like eagles, looking out over the Wisconsin River, and drink "two tree beers." She laments if it were warm enough to drink some beer up here, we probably would be plagued by bugs, and we laugh out loud. It is inevitable here in Wisconsin. If it's nice

Tower Hill State Park

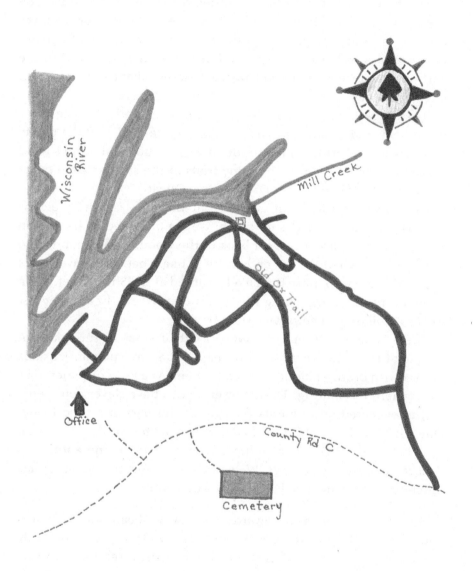

enough to do something fun outside, then you better make sure you have your bug spray with you.

The hike down to the Shot Tunnel is markedly stunning. The rounded sandstone bluff, which juts out over the Wisconsin River flowage, is a picturesque monolith next to a curve of smooth green-blue water. A walk to the gated end of the tunnel, deep within the cliff, is replete with bats and microclimates, silent coolness, and ancient echoes.

It is difficult to get in my mileage in this small park. We hike many loops back and around the Old Ox, the service road, and the picnic area. Given the terrain, it is a moderately strenuous hike and a good workout. Wandering over the same trails in the smaller state parks is going to be the norm as I continue my Quest.

Upon leaving Tower Hill, we stop at the little cemetery across Highway C near the park's entrance. We are intrigued by its hidden nature along a gravel drive set back in the woods. It was connected to the little town of Helena and is still in use. There are gravestones of people here who more than likely worked at the Shot Tower. It is a splendid place—burgeoning wild irises everywhere. In another few weeks it will be gorgeous with their flowers.

There is, as my friend observes, "a bit of sass" in this place! A couple of the stones are rather unusual. They are substantial slabs of rock with bronze plaques affixed to them. As a lover of cemeteries, I find them fascinating. These newer stones have clever comments and unexpected adornments relating to the person buried below. One, for a teacher stating she had encouraged her students to "read your brains out." One has an incongruent alligator, and another is decorated with happy frogs. We smile about how this location has much to investigate. It's definitely worth a stop!

For me, visiting a graveyard has always been life-affirming. Someday, in the not-too-distant future, I will be gone, my body returning to the earth. Cemeteries are a visceral reminder to live, to be, to love while you still can. Make peace with yourself, first and foremost, because even with loved ones at your side, you will be alone on your final journey into the unknown.

Growing up on the farm, I would ride my stingray banana seat bike to nearby cemeteries to make charcoal rubbings of the designs on the stones. I found the images of weeping willows, resting sheep, and the myriad of flowers surprisingly expressive. I enjoyed reading the poetry etched upon them and the different shapes and textures of the materials used to create them. There was a time when my mom became somewhat concerned about me, what with tombstone art decorating my childhood bedroom alongside my Beatles posters.

I grew up to become a hospice social worker, where death and dying were a daily occurrence. At times, it was poignant and sad, but for the most part, it was a fount of strength, a place where the spiritual connections between us as humans were nothing less than miraculous. During my time at such a job in Rogers, Arkansas, I remember one woman who was close to the end of her life. Waking from a slumber that had lasted several days, she sat up in her bed and obstinately declared to me she was not going to die until her family arrived from St. Louis. I knew her two daughters were returning to Rogers to be with her. One had arrived a few days prior. I spoke with the first daughter and asked about her mother's statement. She related the other sister lived in Houston and was on a direct flight expected to land later in the evening on Christmas Eve. There was a rare snowstorm, and their plane got diverted ... to St. Louis. The second daughter and her family were finally able to enter her mother's room in the wee hours of Christmas morning. Death came swiftly after for the old woman. Mysteries happen all the time in hospice.

Tower Hill State Park is close to the American Players Theatre. Petra and I reminisce about the shows we've seen there as we drive home past the road to APT. I like to be generous with my friends, and for several years I have purchased six tickets and brought whichever of them could come. We picnic and drink champagne before taking in a Shakespeare comedy or anything by Oscar Wilde, my favorite author. I will have to check out their lineup for next summer. This summer, to paraphrase the Bard, the Quest is the thing!

"Death must be so beautiful. To have no yesterday and no tomorrow. To forget time, to forgive life, to be at peace."
—Oscar Wilde

Tower Hill State Park

The Questions

1. What about this chapter resonated with you?
2. What are some things you remember having or doing that are no longer a part of general societal knowledge?
3. In what ways have you considered how your body will be handled after you die? Do you want a burial, a cremation, or have some other idea?

The Particulars

Sticker Required: Yes

Map on the State Park's Website: Yes

Bathrooms for Day Hikers: Yes, but in the office

Office or Kiosk: Office which is frequently closed depending on the day or season

Trail Markings: Infrequently marked

Seasonal Closures: None

Flooding Concerns: Picnic area may be flooded at times of high water

Five Miles: Circles required

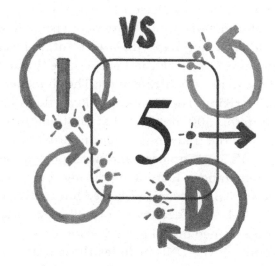

Nelson Dewey State Park
Cassville

5.12 miles
Highest Point: 849 ft
Lowest Point: 583 ft

May 4, 2022
Privilege and Gratitude

On the way to this park, as I drive on Highway 18 West, I pass through the town of Lancaster, the seat of Grant County. The courthouse is truly a work of art, built of red sandstone in the Classical Revival style. It has an astonishing amount of intricate glass and copper work on its spectacular Victorian-era dome. I definitely should stop and tour it, but I got into bed after midnight, leaving my house late this morning. I will have to come back to experience its beautiful architecture, perhaps stopping for lunch in one of the little diners on the square. Today I must continue on, because my Quest is the goal.

The park office is in a delightful, old building, an original to the Stonefield Farm built here by Nelson Dewey, the first governor of Wisconsin. It is closed, but I find a state park visitor newspaper in an outdoor bin. It has a nice map with large print, so I won't have to use my reading glasses to check the trails. I drive through the park until the end of the road, my starting point. The views here from this elevated spot are striking. The Mississippi River flows broad in the distance from atop this 500-foot bluff. I start off on the Cedar Trail. I will have to hike all the trails in this park multiple times to get in my five miles, but it's lovely up here, and time rolls out before me.

One thing to remember when hiking during this time of year is that many of the state parks have prescribed burns. Two weeks after I hiked Governor Nelson, they burned off all the prairies. It looks like there was a prescribed burn here at Nelson Dewey two or three weeks ago. I wonder if the DNR includes these burns under their "Conditions" tab on the state park websites. There are probably many like me who do not want to be surprised by clouds of smoke upon arrival at a park, especially as an older hiker with respiratory concerns.

Coming to this park is the longest drive I have undertaken thus far on my Quest. Because of this, I spent my time driving here thinking about privilege. I have the privilege of having a day off and a car I trust to drive me hours to and from a place I've never been before. I have privilege in our society, and it is important for me to recognize and acknowledge it. I am a third-generation immigrant. My father's parents came here dealing with only the oppression of poverty and a language barrier, not compounded by how they looked, who they were, what they believed, or who they loved. I use my privilege. I am not talking about trying to get a discount on an expired coupon or complaining about the price of a meal in a restaurant. I am referring to using it against injustice in the world.

Amplifying the voices of those without such privilege can be an agonizing choice. Will we simply keep going along to remain in our jobs, or will we defy the wrongdoing and risk the consequences for the rights of others? Can we honestly have integrity if we are complicit? If we help design the emperor's new clothes? I don't think so.

Nelson Dewey State Park

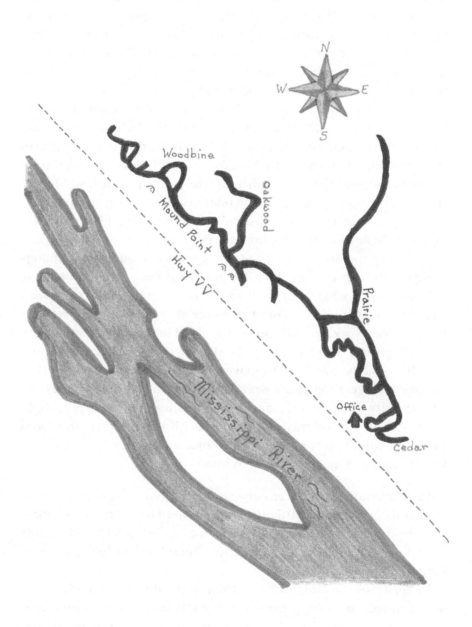

When I left my career, it was not the way I wanted to leave: no parties, no speeches, no accolades. Instead, I got what I have come to refer to as a "Stormy Daniels deal." I got fucked. I got money. I had to sign a non-disclosure agreement, unable to speak about what the injustice I reported entailed. The getting fucked part was decidedly not in the fun, sexy way. However, I would much rather have my honor, have as my history that I stood up for the rights of children than a piece of "Happy Retirement" cake.

My work laptop sported a yellow sticker with a quote by Ida B. Wells: "The way to right wrongs is to shine the light of truth upon them." I was frequently intrigued by those who averted their eyes after reading it. I have never been one to follow the idioms of cowardice when confronted with injustice: "Keep your head down," "Don't make waves," "Don't ruffle feathers." I may be geographically challenged, but I have a strong, definitive moral and ethical compass. I sleep well, knowing I did what was right.

Do I have regrets? I regret not being powerful enough to change things for those I stood up with, stood up for. I regret not being able to ensure what happened to them never happens to anyone else. As I do this Life Review, it gives me an opportunity to reframe regrets and work toward resolving the feelings associated with them. Thinking of it now, I realize the untenable situation I found myself in only allowed me to make one choice to avoid giving tacit approval, protect my social work licensure, and be able to preserve my integrity. As a result, I don't regret using my privilege to fight the battle, to try and make a difference. All I can hope is the seeds I planted will continue to grow into more and more, and they will keep fighting to make all children safe.

I became a social worker because I felt a bone-deep need to pay back and pay forward all this life has given me. I have had my fair share of hard days and hard times. Even so, gratitude and thankfulness are essential to maintaining integrity. Those feelings help us to find light and hope in the darkness.

Integrity versus Despair is the final stage of Erik Erikson's theory of psychosocial development. His work is one of the foundations of my social work practice. It speaks to how our personalities develop as we move through our lives, meeting challenges, making decisions, and resolving conflicts. Each stage has a positive strength and a negative maladaptation. The strengths build a sustainable life. The maladaptions build a fragile structure prone to collapse. As a school social worker, I used as a guide his stages of Industry versus Inferiority and Identity versus Role Confusion. In my work with elders, I used his final stage, which I now exist in myself. We begin the functions of this one around 65 years old and work on them until we die. Understanding our privileges, failures, traumas, and achievements is the important task as we age. Do we feel we had a good life, all in all? That's the question at the heart of the aging journey.

With its long drives and miles of hiking, this Quest provides a substantial amount of time for processing. It's a type of therapy being out in the forest. I am able to think, look back, and search for clarity and purpose. Maybe I find regret, too, but I work to locate a place for it. One of the biggest responsibilities of aging is this reflecting and making sense. It is the crux of our coming-of-age stories.

Therefore, I wander today, enjoying the views from these Mississippi bluffs, the river high and inundating the tree lines. It is why I hike clockwise and counterclockwise, *deasil* and *widdershins*, around and around these short trails. The Prairie and the Cedar Trails with their rocky slopes and stunning panoramas. The Mound Point with its steep grades and remaining conical effigy mounds. The Oakwood with its densely wooded and gentle saunter. The Woodbine with its self-guided tour through the mixed prairie. I am processing. I am coming to terms with my life and its many facets. I am reclaiming my identity not only as a Hiker but also as a Gardener. One of the crucial aspects of being a Gardener is knowing that even if the soil is poor, the seeds you plant keep growing and can still become mighty and powerful.

Nelson Dewey State Park

The Questions

1. What about this chapter resonated with you?
2. In what ways do you experience privilege in society? In what ways have you lacked privilege?
3. What are your initial thoughts on the idea of Integrity versus Despair as the central conflict of aging?

The Particulars

Sticker Required: Yes

Map on the State Park's Website: Yes, and nicely detailed

Bathrooms for Day Hikers: Yes, but in the office

Office or Kiosk: Office which may be closed depending on the day or season

Trail Markings: Well-marked on short trails

Seasonal Closures: None

Flooding Concerns: None

Five Miles: Circles required

Blue Mound State Park
Blue Mounds

5.50 miles
Highest Point 1,706 ft
Lowest Point: 1,217 ft

May 9, 2022
Scars and Tattoos

I am frustrated this morning trying to fasten my sports bra. Life is too short to deal with unruly bras! Maybe I simply have unruly breasts, but that is a whole different story. It goes back to my love-hate relationship with outdoor sporting goods stores. I hiked over 30 miles in the last couple of weeks, yet all I can buy in most places, clothing-wise, are hiking socks. Most stores mainly stock extra small and small sizes of women's clothes. If I can find a large, it is more of a junior size large, which will not fit over my size D cups. I am over the moon that I found a backpack specifically designed to accommodate breasts. The straps across the front can be arranged and adjusted and are marvelous!

The office is closed at Blue Mound, but I find a map in an outdoor brochure slot. I miss being able to stop into park offices to get more historical information, check out the merch they usually have, and use the bathroom.

I park in the lot near the swimming pool, devoid of crowds, on this early spring day. I start on my five miles by taking the Gneiss and Smooth Mountain Bike Trail. I plan to stay on it until I can link up with the Pleasure Valley Trail, a name calling to my mind images of half-naked firefighters. As I go, I am listening to a book about a man who can control the weather with his emotions. It is surprising and fantastical, just like these trails. The Weeping Rock Trail branches north off the Pleasure Valley and rejoins it to make an outstanding loop full of wonders.

The trees are still leafing out, making the trails a fusion of sunshine and strange shadows. The Weeping Rock Trail follows a spring-fed creek bursting with effervescent rivulets and waterfalls. The trail intersects it several times with low bridges and jumping steps across. It's a perfectly lovely hike. The trail meanders around to its namesake, a bold rock face dripping with fresh spring water. This forest is full of moss-covered rocks and early wildflowers. It's one of the prettiest places I've been to so far, especially with all the delightful hepatica, its white petal stars suspended over tri-lobed leaves of darkest green.

On the way here, I started thinking about scars. I was set to have some of the windows in my house replaced today. However, at six o'clock this morning, I got a call saying the contractors weren't coming. It's frustrating, all in all.

I planned to go hiking on Wednesday this week, but now I am hiking on Monday. I am thinking about the universe, perhaps protecting me from a more significant hurt. Sure, it "hurt" not to have my windows taken care of today, but it is primarily a maddening inconvenience. However, maybe it happened so I could hike today instead of Wednesday and keep myself from something worse. This kind of thing happens all the time. It is the weird phenomenon of being in the wrong place at the right time. For example, when someone is running late and misses their flight on what becomes a doomed plane, or when they are stuck in traffic avoiding a deadly

Blue Mound State Park

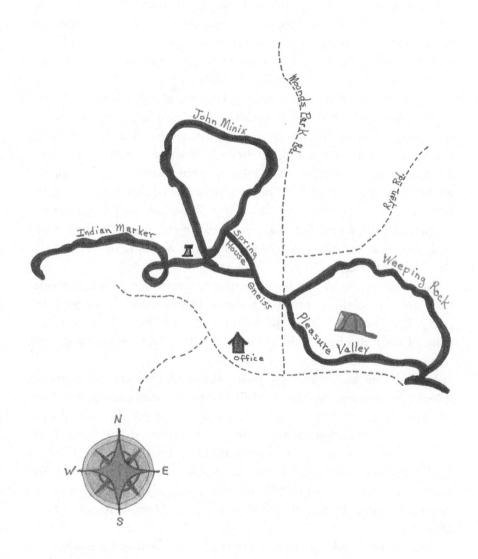

car accident, or when they call in sick on the day a shooter decides to devastate their school. Mine, though less intense, has to do with a scar.

I have a scar on my right middle finger from an injury I got in my late twenties. I was working as a floral designer and slammed my finger in the delivery van's door. It was a freak accident, and I got irritated with myself. *What the hell? Why didn't I pull my hand all the way out of the door? Why did I misjudge the distance?*

I had been delivering wedding flowers along with the store's driver, Malcolm. Malcolm is another bottle of wine, but anyway, I ended up bleeding profusely. I went inside the church and found the bride's mother, having met her when she came into the flower shop with her daughter. The grooms rarely came to the shop, and we never kept track of their names, only the brides. I informed her what had happened as drops of my blood fell to the parqueted vestibule floor. I told her Malcolm and I were going to leave, but I would send someone else to help set up the wedding flowers, pin on the corsages, etc.

Malcolm drove me to the emergency room. He called our boss to relate the dilemma and the need to follow up with the wedding party. The doctor numbed my finger, and I watched him sew it up, a total of four stitches. Malcolm watched, too, and ended up getting queasy as he drove me home.

I didn't think significantly more about it until around a month later. I was studying the wedding announcements in the local newspaper as the shop maintained a list of all the ceremonies we did. As I browsed through them, I recognized the bride I was delivering flowers to when I accidentally injured my finger. Looking at the photo in the paper, I saw the groom standing beside her. Her groom was an ex of mine. When I said I was leaving him, he held a gun to my head. I honestly didn't think I would make it out of there alive.

Thus, I am thinking about scars today. If I had not smashed my finger in the door, I would have been responsible for pinning a boutonniere on that groom. It would have hurt a hell of a lot worse! I learned from the experience sometimes you never know why things change at the last minute. Maybe it's the Divine saying, "No, you need to do something else today." I decided to take advantage of the change in window installation and go for a Quest hike.

I finish the Pleasure Valley Trail with, sadly, no firefighter sightings. I set out on the John Minx Trail. The trees here become denser, the forest floor sparkling with blood roots in bloom, additional white stars on the ground. This trail is an easy loop on which I could make up some time if I were in a hurry, but then I would miss the unfurling ferns with their enchanting and sacred spirals. The John Minx takes me back to where my car is parked and the beginning of the Spring House Trail.

I have to say, I don't know anyone who gets to be 65 and doesn't have scars. I have several—from farm machinery, from glass where it should not have been, and even one from a fall while hiking (another park holds that story). Some are ones I wanted in the form of tattoos from my different hiking adventures.

Tattoos are scars, after all, colorful as they may be. I have four so far. One is of a fencepost trail marker for my hike of the C2C. One is of a bright green snake surrounded by chamomile flowers for my hikes in Ireland. One is of a paisley with Virgo in Sanskrit from my hikes in India. My favorite, though, is of two black birds flying on my wrist. It is in the same place where my beloved child has the exact same tattoo. Whenever I look at it, I remember the day we were inked, and I am filled with joy.

There are people with self-inflicted scars. As a social worker, I had many clients with these types of scars, the feelings related to them—overwhelming. Some returned and showed me the tattoos they had obtained to cover the wounds. What an intense, emotional healing it is to take sadness and pain and transform it into beauty.

The remnants of the Spring House sit in an open bowl of prairie surrounded by the forest. I follow the trail to the daunting steps of the East Tower. I have resolved to climb every tower I encounter on this Quest, even if they are difficult. I must see the views from their summits. At the top of this tower, there is a selfie station. They are unique wooden structures placed at many picturesque locations throughout the Wisconsin State Parks. The wind is markedly fierce up here, though, and I am afraid to use it. I am fearful my phone will blow off the side, crashing to the ground far below. Instead, I simply enjoy the scenery and congratulate myself for not thinking because I am old, I can't climb this many steps.

After the walk down, I head off toward the Indian Marker Tree Trail. Here is where the huge dolomite boulders live! The trail winds around and over, showing off all the microclimates created by them, the sun and the shade influenced by their grand aspects. The flowers on this trail clinging to the sides of the boulders are dazzling. Many of these precocious wildflowers are white; the hepatica, the bloodroot, and the Dutchman's breeches are a pretty contrast to the lichen gray rock and the kelly green moss. With their remarkable spotted leaves, the trout lilies are in full riot. I return to my car, a happy hiker with five miles on my GPS. I plan to revisit this park and do several more of these fantastic trails.

While driving home, I think again of scars, a bizarre subject on a fine day. I had the ramifications of a childhood scar come up last year in the form of an acutely fast-growing cataract in my right eye. Apparently, when you get an eye injury, it can come back to haunt you.

That scar was a life changer. It happened the summer before I was to start third grade. I was playing outside at the Van Dyne Volunteer Fireman's picnic with my friends and siblings. My father was a member who helped with several local house and barn fires. Playing tag, running and laughing, I was not watching where I was going, instead looking backward. Turning forward, I ran straight into a barbed wire fence. The flesh around my eye was slashed, jagged and rough, leaving me with scars through my eyebrow and above and below my eye. I was self-conscious about them for many years, wishing my parents would have found someone other than a chain-smoking country doctor to stitch up the face of my little girl self.

Being older and having grown to accept them, they mingle with my ever-increasing wrinkles. I was shocked when the injury came back to me. Cataracts are often a rite of passage as we age, but I thought it would not be for another 10 years or more. I was told because of a dang barbed wire attack long ago, I needed to have eye surgery. It had to be put off because of the pandemic, allowing me to experience the world as Monet and Degas eventually did, blurry and muted. I finally got in, and everything worked out wonderfully. I took advantage of having to wear an eyepatch after by decorating it with a Jolly Roger and pretending to be a pirate, at least for a few days. It is not something one gets to do often in this life! It is helpful to find creativity and mirth when confronting such a procedure.

Avast me hearties, alas, it was the eye able to see well up close. I went from needing glasses to drive to no longer requiring them for distance, changing to relying on them to read. Another coming-of-age issue is having a pair (or two) of reading glasses in every room of my house and even in my backpack!

Blue Mound State Park

The Questions

1. What about this chapter resonated with you?

2. What do you remember about your injuries that resulted in scars? How have you incorporated those changes into your body image?

3. Do you have any tattoos? What do you think about tattoos and those you encounter with them?

The Particulars

Sticker Required: Yes

Map on the State Park's Website: Yes, and nicely detailed

Bathrooms for Day Hikers: Yes, but in the office

Office or Kiosk: Office, which may be closed depending on the day or season

Trail Markings: Well-marked

Seasonal Closures: None

Flooding Concerns: Possibly in heavy rains

Five Miles: Easy to get with no circles

Natural Bridge State Park
North Freedom

5.09 miles
Highest Point: 1,095 ft
Lowest Point: 788 ft

May 12, 2022
Lost and Found

This morning, I was awakened from a dream by what I thought was a weird, electronic tone coming from my phone. It was a curious sound in my rousing slumber. As I became more fully awake, I listened to the pattern of the notes and realized it was a beautiful, singing bird! It has been eons since spring has been here, causing the sounds of a lovely, warbling bird outside my bedroom window to seem alien. A few seconds later, the rhythmic trill of my alarm went off, telling me it was time to get out of bed. I hit the snooze button as my psyche slowly rose to the surface. It's one of the things I love about my little clock. It's not pretty in any sense but is exceedingly functional. It allows me to go back to sleep for four minutes and then another four minutes as many times as I want. I love hitting the snooze button even when I have to get going, expressly because it feels indulgent to doze; it's definitely one of the best perks of being retired.

I got slightly turned around trying to get to Natural Bridge. I am one of those people born without a sense of direction. Like the meme which plays on the Robert Frost poem: "I took the road less traveled, and now, I don't know where the fuck I am." That's me! I choose to refer to it as being geographically challenged. I think it's truly curious how, when I've hiked in the past, especially at popular state parks such as Devil's Lake or Governor Dodge, people have come up to me and questioned if they're going the right way. Due to the aforementioned challenge, I invariably carried a map with me and was able to tell them where they were and how to proceed. I wonder if they knew they were appealing to the least geographically grounded person they could possibly ask to tell them if they were lost.

It is a wise thing I downloaded and brought a park map with me today, as there is nothing out here. At this state park, there's not an office of any kind. There is only a weathered, worse-for-wear kiosk and a can station to deposit fee money. There are no maps, brochures, or newspapers—all those things I have usually been able to find. There is a rustic restroom building covered with graffiti, but otherwise, there are no improvements for visitors.

I think Natural Bridge will be one of the parks where it's a back-and-forth hiking situation to get my five miles, the bizarrely rigid goal for this Quest. The thing about a Quest, though, is the Quester gets to decide.

As I ready myself in my hiking boots and backpack, I'm enamored with the marvelous symphony of songbirds and the delicate fragrance of blooming thornapple trees. The area is splendid and nearly devoid of human noise. Mine is the only car here.

While I am getting my act together to hit the trails, a truckload of older people pulls into the parking lot. They get out and venture over to spy at the sorrowful kiosk. Not finding what they need but seeing

Natural Bridge State Park

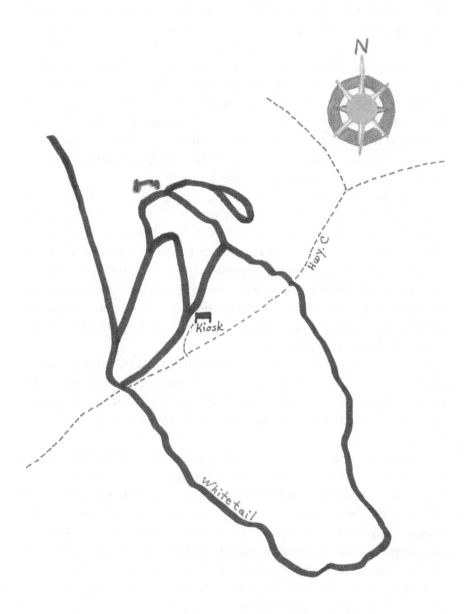

I have a backpack and poles, they come over to inquire of me which way and how far to the bridge. This is what I mean! Perhaps I have an air of confidence and knowledge about me that my geographically challenged brain doesn't really possess. I show them my map and estimate it to be about one-quarter mile to the namesake feature. They smile thankfully at me and go on their way. I think they made it up to the bridge, but I am starting on a different route today.

The Whitetail Trail is the only named trail in the park. It leaves the parking lot and crosses the road through a farm field, leading to a steep forested hill. This trail is a challenge today with the over-90-degree temperature, but I have nothing else needing to be done. I keep a good pace and stop as I need.

There are no park benches along the trails, no picnic tables, nothing to sit on but the bench attached to the lonely, rough kiosk. As a result, I hike for over four miles without a break before I finally get to the bridge, having taken the long way around. It has me thinking about some of the benefits of hiking. It's great for cardiovascular health. Our hearts benefit from the aerobic workout and the endurance it takes to put in the miles. Hiking also improves balance. Navigating over roots and dodging boulders like I am today especially benefits us older hikers.

It is exquisitely cool inside the cave under the Natural Bridge on this hot, humid day. I find it no surprise the original people used it to shelter under 11,000 years ago. Excavations at the site date it as one of the oldest places humans called home in this part of North America.

I climb up and sit in the shade under the curve of the bridge for a snack. It is a stunning view, looking out across the forest. I even spot a rose-breasted grosbeak! The sky is adrift with turkey vultures, casting shadows as they soar high above. I am serenely happy underneath this incredible stone monolith of nature's architecture. I like Natural Bridge. It reminds me of places out West where prominent stone features are the norm. I'm looking forward to visiting more of the state parks in the unglaciated region, which feature similar geological marvels.

After all my roundabout hiking, I think I am over five miles. However, back at my car, 4.94 is all I have. The backpack goes on again, and I take off on another trail to finish. I know it's a random boundary, but I want to stay true to myself.

As I'm leaving the park, I find my car's GPS isn't working. I will need to use my maps to find the way home. I laugh out loud at myself recalling how I would go on adventures with my child when they were little. I didn't have GPS then. I was constantly looking at maps and trying to figure out how to get where we wanted to go. Sometimes (okay, oftentimes), I would get frustrated and lost. My child would start singing a song from one of our favorite movies. Instead of singing, "Just keep swimming," we would sing, "Just keep driving." We would get the silly giggles, and I would drive on because, after all, it's about the journey; it's about the adventure.

Big deal if I get a little turned around. I am resilient. I have maps in my car, and I can figure out where I'm going. I have many skills. I am tenacious. Hiking and the challenge it provides increases my self-esteem. I have to remember that my drives to the state parks are similar to my life—sometimes knowing exactly where I'm going, and other times, having absolutely no clue, getting lost, and discovering new things because I didn't know what I was doing. I think it is one of the gifts of being almost sixty-five. I know from experience, even if things are tough, I will be able to find my way.

Natural Bridge State Park

The Questions

1. What about this chapter resonated with you?

2. If you are retired, what are some of the perks of your unstructured time? If not, how do you anticipate you will use your unstructured time?

3. In what ways do you feel resilient when confronted with a challenge?

The Particulars

Sticker Required: Yes

Map on the State Park's Website: Yes, but minimally detailed

Bathrooms for Day Hikers: Yes, but in frequently locked building

Office or Kiosk: Kiosk with no additional information available

Trail Markings: Not well-marked

Seasonal Closures: None

Flooding Concerns: None

Five Miles: Circles required

Buckhorn State Park
Necedah

5.32 miles
Highest Point: 924 ft
Lowest Point: 891 ft

May 15, 2022
Hair and Hiking

I had difficulty with my hair while getting ready to go on this hike today. I was attempting to form trendy side buns but couldn't get them to work. I settled for my usual braided pigtails with a bandana. This morning's struggle has me thinking about how hair is another coming-of-age issue. For men, of course, male pattern baldness. For women, there are a great deal more societal forces at play.

The first issue, I think, is one of the most important. It is the expectation as women get older, we are supposed to cut our hair short. It stems from historical, patriarchal thinking about how only maidens could have long, free hair. Women of a certain age are constantly barraged with articles about how to dress after 65, what makeup is allowed, and what hairstyles are suitable. At this age, I am sick of having my looks policed by society. The only thing those of us over 65 should stop wearing is the weight of other people's expectations. We should stop letting the judgments of others dictate our behaviors.

I decided long ago not to cut my hair short. At least until I absolutely had to due to complex aging or health issues. My hair, therefore, is a bit beyond shoulder length. During the first year of the pandemic, I dyed it a fabulous indigo. I figured I might as well take on the whole "old blue-haired lady" vibe. I really like it and have kept up the color. I find it makes me less invisible as an older person.

It is a substantial drive from Madison to Buckhorn, especially now when it's construction season. I will have to decide how far I will travel in a day in pursuit of my Quest—maybe two or three hours? As I near the park on Highway G, I cross a lengthy, low-water bridge over Castle Rock Lake. The lake was formed by the damming of the Yellow and the Wisconsin Rivers. It is captivating on this vivid, sunny, perfect hiking weather day! No mosquitoes yet, but I still need to practice the diligence required regarding ticks.

I stop by the park office, hoping to find it open. As I walk toward it, a man comes forcefully right up to me, getting way too close. He asks me how to deal with the required day sticker and how to get information, because the office is closed, even on a Sunday. I tell him about it quickly and hurry back to my car, lock the doors, and drive off into the park.

The scariest thing in the woods, for women, is not snakes or bears; it is men. Yeah, yeah, blah, blah, "not all men." How the hell are we supposed to know which kind they are? I have to be suspicious of a man who comes up to a woman out in the middle of nowhere to ask for directions. It's not something men usually do, so, in and of itself, it is a red flag. For men reading this, don't approach women at isolated state parks. If you legitimately need help, stand back— don't invade a woman's personal space. Every man needs to use their societal power to be a part of the solution. I dream of a world where none of us ever have to worry about being sexually harassed or violated while out hiking.

Buckhorn State Park

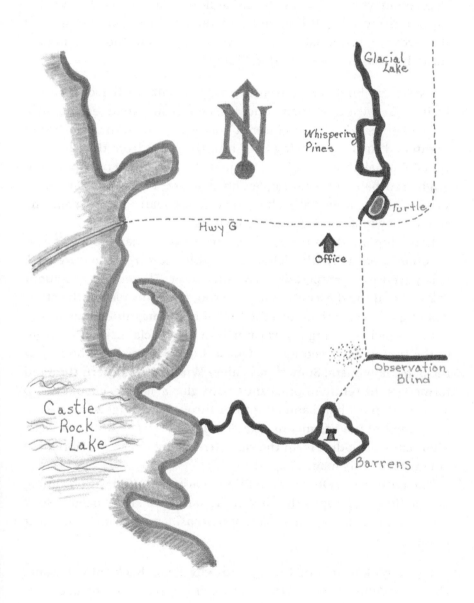

Anyway, back to the coming-of-age issues related to hair. Besides having to deal with societal pressures, there's also the sad and common fact our hair thins as we age. Ah, for the lush locks of pregnancy! Mine is not the same lion's mane it used to be. My hairline is receding. If I do end up bald someday, I wonder if I will start wearing fashionable hats, or would I get a tattoo covering my entire head with a verdant, floral jungle.

I start my Buckhorn adventure with a walk on Barrens Nature Trail. I hike west to a small pond. It's a gorgeous circle resembling a glacial kettle. When I get closer, it comes alive with the splashes of frightened turtles scurrying back into the water from their basking spots. The oaks surrounding it are just starting to leaf out, their tiny, bright red baby leaves—fragile and delicate. I continue on to the shore of Castle Rock Lake, checking out the nearby hike-in camping spots. They look to be genuinely inviting.

Retracing my steps back on the Barrens to my car, I follow it as it becomes a partially wheelchair-accessible interpretive nature trail. It is paved to a ramped Observation Tower. There is a sign about oak wilt and the devastation it has wrought in this part of the state. Reading it makes me mourn the loss of these magnificent giants.

I am slowly working my way north to the Glacial Lake Trail to get in the five miles I need for my Quest. I drive toward it, stopping at the Sandblow Vista. Sometimes called Wisconsin's desert, the sand formed as the remnant of an enormous glacial lake receded. I scoop some of it in my hand and let it filter through my fingers, marveling at all the minute organisms' skeletons from over 10,000 years ago. Their ancient bodies form the sand stretching out to the horizon. I am in awe of this magical spot!

The path to the Observation Blind nearby is dotted with beaming purple flowers, happily thriving in the sandy soil. I will need to look them up in my book, *Wildflowers of Wisconsin*, as they are unfamiliar to me.

I am thinking about hiking and why I got back into it again. Hiking occupies time. A vital component of reaching the age of 65 is figuring out what to do with all the time you have. If you're lucky enough, you will live to the age when you are living alone. Maybe, like me, you are divorced. I can't say I like it, but there are far worse things. Perhaps you are alone because you were never able to find someone to partner with. Possibly you did find someone and were happily together for 50-plus years until they died. You must have an idea, a plan. You must have things you can do to cope with the time rolling out before you, time you will spend by yourself.

Give earnest thought to how you will occupy this alone time as you age. It is truly important. Start making a list of the positive things associated with it. You can leave the bathroom door open, turn up your music as loud as you want, not have to adjust the shower head or the driver's seat, think only your own thoughts, turn up the heat and turn down the air conditioning, have time to create art, to write, etc.

I park by the beginning of the Turtle Trail, taking it to the Glacial Lake Trail. I'm glad I came here on a cooler day with intermittent clouds, as many of the trails are in the sun with no prolonged tree cover. The trails at Buckhorn are easy, nothing really uphill or down, mostly level ground in this beautiful park. I would have liked to have seen it before oak wilt decimated the mighty trees. I am heartened the DNR is working on restoring as much as possible, even with the Sisyphean task of battling a fungus spread by flying beetles.

Reaching the Whispering Pines Trail, I follow its loop to the east. I have the odd sensation I am the only person in the entire world, my reverie seldom broken save for an occasional plane sound overhead. It's spiritual and tranquil among the scrubby oaks, pines, and spruce. I drink in the isolation, and in the process, I become part of an even bigger world. I embrace the aloneness of this place and find in it a profound connection to nature and to the Divine. I wander farther to the edge of the park boundary before retracing my steps back to my car for the drive home.

As we age and spend more time by ourselves, we cannot sink into despair and loneliness. We must accept the aloneness. One of the reasons why I like Agatha Christie's character Hercule Poirot is because he appears to be happy by himself. He sets out fabulous gourmet dinners replete with decorative china and elegant stemware. He buys himself fancy Belgian chocolates for dessert. He fully embraces his aloneness like I am endeavoring to do. I wasted many years fearful of this state of being, but when I ultimately left my marriage, it was as if an enormous weight was lifted off me. Instead of spending my kindness and love, care and tolerance, patience and compassion on someone who did not reciprocate it, I now spend it on myself.

Buckhorn State Park

The Questions

1. What about this chapter resonated with you?
2. How has your relationship with your hair changed as you've gotten older?
3. If you live with a partner, what plans do you have to address your future without them in it? If you live by yourself, in what ways do you cope with the time spent alone?

The Particulars

Sticker Required: Yes

Map on the State Park's Website: Yes, and nicely detailed

Bathrooms for Day Hikers: Yes, but in the office

Office or Kiosk: Office which is frequently closed depending on the day or season

Trail Markings: Well-marked

Seasonal Closures: None

Flooding Concerns: Possibly from the Castle Rock flowage of the Wisconsin River

Five Miles: Easy to get with no circles

Hartman Creek State Park
Waupaca

5.14 miles
Highest Point: 1,323 ft
Lowest Point: 986 ft

May 19, 2022
Sex and Snakes

As I am preparing to leave my house this morning, I'm thinking about the musical I saw last week at the local performing arts center. Through the music, the main character conveyed an imaginary friendship he wished he had. He spoke of how they delighted in being together, talking and enjoying an endless sky. It is what Petra and I do whenever we hike together.

Over the years, we have helped each other navigate tremendous life changes. Her house is one street over from mine, making it easy to get together when we want to borrow ingredients, take a walk, or share a glass of wine. It is said one of the reasons women live longer than men is because we have closer friendships and deeper connections. I believe this is true, and I am honored by my wonderful group of supportive friends.

When I pick her up for this hike today, Petra gives me an adorable miniature compass to attach to my backpack and includes this note: "For my friend, who always knows the path she needs to take. Offering a chance to know the direction." I absolutely love it! All I need at this stage of my life is a compass to help me on my journey. I have a different relationship with time now. No more wearing of watches for me!

This is the first park I have come to on my Quest where the office is open! The ranger working here is gracious and helpful. The building is full of information and has a pleasant bathroom. I pick up several brochures and a great colorful map made of sturdy paper, the best one of the previous eight parks. They even have fun Hartman Creek merch for sale.

After leaving the office, we drive to a parking lot with several trailheads. One is an equestrian trail. When there are horse trails, I know it will be a great park! We start off on the Dike Hiking Trail around Hartman Lake. It is a gorgeous day, and it looks like a splendid spot.

Crossing a low-water bridge, we see a large and fantastic snake sunning itself. Surprised, it hurries off the shore and into the water weeds. As it peeks back out, we see it is a unique black snake with interesting but subtle markings. We keep a healthy but curious distance as we study it.

Along this trail is a loud chorus of bullfrogs, clamoring for territory and betrothal. There are scores of baby goslings with their needfully protective and hissing parents. Many of the babies are still yellow and downy, but some are gray, gangly teenagers. They are so tender and beautiful! I love the sound the mother and father make to collect their offspring when a human gets a little too close. They make a noise, not at all like their regular tones. It is a vibrant baritone honk, signaling their wee ones to come together and swim fast away.

At the western tip of Hartman Lake, we take a spur trail to connect with the Pope Lake Hiking Trail loop. It passes through a simply

Hartman Creek State Park

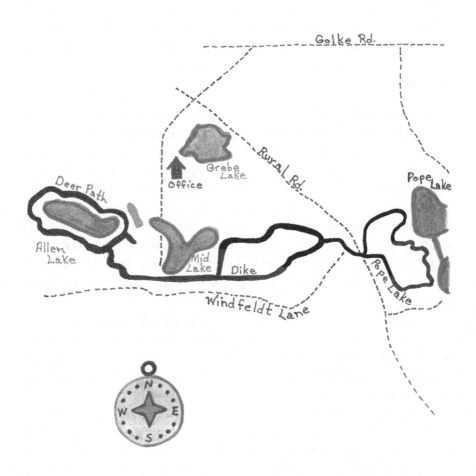

magnificent, wooded meadow. This part of our hike brings us to Pope and Marl Lakes, with Manomin and Knight Lakes off in the distance. This park has seven lakes, with an additional one marking the boundary of the northeast corner. One is even named for my favorite water bird, Grebe Lake. I am eternally grateful to the people who preserved this area for public use.

We notice dozens of people fishing around Hartman Lake as we complete the loop. I am pleasantly surprised so many cars are in the parking lots. I did not realize Hartman Creek is such a happening place with so many things to do! There is a place to rent kayaks and bikes, a swimming beach, and an abundance of camping sites. It is markedly unlike my recent hike at Buckhorn, where I was perhaps one of only three people in the entire approximately 7,000-acre park.

My Quest is bringing me to amazingly diverse landscapes in Wisconsin, places I would not have thought of necessarily because they are such a distance from my house. Usually, when going out for a day hike, I go to one of the state parks I love, like Devil's Lake or Governor Dodge, or hike on nearby segments of the Ice Age Trail. Doing this Quest has allowed me to see many different and awe-inspiring parks, and I am only on number nine! Another benefit of hiking as an older person is the experience of the novel and the new, which are good for our brains.

We hike from Hartman Lake to the family campground area to investigate the restored 1864 cabin, Hellestad House. Sadly, it isn't open, but we peek inside and marvel at the fully livable size of the place. Petra and I live in small ranch houses, and seeing this cabin, we simultaneously break into tirades about the enormous houses being built on the outskirts of Madison and the extreme overconsumption they signify. The whole downsizing as we age thing was certainly not an issue in the 1860s.

From the cabin, we start off on the Deer Path Trail around Allen Lake. Sections of this trail are being rebuilt by a crew of volunteers working to reroute it to ameliorate erosion. The trail is washed out in a few areas, with several downed trees. How great to see people working to fix it. We thank them wholeheartedly for their service and for helping to improve this state park.

Dark clouds have rolled in, and we get caught in the drizzle on the Deer Path Trail. The forest is musical, filled with the harmony of raindrops and birdsong. The gray, glassy surface of Allen Lake rippling with wind and rain is stunning.

All day, as we hike, Petra and I discuss the merits and drawbacks of small-scale campers. Both of us have toyed with the idea of getting a little pull-behind. We talk about videos we have seen, the various kinds, and the upsides and downs of owning one. Thinking of the van life has us remembering our younger days. Before we knew each other, we both had done a great deal of tent camping and backpacking, trips lasting for several days.

She announces, "I would not go backpack camping again unless I had a muscular, six-foot-tall man with me to carry all the stuff."

I chime in, "Oh yes! I want one too! Then, after he carried most everything and we set up the camp, I would provide him with sexual favors to make sure he felt all his hard work was worth it." We both laugh! Talking about fictional hot men helps us stay warm as the cool rain continues to fall.

Relationships are similar to building a fire. If you don't build it right, it doesn't last long. If you burn flash and papers—physical beauty and sexual attraction—it will ignite quickly, bright yellow and warm. Without the addition of enough kindling, like caring gestures and kind words, it ignites and dies. However, if you build it right with these things that flame, followed by those that burn red—honesty and feeling—and fuel that burns blue—grief and love, sadness and joy—your fire will continue. It will be a fire you can bank against the clock, against the cold. Because you've built it correctly, you'll have coals deep down under the ash to keep you warm forever with abiding genuineness of spirit and trust so you can start the fire again anytime you need it.

When we finish the Quest's required five miles, we stop back at the park office to use the bathroom before the long drive back home. The helpful woman is still there, joined by another ranger. Petra tells the new ranger about seeing the snake. He pulls out a great, old DNR brochure titled *Snakes of Wisconsin*. He is a decidedly handsome man talking to us about large snakes, so, of course, my mind goes there!

I giggle to myself, thinking about what Mae West would have said about our current situation. He shows us several different pictures of the ones he thinks it might be, and we are in no hurry to decide. Eventually, we all concur it is a gray rat snake. He kindly lets me keep the brochure, as a hard snake book is good to find.

Walking back to the car, we start laughing, and I muse, "I wouldn't mind having him take me backpack camping, followed by the sexual favors!" I always have appreciated a good-looking man. Even though I am turning 65, it is one thing that isn't going to change.

On the way to the car, Petra tells me about the audiobook she's been listening to, bringing me up to speed on the story. We enjoy it during our hour-and-a-half drive. It is a wonderful tale about a teenage girl, mother loss, women friends, and bees. It is a splendid way to finish our day together.

Hartman Creek State Park

The Questions

1. What about this chapter resonated with you?
2. Who do you have in your life with whom you can share major life changes and experiences?
3. How do you define your past and present sexual relationships?

The Particulars

Sticker Required: Yes

Map on the State Park's Website: Yes, and nicely detailed

Bathrooms for Day Hikers: Yes, but in the office

Office or Kiosk: Office which is frequently closed depending on the day or season

Trail Markings: Infrequently marked

Seasonal Closures: None

Flooding Concerns: Trails may be wet, but no flooding issues

Five Miles: Easy to get with no circles

Mill Bluff State Park
Camp Douglas

5.06 miles
Highest Point: 1,127 ft
Lowest Point: 910 ft

May 28, 2022
Empowerment and Orchids

One of the exceptionally great things about being older is the formal adoption of the "I don't give a fuck" mindset regarding appearance. I feel confident in who I am and how I look. Yes, I could someday be thinner or in better shape or have my makeup perfect, etc., but hell, I will also be older! There is no winning on this societal construct. It is better to be happy where you are and thankful to be living your best life, one denied to the many who die young.

As a result, today I am wearing my blue hair in pigtails with multicolored rubber bands and my REI Adventures bandana. I got this bandana when I went on a trip with my friend Diana. It was 10 days of hiking in Ireland: the Wicklow Way, the Beara Way, the Wild Atlantic Way, and the Cliffs of Moher. The tour included hiking trips to these and other areas for a total of 75 miles. It makes me smile to wear it as it reminds me of a wonderful trip with a cherished friend.

I arrive at Mill Bluff after the two-and-a-half-hour drive. It starts to drizzle, and I put on my trusty Marmot rain jacket. I take it with me everywhere I hike as it folds into its own pocket, making it easy to keep in my backpack. Today reminds me of a past cold Memorial Day weekend.

When I was in my early 20s, I worked in a Quonset hut selling bedding plants. Working a number of different jobs, trying to make ends meet, I was there only on Saturdays and Sundays. During that time in my life, I would go for several months without having a day I didn't work. With a high of 42 degrees, it was cold on the rain-soaked concrete under the thin plastic of the makeshift greenhouse set up outside a grocery store. The smells of the petunias and the geraniums seemed to be extraordinarily fragrant on those dreichy days. I remember suffering from horrible boredom as much as from the weather. On this Memorial Day weekend, I may not be enjoying the light shower, but I am definitely not bored!

Mill Bluff has no park office, only a box with trail maps in front of the façade of a cabin near the parking lot. Undaunted, I am happy to be on hike number 10 of my Quest. A somewhat dilapidated brick shelter is here as well. There is a hole in its chimney, and from it sprouts a heroic, white pine sapling. Life grows anywhere it can!

I start off on the Mill Bluff Trail, reaching the stairway up to the top. The stairs are wicked and a bit slippery with the rain. It brings to mind when I was hiking at Devil's Lake State Park, and it started storming. It was a treacherous experience, but I will save the details for when I hike there as part of this Quest. As I climb the stairway, I recall a sticker I bought for myself several years ago. It says, "I'd rather die on an adventure than live standing still." Better to die falling down the stairs at Mill Bluff than in my house, tripping over my cat and careening down the basement steps.

I forgot my audiobook before starting on this trail. It is strange not because I am missing the fiction but because all I hear are roaring

Mill Bluff State Park

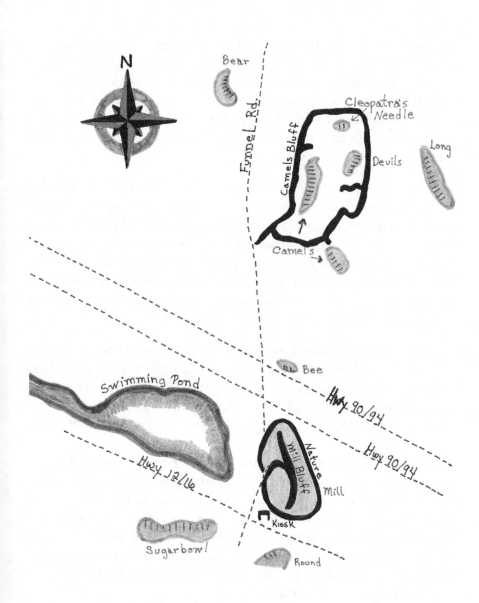

engines and Doppler effects instead of being serenaded by birdsong and the rustling of trees. There are major highways on both sides of this bluff. In fact, this state park is located between them, and I sense the sorrow of this forest as a result.

At the top of Mill Bluff, elevation 1,123 feet, is a surprising little trail, including a picturesque overlook. I reach it as the sun peaks out and the rain starts to ease. There is a sign here describing the bluffs of the surrounding terrain as "the islands of the great Glacial Lake Wisconsin." It is mind-boggling there was a vast inland sea here 10,000 years ago, a sea 72 miles long and over 150 feet deep! A fitting reward for what can best be described as a medieval flight of stairs is the breathtaking view of the sandstone islands rising high above the surrounding trees.

As an aside, I read some advice the other day, and sadly, it's what we need to do as women. Never say you're hiking alone to men you meet on the trail. Always say someone's right behind you, or you are catching up to someone if they ask. You won't appear as vulnerable. It makes me angry, though, to not just be safe hiking. Another thing that makes me irritated as an older hiker is I have to get to know all the moles and dark spots increasingly finding their way onto my aging skin so I don't misconstrue them as ticks!

On the way back down the gothic steps, an older couple walking up notices my fantastic LEKI hiking poles. I give them a brief sales pitch because the poles are superb. I must have sold many pairs of these with all the hikers I have spoken with about them. At the bottom of the stairs, I can finally hear the birdsongs as well as the traffic noise.

Because of where it is, this bluff must have been a holy and sacred place back before colonization. Its atmosphere is of foregone, green forest and Earth magic. The highway cutting around it makes it feel like most of the power has left. As I come around to the other side of the bluff on the Nature Trail, I can tell it hasn't. The magic is merely sleeping, merely waiting. Soon, the highways will be gone, it seems to say, as it rests quietly for thousands of years. The Earth's sense of time is fundamentally unlike our own.

After I finish circumnavigating Mill Bluff, I return to my car, driving under the highway to the other side of the park. There, I will be able to hike closer to several of the "islands": Wildcat, Camel, Bee, Devil, and Bear. They range in height from 60 to 170 feet. The start of Camels Bluff Trail is located at an unimproved parking area, only big enough for three cars.

It would be marvelous to come here in late March or early April before all the trees are leafed out. It is a time of year when the bluffs could possibly be viewed from the ground all the way to their peaks. Even now, though the greenery shields their countenance from full view, they still appear utterly magnificent.

Hiking on the Camels Bluff Trail, I take each short spur branching off and am rewarded with an incredible bluff each time. My favorite looks like a ruin from a bygone civilization. Its bestowed name is Cleopatra's Needle due to its obelisk shape. It reminds me of the ancient sandstone temples I saw in India built between 600 and 1000 BCE. They were the Khajuraho Temples in Madhya Pradesh. Only about 20 remain out of over 100 originals. All were left to ruin over the centuries after the invasion of the Mongols. The striking, erotic carvings on several of them were seen as deviant through the lens of the invaders' severe, patriarchal culture. No Goddesses and their sexual powers allowed! Not until they were rediscovered in the mid-1800s, underneath the encroaching jungle, did they become known again. All align with the sun, their doorways facing the dawn. They were cool inside, even though I visited them on a 90-plus-degree day. The interiors smelling of dank bat guano did not, in any way, take away from their beauty. The spires of the temples were formed by concentric circles and rotating squares, preternaturally like the shapes in this bluff.

I hike the Camels Bluff Trail two times, once clockwise and once counterclockwise. It is during the second time around I see a magnificent sight. Exactly where they should be, in an oak-pine forest—pink lady's slippers galore! I count 58 of them in bloom. It is unbelievable! I've never seen them in the wild before. I stand in admiration, a witness to the colony of bumblebees swarming around them. I try to think of an appropriate term for this incredible cluster of lady's slippers. An epiphany of orchids? A conflagration of orchids? An orgasm of orchids! I like the last one the best as it seems the most fitting. They are, after all, named after a scrotum, "orchid" in Greek, translating to "testicle."

Hiking it in both directions, I see a myriad of different things, including more pink lady's slippers and two lilac bushes. There must have been a house many years ago for lilacs to be here. Purple lupines are blooming along with orange columbine and wild strawberries. The strange purple flowers I can't seem to identify, the ones I saw at Buckhorn State Park, are growing here, too.

I make it to 4.5 miles with my two loops around Camels Bluff Trail. I drive back to Mill Bluff Trail to get the last half mile, taking in the swimming pond and beach this time. Like every park I have visited so far, I am smitten by the uniqueness and beauty I never knew I would find, especially in a park located between two busy highways. It is by the spending of time, by having a minimum mileage at each park, I am afforded wondrous things!

Mill Bluff State Park

The Questions

1. What about this chapter resonated with you?
2. How has your need to be overly concerned with your appearance changed as you've gotten older?
3. What surprises have you experienced while out in nature?

The Particulars

Sticker Required: Yes

Map on the State Park's Website: Yes, but minimally detailed

Bathrooms for Day Hikers: Yes, but in frequently locked building

Office or Kiosk: Façade of an office with trail maps available

Trail Markings: Not well-marked

Seasonal Closures: None

Flooding Concerns: None

Five Miles: Circles required

Belmont Mound State Park
Belmont

5.16 miles
Highest Point: 1,349 ft
Lowest Point: 1,081 ft

June 1, 2022
Invisibility and Divorce

This past weekend, I went to several rummage sales looking for interesting things to use in my art. At one of the sales, I found a glass juicer circa 1940. I went to purchase it and started a conversation with the women of the house about how happy I was to locate one. I learned the two white-haired women were a mother and daughter— the daughter in her seventies and the mother in her nineties. They both commented on how they loved my blue hair. I told them one of the truly positive things about having brightly colored hair as an older woman is it makes me less invisible. "You know what I'm talking about," I said. "How after 60, it is like no one sees us anymore?" They both nodded knowingly in agreement.

The daughter pointed out, "Sometimes it can be a good thing. People don't bother you, and you can eavesdrop a great deal easier." We laughed in our shared experience. I told them about the hair dye I use after the daughter said she had been wanting to have her hair bubblegum pink. It makes me happy to feel I've inspired another older woman to break free of the mold and live her best colorful life.

I know it might sound funny to people who aren't in their 60s, but there really is an invisibility that happens when we age. Now, turning 65, I'm totally done with moving out of the way of people who pretend they don't see me, their perception marred by their value judgment of my appearance. I have as much right as they do to walk where I'm walking.

Case in point: I was moving through a big box home improvement store yesterday. I was on the right-hand side of the wide main aisle, proceeding toward the exit, carrying three six-foot cedar boards the long way on my right shoulder. Several men walked directly toward me. When I didn't step aside, the ends of the boards almost hit them! They were all waiting for me to give over my space. It wasn't until those boards were within 10 inches of their faces that it dawned on them they needed to get out of my path. The fact this happened with at least five different men as I walked the length of the store was comical. When I told my 85-year-old friend about this, she proclaimed, "As we age, we have to be fierce. We have to stand loud and proud for ourselves, for the bus driver to lower the stairway, and for young folks to move out of our way. You will be discounted, and to counteract it, be ferocious!"

I refuse to step out of the way for men who are younger than me. I have not for years now. I have found if I look away, pretending I don't see them, they will move to the side. If I make eye contact, they expect me as a woman, especially as an older one, to give deference and concede my space. Sometimes, their expectations are overwhelming to the point they smack full force into me. Again, I am walking on the right side of the walkway, and there is plenty of room for them to pass if they simply step slightly to my left. As an almost 65-year-old, I am getting even less patient with this crap. So, get out of my ferocious fucking way, especially when I am carrying lumber!

Belmont Mound State Park

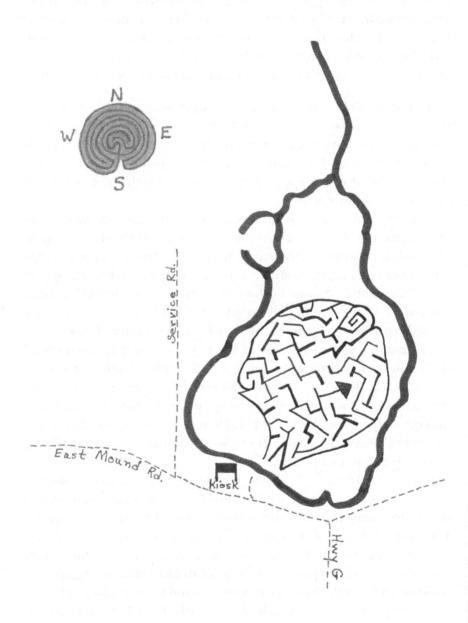

Alright, I am done ranting—back to hiking. Belmont Mound is another sandstone "island" from the ancient inland ocean, its dolomite cap keeping it from weathering away. The land around here reminds me a bit of when I hiked in the Yorkshire Dales in England, with beautiful rolling hills undulating out to the horizon line. Instead of being covered with heather and bracken, these are covered with burgeoning corn and occasional tree lines.

There is no park office, merely a kiosk with a posted winter hunting/trapping map. No one has been caring for this place for many months. I'm glad I brought my own map, downloaded off the DNR's website. Run by the local Belmont Lion's Club, it has the quality of a county park and is way outside my Quest parameters! I didn't catch it while I was researching, but since I am here, I will endeavor to persevere.

Having this Quest allows me to look forward instead of looking back. Dwelling in the past is never beneficial. No matter how peculiar and arbitrary the boundaries, having a Quest is a genuinely good thing to keep us turning toward the future. This is especially significant today.

Even when you're divorced, as much as you try not to, the day you got married still means something. I'm not sure what exactly, but it does. No one remembers it as your anniversary. No one celebrates it anymore. It's a date remembered, which signifies nothing to anyone else but you. For me, it means on this day, I will do whatever I feel like, whatever I want to do for me, only me, and that's it. Therefore, I slept late this morning and treated myself to a cherry Danish for breakfast. I will sing and dance in my garden when I get home from this hike. I will dream of what I will do in the days ahead, without the presence of that person, on this day that no one else remembers.

This park's trails aren't marked at all, aren't named, and don't match the map. The only sign is at the entrance to the forest, off to the right of the Lion's Club shelter building. On my map, the three trails are loops: one high, one low, and one out to a woods. There is supposedly a fire tower here, but it is not marked on the map. The park website says it is closed due to several recent suicides, lending a pall over this place. I do find the arches of the abandoned limestone quarry, but only by chance.

Following a section of the trail brings me around the bottom of a sheer rock face next to a low spot, which may be an ephemeral creek. Again, no signage here and not on the map. It is beautiful, nonetheless, and lovely shadows are cast upon it from the surrounding tree canopy. I continue along the ill-maintained trail until it comes to a junction also not on the map. I take the right-hand fork and end up on a far-off service road. I retrace my steps and try the left fork instead. This trail crosses a different creek, and my geographically challenged brain is righteously grateful that today is a bright blue sky, a verdant green day, as I have no idea where I will end up.

The trails in this park are labyrinthian! There's no rhyme or reason. Were they put in place by the Byzantines? They don't match my exceedingly basic map or the posted one of the hunting and trapping areas. They are completely all over the place! Everything looks similar. It would be easy to get remarkably turned around and lost in here. I am glad I have my GPS tracker to help me figure out where I am. I am especially pleased I have the little compass my friend gave me. Belmont Mound is a convoluted, curling cul-de-sac of trails going everywhere at once.

Needing to obtain my five miles, I hike on and mindfully seek a lesson in all this craziness. I don't know where the trails are going to go. They might make a loop, or they might disappear, forcing me to turn around and go back. I might see something exceedingly wonderful, letting me know I'm heading in the right direction. This is analogous to the whole process of growing old, which is quite honestly a maze needing to be navigated. It is good to have tools to help us find our way through and good to have friends to rely on.

Belmont Mound State Park

The Questions

1. What about this chapter resonated with you?
2. What has been your experience with the "invisibility" that comes with growing older?
3. What special dates—good or bad—are significant to you?

The Particulars

Sticker Required: No

Map on the State Park's Website: Yes, but it does not coincide with the trails

Bathrooms for Day Hikers: Yes, but in a frequently locked building

Office or Kiosk: Kiosk with minimal upkeep

Trail Markings: Not marked at all

Seasonal Closures: None

Flooding Concerns: None

Five Miles: Circles required

Rocky Arbor State Park
Wisconsin Dells

5.27 miles
Highest Point: 984 ft
Lowest Point: 847 ft

June 2, 2022
Elders and Objects

When I got home from the bookstore last night, I decided to work on my art. I went to the basement to bring up some supplies but got distracted by a box I had set aside during some recent purging. I knew it would contain emotional power, and I had decided to wait to go through it. The objects inside were from my mom.

In it, I found her signature scent, Opium by Yves Saint Laurent; several super cool steampunk buttons; a fabulous, cultured pearl necklace; a handful of single earrings; two broken watches; a wolf's tooth; and more. I took out a pin of a mother and baby owl, leaving the rest to find again in the future. My mother's name meant "blackbird." She definitely passed on to me her magpie tendencies to collect quirky, eclectic ephemera.

I woke this morning to perfect weather, making it impossible for me to refuse to do two parks in two days. I review my checklist, text my hiking safety buddy, and head out to Rocky Arbor. The main gate is closed until the end of May, making today a timely choice to take on this park.

Like Belmont Mound yesterday, Rocky Arbor does not have five miles of hiking trails. At the smaller parks, I hike the trails forward and backward and, occasionally, forward again. It's fine with me because it is all part of my Quest. It will be easy to reach my mileage at Kinnickinnic and Willow River, the state parks I am doing next week. For the ones like today, I need only to enjoy being outside and doing what I love.

The park office is open and staffed by a wonderful older woman. She tells me about the park, and I tell her about my Quest. She suggests hiking the mile loop around the campgrounds would help, as the main trail is only about 1.5 miles long.

The map available in the office is an unusual one, four-by-five inches in size. This unassuming map is the front page of a quarter-inch-thick advertising brochure for places in Wisconsin Dells. I wonder why the state is using ad dollars to pay for Rocky Arbor's maps. I haven't seen anything like it. No maps? Sure. Small maps? Yes, but nothing this blatantly commercial.

When I park my car and step out, I am taken aback by the captivating smell of fragrant white pines. It is a beautiful, welcoming smell—pungent and life-affirming. The sky is unencumbered by clouds, and I am surrounded by striking shades of green, sunlit and inviting.

I start off on the only trail, going clockwise. It doesn't have a name. I am mildly annoyed about state park trails not having names. With all the descriptive words in English, in Menominee, and in Ho-Chunk, surely one could be found to describe this trail. This is but a 244-acre park with a short hike, but in the first quarter mile, I step over three trees across the trail. With the tourist season coming up

Rocky Arbor State Park

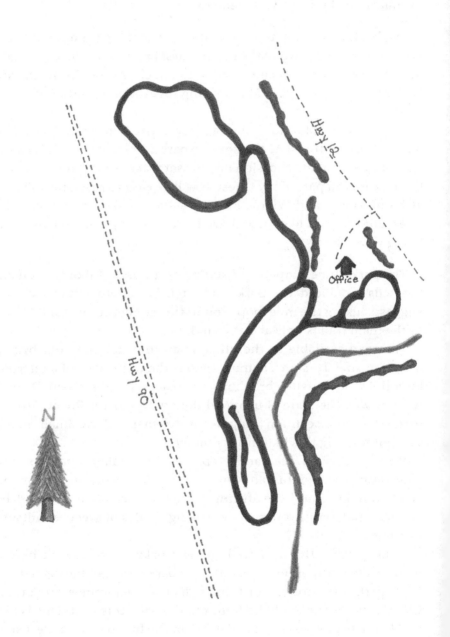

at the Dells, this seems odd. Perhaps a large storm went through recently, or the funds aren't there to maintain it when the main gate is closed.

By the time I finish my first hike loop of the day, I count nine trees down over the path. Some completely block it, requiring a big walk around through groves of poison ivy. I am happy I have my high boots on! I make a counterclockwise loop and am pleased to encounter a kindly ranger with a chainsaw working to remove a precarious tree, broken and hanging over the trail. I thank him for his service, and he remarks he has his work cut out for him to get this trail cleaned up, laughing at his play on words as he roars his chainsaw back to life.

No matter the obstacles, this is truly a dazzling little park! The sandstone ledges are abundant with unique microclimates, full of ferns of all sizes and multitudes of spring wildflowers. I find six pink lady's slippers on my counterclockwise circuit I had missed the first time around. In one area, the trail hugs a creek, alive with green frogs and (yes, they are back!) mosquitoes. In the center of the stream is an immense, balanced rock outcropping. Baby trees fight for purchase on its flat summit. I return to clockwise and hike around again, planning to take the stairs to the campground this time.

Being at Rocky Arbor reminds me of a place from my past. I lived on the outskirts of a small town, Rocky Comfort, Missouri. Out in the middle of nowhere, in the farthest southwest corner of the state, it was where I lived when my child was born. An uncommon and interesting place, there was a pond brimming full of colossal bullfrogs on my property. When I caught them to hold, they filled up the palms of both my hands. I frequently visited it at night to take in the deep baritone symphony. I would shine my flashlight along the edges of the water. It was as if stars had fallen to the earth, their countless amphibian eyes reflecting my light back to me.

I had purchased a 1920s farmhouse with two barns and 80 acres from a great aunt and uncle. They became my fast and loving friends, expanding my acquaintance within their circle of life-long buddies. It was a peculiar time in my life when most of my close friends were over eighty! I remember sitting back and trying to absorb their wisdom and life stories, all the ups and downs of living through the Great Depression and World War II. I would unwind with them over games of dominoes, hot decaf, and freshly popped corn after my intense days working at the nearby community mental health center. We would discuss all the innovations they had seen in their lifetimes: motor cars, store-bought white bread, votes for women, and rockets to the moon. They lived through remarkably changing times. Never changing, though, are the needs of people. Our desires for love, connection, purpose, beauty, and an understanding of loss stay the same. These are, and will always be, our link through time immemorial with other human beings.

The clients I worked with at the mental health center and the experiences I had with them have stayed with me my entire life. One of the most memorable events occurred when I let the ones who came to the day treatment center know I was pregnant. I had an inkling it would be traumatic for some of them to hear such news, but I was not prepared for the uncommon responses that came about as a result. One woman had a panic attack, screaming that it would be like the movie *Alien*, where it burst out of my chest. Another loomed over me in a markedly threatening manner, warning me to "Never hurt that baby!" before she collapsed on the floor in a fetal position. The most incredible and mysterious response came from a young man named Jeremy. He suffered from schizophrenia and spent his days self-isolating in a corner of the open treatment room, facing the wall, rocking back and forth, and softly mumbling to himself.

His view of the world was decidedly unlike anyone I've ever met. In the day program, we always had a huge 1,000-piece puzzle going. We would sit and talk and work on it as a group. Occasionally, he would come out of his corner, look at the design, grab a random piece, and put it exactly where it needed to be. He would then scamper back to where he had been, giggling with glee. Jeremy was a puzzle wizard!

On the pregnancy announcement day, he turned from the corner and walked right up to me. He announced the sex of my child and the date they would be born. It was so bizarre, I decided to write it down on a sticky note and put it in my desk. My child was not born on the due date my doctor predicted, but twelve days prior on the date that Jeremy had. Having decided to let the sex of my baby be a surprise, I was astounded to have his knowledge of that be true as well. I put the yellow sticky note in my baby book, and on my child's birthday, I always remember him fondly and with wonder, knowing some of us see things no one else does.

I reach the stairs up to the campground and head in the direction the ranger had suggested. It looks to be a nice place if you don't mind the traffic noise. The wander through the area and back to the trail added sufficient distance to my hike. As I retrace to my car, I find another orgasm of orchids; 17 pink lady's slippers are blooming this time. I have come to believe finding orchids invariably makes it a phenomenal day! Rocky Arbor is infinitely more pleasant than wandering around in the bewilderment of Belmont Mound yesterday.

This evening, having had a grand forest bath, I have the emotional energy to revisit the box from yesterday evening. It is, after all, part of my Life Review and part of accepting I am an orphan. It contains a thick envelope, inside which are nearly 60 cards I sent my mom over the years. Reading them takes a couple of hours—all the thoughts I had sent her, all my loving words. The cards are heavy with memories. I decide to bring them outside under the light of a waxing crescent moon and burn them. I include in the fire dried lavender and sage from my herb garden, sending the smoke to the heavens, remembering her with love and sorrow.

Rocky Arbor State Park

The Questions

1. What about this chapter resonated with you?
2. What experiences have you had with those older than yourself?
3. From what sources do you gain emotional energy to do the work of addressing difficult memories?

The Particulars

Sticker Required: Yes

Map on the State Park's Website: Yes, but minimally detailed

Bathrooms for Day Hikers: Yes, in a separate building

Office or Kiosk: Office which is frequently closed depending on the day or season

Trail Markings: Infrequently marked

Seasonal Closures: The main gate is closed Labor Day through June 1

Flooding Concerns: The trail along the creek may be flooded in parts during wet times of the year

Five Miles: Circles required

Kinnickinnic State Park
River Falls

5.11 miles
Highest Point: 903 ft
Lowest Point: 813 ft

June 7, 2022
Responsibility and Mosquitoes

This is my first time doing an overnight as part of my Quest. I arranged for a hotel room in Hudson, and plan to hike this park today and Willow River tomorrow. The distance is too far to drive twice. My friend Petra is accompanying me once again.

I was in a quandary last night, thinking about how hard it is to be accountable to another person after only having to take care of myself for the last several years. I spent the vast majority of my life being accountable to siblings, boyfriends, neighbors, friends, my ex, and my child. I am sincerely happy I have a friend coming with me, but I forgot how much can be involved in coordinating times and logistics. It used to be commonplace for me to finish work, drive across the city during crazy rush-hour traffic every week, sometimes every day, doing something for someone else. It has taken me quite some time to become comfortable with not being responsible for anyone. It is something I never imagined experiencing. I suppose it is yet another of the double-edged swords of being older and being alone.

The sense of only having personal accountability is one of the reasons why I like hiking. I can get up in the morning, early or late. I can mess around, entertain distractions, maybe have an extra cup of coffee. I can head out of the house, and it doesn't matter because I'm only responsible for getting myself out there to enjoy the day. To sum it up, though I absolutely love having my friends go on hikes with me, it does force me to do something I am not as used to anymore.

When we arrive, I step out of the car to get my Quest required entry sign photo. The air is redolent with fragrance. Black locust, blackhaw viburnum, and fields of phlox are heavy with pollen, creating remarkable and wonderful smells!

I am disappointed the park office is closed. I want to know how to pronounce the name of this place correctly. I wonder what it means and from which Native American language it originates. There is a nice brochure/map in a slot outside the office, but my questions remain unanswered after reading it.

We park by the trailhead for the Blue and the Pink Trails and bring out our haul of goodies for lunch. Petra knows how to put on a good picnic! She tells me she learned it from her mom and all the travels they would go on as a family when she was growing up. I am envious, as that did not happen for me as a kid. My father was tied to his cheese factory and the perishable nature of the work, and my mother didn't drive until I was a pre-teen.

As we begin our trek into the dark forest on the Blue Trail, we immediately encounter mosquitoes in intensely horrible amounts. Mosquitoes don't usually bother me much, especially when I am with Petra. She is a mosquito magnet. I tease her and say she is on my zombie apocalypse team for that very reason. Today is a whole new world of mosquito hellscape! We apply my heavy-duty DEET

Kinnickinnic State Park

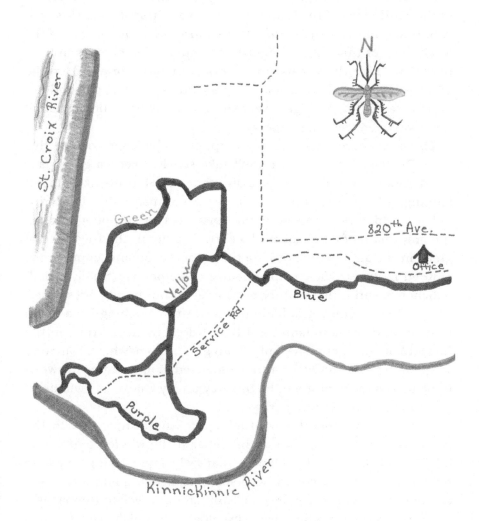

every 15 minutes, and still, we have a personal, bloodthirsty horde buzzing around us the entire time.

There are a few brief respites. We hike from the Blue Trail to the Yellow Trail to the Purple Trail, ending up at the incredible overlook of the confluence of the Kinnickinnic and St. Croix Rivers. This spot is breezy, and the sadistic insects are blown away as we take in the lovely view of the rivers' delightful meanders. The open prairie we find as we hike the Green Trail offers a further reprieve from the barrage of the family Culicidae. In these areas, though, emerald ash borers are glinting in flight everywhere, and my heart breaks for all the devastated trees in the park.

The mosquitoes make it an exceptional challenge to hike this park. Don't get me wrong. I don't hike slowly. I keep a good pace for the most part, but I love taking time for Shinrin-yoku—forest bathing. It helps keep me in the present and maintain calm in this hectic world. I try to engage all my senses as I go, stopping to touch the gray shards of a shagbark hickory, reveling in the fragrance of green in the air. Phytoncides are the aromatic, organic compounds emitted by trees. Their resplendent green smell is actually mood-enhancing, anti-inflammatory, and increases our immune response! When I hike, I enjoy indulging my curiosity, searching for a bird I hear or studying a mushroom I find. I don't want my time in the forest to be transactional—only about getting somewhere. I am fond of spending my time with nature, immersed in it, standing in awe of it. I am even more prone to be this way on my Quest, as I will likely never hike many of these parks again.

As such, it is relentlessly grueling at Kinnickinnic due to the dreadful mosquitoes. I end up hiking as if the whole point of the hike is to be done. I hate it! In fact, that's why I quit hiking for a long time. I was with someone whose sole purpose of going was to get to the end. I have always been a "stop and appreciate the beauty" hiker, not someone whose exclusive goal is to finish. This became unbearable when including our child because children don't walk fast. He would be miles away from us on the trail, petulant and terse. To avoid that situation, I began hiking intermittently with only my child. Eventually, I found myself alone, with no one to be upset with me because I wanted to hike in a way that allowed for the appreciation of beauty. Sometimes, it takes many years to reclaim your own heart. Suffice it to say, this isn't an enjoyable place for me today on many levels. Mosquitoes and memories of emotional trauma are not quality companions.

I realize I must include some positive points about this park. It has the best-marked trails I have seen, to this point, on my Quest. Every junction has a "You Are Here" sign. All the trails are labeled with fence posts, the tops painted in the colors of their names. Our hike varies in intensity from easy to moderate. Petra says the trails, at times, mirror the yellow brick road weaving through the mysterious and foreboding forest in *The Wizard of Oz*. It is, all in all, a beautiful park with almost no human noise. I heard a plane go over once and a couple of gunshots off in the distance, but nothing else. There is no other sound save for birdsong and ceaseless mosquito droning. We accomplish the five miles and breathe sighs of relief as we jump into my car, finally safe from the predatory multitude. This would be a pleasant park to hike in early spring or after a hard autumn freeze to escape this bloodlust.

After the hike, we drive into Hudson to find our hotel. It is a picturesque river town seemingly exploding with wealth. As we enter the city, we see two brand-new schools and subdivisions of mega houses. We take time to change and regroup before venturing to the historic downtown. On the way, we ask several locals how to pronounce Kinnickinnic and get varying responses. I decide the frequent use of "Kinni" is the best. Safer to say it fast as you run away from the park's mosquitoes!

The St. Croix Riverfront is gorgeous and has a trendy vibe. I see an old mansion for sale close to the river and dream of buying it, fixing it up, and making it into a destination blues club; a place similar to one I visited in the Gothic Quarter in Barcelona. The building here is possibly three stories and has columns across the front. I predict it would have great acoustics.

We end up in Lakefront Park, where we had arranged to meet Petra's son. He goes to college in Saint Paul, Minnesota, and with Hudson so close, it was a welcome chance for her to spend some time with him. We eat dinner by the river and walk the Hudson Dike out to the Pier Beach and back. Many others are strolling, enjoying the warm evening and the casual flow of the river. It is stunning and tranquil, with abundant shades of blue and green and gray shimmering in the setting sun. Sailboats bob and reflect on the smooth surface of the water. As we walk, our conversations range from Harry Styles to the history of concrete, all the while listening to a bagpiper incongruent on the shore. The whole riverfront scene is buzzing even on a random Tuesday night. I can see myself coming back to Hudson as a tourist, and I smile, imagining moving here to start a music venue.

Even though I complain about being accountable and responsible on occasion, I am happy and thankful to have people in my life for whom I can be.

Note: When I got home, I learned how to pronounce "KIN-nick-in-nick." It is an Algonquian word meaning "that which is mixed" and refers to combining dried willow bark, tobacco, and other plants to smoke. This mixture was used for spiritual ceremonies and prayers.

Kinnickinnic State Park

The Questions

1. What about this chapter resonated with you?
2. Who do you feel accountable to in your life? How has that changed as you've aged?
3. What are your experiences with "forest bathing"? How can you incorporate them into your routine if you haven't had any?

The Particulars

Sticker Required: Yes

Map on the State Park's Website: Yes, and nicely detailed in color

Bathrooms for Day Hikers: Yes, in a separate building

Office or Kiosk: Office which is frequently closed depending on the day or season

Trail Markings: Extremely well-marked and color-coded

Seasonal Closures: None

Flooding Concerns: None

Five Miles: Easy to get with no circles

Willow River State Park
Hudson

5.39 miles
Highest Point: 922 ft
Lowest Point: 740 ft

June 8, 2022
Campers and Friendship

I woke up early this morning with a charley horse in the front of my leg. I've had them occasionally over the years but never in my thigh muscles. As Bette Davis famously said, "Old age is not for sissies." It definitely was painful enough to wake me up and keep me awake for a while. For the most part, I slept fairly well at the Holiday Inn Express in Hudson. My friend Petra and I have a nice, reasonably priced room with two queen beds. It was easy to access the riverfront on our way to and fro last night, and we get a free breakfast. After checking out this morning, we stop at a nearby Caribou Coffee for more hiking fuel before we hit the highway up to Willow River.

I take my obligatory selfie in front of the grandest and most impressive sign of any park I have seen so far. It is a monumental entry shot for this one! The park office is open. With a sign that commanding, how could it not be? There is a wealth of information in this office. There are many wonderful brochures about the park, from the birds and wildflowers found within, to the natural and geological history, to the mechanizations of the Little Falls Dam. There are several others as well about bears, raccoons, and snakes. Their map is a mate to the entry sign—27-by-20 inches on sturdy paper with detailed descriptions of all the trails.

The ranger working at the office today is a handsome young man. Petra mentions to him how we had hiked through a mosquito warzone yesterday. He relates it is known—"Kinni" is incredibly buggy. He reassures us they are not nearly as dreadful at Willow River. Petra says she is highly skeptical and will hold him personally responsible if they are. She smiles when she says it, and we all laugh. We begin our hike and discover he is absolutely honest and true as we encounter only a few mosquitoes.

The experience here, compared to yesterday at Kinnickinnic, is like being on a different planet with the bugs. There is a nice breeze throughout this outstanding park. We wander over to see the Little Falls Dam and find a two-foot diameter, slow-moving, snapping turtle. They are indeed prehistoric marvels! The dam is an engineering feat, recently rebuilt to, once again, create the Little Falls Lake of the Willow River. I am surprised to learn it wasn't designed to be energy-producing as vast quantities of water are moving through it. Perhaps it could have supplied the park with electricity, but it is only there to create recreation.

We are here on a random Wednesday morning at the beginning of June, and it is already busy. I can envision in the height of summer, on any given weekend, it can become a highly crowded place, what with the swimming beach, the picnic areas, the campgrounds, and the numerous trails.

To get my five miles, we start off heading east on the Little Falls Trail, marked in green on the impressive map. It follows the shore of Little Falls Lake and is well-marked and well-maintained with "You Are Here" signs along the way. As we hike, we see several trumpeter

Willow River State Park

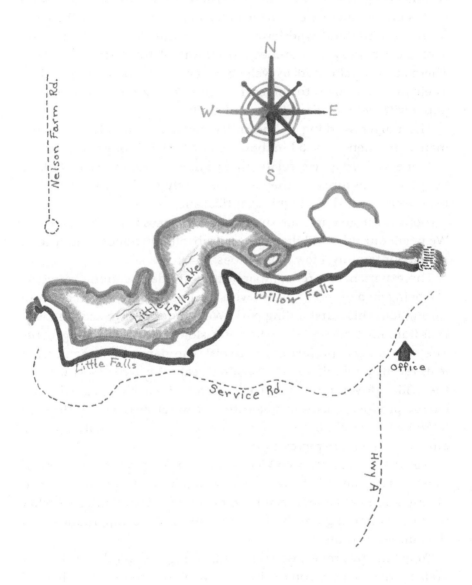

swans, great blue herons, and bald eagles. They obviously love this place as much as I do!

To reach the connection to the Willow Falls Trail, we circumnavigate the 300 Campground. It looks decidedly posh. The bathrooms available to this camping area are in clean, modern buildings, not the simple, rustic brown ones of many other parks. This is a wealthy park, especially compared to some I've been to on my Quest, possessing only rough kiosks like at Natural Bridge or Mill Bluff. No wonder Willow River is in the top 10 on most lists of the best Wisconsin State Parks.

Finding the Willow Falls Trail, we continue to follow the lake's edge leading to the falls. Along this trail, we spy numerous deer with their accompanying fawns. As we hike silently together to avoid disturbing them, a man comes up quickly behind us. Petra chastises him for not announcing himself, as he is acting too similar to a bear. She used to do considerable backpacking out West and has a history of bear surprises. Rather than apologizing, the man tells us about seeing a large black bear ambling along the road to one of the campgrounds. Willow River is definitely in bear country, and this man was definitely a rude hiker. No one should come up silently behind anyone on a trail. Men must do better and not allow their male privilege to cloud their understanding of how frightening this can be for women, especially if we are hiking alone.

This trail brings us right to the front of the falls of the Willow River, and it is absolutely stunning! It is a series of low cascades cutting a deep gorge through the surrounding cliffs. We sit, absorbing the wonderful sounds of it rumbling and crashing and burbling over the remaining stone ledges. There is a selfie station at the falls. I sincerely appreciate how Travel Wisconsin has installed these at many state parks. We naturally take advantage of it for a photo. There is access to the water on both sides, created by a small bridge crossing the lower reaches of the deluge. The bridge is the beginning of the Burkhardt Trail, which follows the bluffs up into the area above the falls. The rockface below this trail is dotted with climbers seeking to conquer.

Off to the right, after we cross the bridge, we find 244 stairs which take us to a sensational overlook of the falls and the surrounding countryside. I reach the top, thinking about how grateful I am to be able to do it. I'm walking up this incredibly steep flight to see a breathtakingly beautiful view. I feel outstandingly lucky. It is a supreme pleasure to be up here above the roaring water. Yet another thing about turning 65, which I think is incredible, is that I get to turn sixty-five. It is a milestone birthday denied to countless people. I take a moment to embrace the gratitude I feel, knowing this is good for my heart and for my soul.

Though my heart is beating fast after the stairway, it is filled with joy, once again, because I have chosen to do this Quest! We descend the stairs and trek back the way we came, on the Willow Falls and Little Falls Dam Trails, to the car. It is simply a perfect day for hiking, and we could've done a good seven or eight miles more. We didn't begin to experience the hiking available here. I would've liked to have done the Pioneer Trail going by the burial site of the Burkhardts, the people who homesteaded what is now this parkland. Even so, the six-plus-hour drive home is the deciding factor, making it best to stay with the five. I will come back here. It's gorgeous! There are an abundance of things to see and do: more hiking, posh camping, and renting boats and bikes.

On the drive back to Madison, we listen to an audiobook. It is the story of the lives of two women across time. One provides medicines for all the things women might need in the 1600s. The other is a mudlarker in London, similar to my desert larker days in Carrizozo, New Mexico. Also, as usual, Petra and I discuss campers and the van life. While we were hiking today through the aforementioned fantastic campground, we saw a tiny Airstream, which seemed spectacular. It causes us to muse as we often do, how extraordinary it would be to have a little pull-behind as a single woman and carefreely hit the road.

Petra tells me she read about a woman who did just that. She would caravan with other single women who had campers of their own. They all went to the same places together, even though they didn't necessarily hang out with each other all the time. What a wonderful group to be part of as an older woman. It touches on another benefit of hiking. It builds community, provides social support, and helps us to create new friendships—all things we need as we age. I don't know if I ever will do the van life, but it's interesting to consider as I drive us back to our little ranch houses. It is splendid to dream of the future again, rolling out endlessly like it did when I was young.

Willow River State Park

The Questions

1. What about this chapter resonated with you?
2. What do you feel lucky to have in your life?
3. What deaths have you experienced that changed your perception of aging?

The Particulars

Sticker Required: Yes

Map on the State Park's Website: Yes, and it is detailed in color

Bathrooms for Day Hikers: Yes, in the office and along the trails

Office or Kiosk: Large, nice office with displays; rarely closed

Trail Markings: Outstanding signage with frequent "You Are Here" maps posted

Seasonal Closures: None

Flooding Concerns: Perhaps in very heavy downpours

Five Miles: Easy to get with no circles

Harrington Beach State Park
Belgium

5.01 miles
Highest Point: 829 ft
Lowest Point: 656 ft

June 14, 2022
Reclaiming and Tornadoes

My neighborhood was torn up by a vortex yesterday. Numerous trees were uprooted and twisted off at the tops. Today, there is a carnage of timber everywhere. The oldest trees in my four-block radius, the burr oaks, are not damaged at all. What a fine example of successful aging! This is the second time my neighborhood has been hit with swirling winds.

The last time was in 2004 when there was a Category One tornado. As a storm, it created even more widespread tree injuries and extensive damage to houses and cars. After all that, I thought our neighborhood was pre-disastered! I thought we would avoid another severe windstorm, but that is not how chaos functions. No human rules, no human constructs can contain or understand its power. Of course, there is Chaos Theory, which seeks to find patterns and connections in the randomness of things. The theory reminds us uncertainty is one of the few constants we can rely on. Something important to remember in the aging process is change comes, for better or worse, and our limited lifetimes narrow our ability to understand the complexity of arbitrary events. Change is often painful, but it keeps us growing and lets us know we are still living in this divine and miraculous world. The older we become, the more important it is to realize change cannot be controlled but we can participate in it. We can decide to embrace rather than fight it. We can choose to be flexible instead of rigid. Change affects us, often like the idiom: "When it rains, it pours," but if we are able to work with it, we can upgrade our skill set and improve our experience as the years roll on.

As a result of this current vortex dilemma, my electricity is out. I am going to Harrington Beach because it is a heat advisory day, with Madison reaching over 97 degrees. I love hot summer days but hiking in a cool spot is in order as I am sans air conditioning at my house.

I am a little discombobulated without my electricity and no coffee this morning. About an hour into my drive to the park, I realize I forgot my map. I need to have a photograph of the parks' maps on my phone in case this happens again in the future.

Upon arriving at the park, I stop to take my entry selfie and am embraced by the refreshing breeze blowing inland from Lake Michigan. Yes, this was a good idea. The park office is open, and they have a brochure/map. I am saved! It even has trail descriptions on it, which is rare and welcome. There are friendly rangers to help me get the best out of my hike today. This office is bursting with merch: Harrington Beach sweatshirts, patches, hats, stickers, pins, and more.

I park by Puckett's Pond Picnic Area and smile about how much cooler it is here than it is back at my house. I chose a great day to come here to hike! There's a funky little observatory by Puckett's Pond run by the Northern Cross Science Foundation, offering public

Harrington Beach State Park

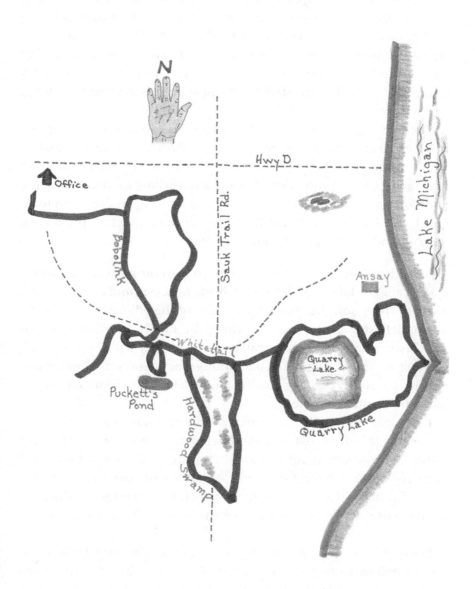

viewing nights throughout the year. The Bobolink Loop is accessible from this parking lot. It takes me through an open meadow bursting with prairie plants.

After hiking this loop, I move on to the Whitetail Trail, which also starts at this parking area. I follow it west toward Quarry Lake. As I hike, I think about everything I'm trying to reclaim during this Quest. Reclaiming how much enjoyment I experience from driving someplace to go hiking has been amazing! I love the freedom of a long drive on a flowing stretch of highway surrounded by rolling, green Wisconsin hills.

There is a great deal of reclaiming to be done—reclaiming my freedom from negativity, workplace bullying, and psychological abuse. I had a job I loved, but it was in a toxic environment. I had a husband I loved who created one. I am working on reclaiming my emotional well-being, reclaiming my desire to stay healthy, and to be able to hike forever and ever. Reclaiming is an important process to help us find integrity at this stage of life.

I exit the Whitetail Trail at its junction with the loop of the Quarry Lake Trail. The lake is preternaturally round, clear, and clean. There's a wonderfully soft, holy cedar grove along the edge of Quarry Lake on the left side of the trail. On the right side is a strikingly green and lush primordial extravaganza of ferns and wildflowers as an understory to the abundant deciduous trees. Numerous waterfalls flow into it, fed by delicate streams. It is a lake out of a fantasy movie, a lake in an elfish kingdom.

I continue to the North Lakeview Trail as I want to get closer to the majestic inland sea of Lake Michigan. The colors of the vast waters are ever-changing and awe-inspiring—greens and blues and browns—dark, rich, and beautiful. What a truly precious gift of a day. A day like today is like the birth of a child. You forget all the pain of the winter when you experience the beauty of such a summer's day.

Sadly, it is alewife die-off season. There are thousands dead on the shoreline among the rocks. In places where the waves have more access, the dead are cycled back out. The situation does lend a distinctive odor to the entire place. Therefore, I leave the beach and return to the Quarry Lake Trail. On the way to the picnic area and the kiosk by the Ansay Welcome Center, I pass by the ruins of the quarry workers' houses and stores. The kiosk tells the story of immigrants from Luxembourg, the Austro-Hungarian Empire, and Italy who came here to labor in the limestone quarry which operated from the 1890s until 1925.

I visualize myself as an immigrant woman living in one of those two-room rock houses. I picture making bread and talking with friends as we collectively tend to our children. All the while, the influence of Lake Michigan mitigates the harshest summer weather, as it does for me today. It would have been a difficult life but a good one, filled with the joy of community, the grief of hard quarry work, and the love of extended family.

Walking back on the Whitetail Trail to my car, I decide to branch off onto the Hardwood Swamp Trail. Given the recent storms, it may be soggy to hike, but I have to get in my mileage. I wore my shorter hiking boots today because it was exceedingly hot, forgetting they are not waterproof. I remember now as they are drenched through.

It had been dry weather when I bought them, and they worked great. However, my feet got soaked and cold the first time I hiked in wet, dewy grass. It has been over a year since I wore my shorty boots, as I usually wear my above-the-ankle Asolos. My socks are getting squishy, and my toes feel pruney hiking to the end of this trail.

I arrive back at my car but still require another half mile. I change into my hiking sandals and walk the park road until I reach my goal. As I do this Quest, I have to occasionally improvise.

I sit in my house tonight, having a cold dinner by the light of one small lantern—my electricity still out. I contemplate the people who used to live on the shores of what is now Harrington Beach and how I am remarkably privileged. I think of the dim lights afforded to the limestone quarry workers who lived in 15- by 20-foot cottages with their families or sometimes with multiple other single men. Their work hours would have been especially hard on these long summer days. By the time the sun descended, they must've come home beat down and exhausted. Their small houses would be darkening, perhaps allowing one little candle they could use to read by or write a letter back to family in Europe. The temperatures along the lake would've been brutal in the winter. Ah, but on a hot summer evening with a full moon reflecting off the lake, it would've been a place for a soul's respite, as it has been for mine.

My time at Harrington Beach today reminds me of a poem I wrote about an aged man I worked with when I was a hospice social worker. He and his spouse had come from Italy to America shortly after WWII. When I knew him, he was grieving the recent loss of his beloved wife:

For Amedio

An old man's hands.
They were a baker's hands as a boy for his father's Italian ovens.
"You see, I had to."
They were a mechanic's hands fixing the engines of airplanes.
"You see, I liked to."
They were a warrior's hands in Germany, World War II.
"You see, I hated to."
They were a carpenter's hands building houses in Myrtle Beach.
"You see, I wanted to."
They were a husband's hands caressing his wife's body.
"You see, I loved to."
They were a healer's hands massaging her after cancer took her breasts.
"You see, I needed to."
Now they are a griever's hands.
"Don't you see, I couldn't help her."
Now, they are a lost soul's hands.
"With all these hands can do, I am powerless."
An old man's hands.

Harrington Beach State Park

The Questions

1. What about this chapter resonated with you?
2. What memories do you have of significant weather events, floods, tornadoes, etc.?
3. What are you working to reclaim in your life as you age?

The Particulars

Sticker Required: Yes

Map on the State Park's Website: Yes, and nicely detailed

Bathrooms for Day Hikers: Yes, but in the office

Office or Kiosk: Office which can be closed depending on the day or season

Trail Markings: Infrequently marked

Seasonal Closures: None

Flooding Concerns: Yes, on some of the trails in wet times of the year

Five Miles: Easy to get with no circles

Wildcat Mountain State Park
Ontario

5.46 miles
Highest Point: 1,284 ft
Lowest Point: 962 ft

June 17, 2022
Identity and Gardening

This morning, I am happy as I go over my checklist and get ready to leave my house. With my blue, braided pigtails and multicolored bandana, I am excited to tackle the 16th park on my Quest.

Driving into the park, I do not see a sign. This is the only park I've been to without a wonderful state park sign. All I find is a nondescript wooden one, not the least bit celebratory—the perfect antithesis of the fabulous one at Willow River. Nonetheless, I take my entry photo to be consistent with the requirements of my Quest.

The park office is open, and, though the sign is less than, the office is not. There is quality merch with t-shirts and sweatshirts boasting a sensational graphic design featuring images of people engaging in all the exhilarating things you can do at this park: horseback riding, skiing, hiking, camping, etc. Their map is larger and more detailed than most, topographic with in-depth descriptions of the trails!

The first trail I begin as I set out on my five miles is the Observation Point Trail. It's a short, accessible trail ending in a breathtaking view of an oxbow on the Kickapoo River, almost 400 feet below.

After this short trail, I drive to the upper picnic area parking lot to catch the trailhead of the Old Settler's Trail loop. It starts with a steep, downhill trek, and I will be burning it up coming back out of this one. It is delightfully shady on this trail, and I anticipate it will be a pleasant time on this marvelous summer day.

Today, as a hike, I am contemplating one of my favorite aspects of myself as part of my Life Review process. I am a gardener. For me, this is about more than planting and working the soil. It is a state of being. Wherever you go and whatever you do, you try to leave seeds of benevolence and hope, and of kind acts to help others move forward. As a gardener, you may never know if those seeds ever come to fruition. You may never get to behold anything you plant, grow. Every once in a while you do, and it's a brilliant thing. It happens when I run into students I worked with during my time as a school social worker. They tell me that through all their times of sadness and despair, I was the person who helped them find their way. The little seeds I planted in them grew. When they thank me, it's an amazing feeling! It doesn't happen often, but no seeds from a true gardener's soul ever go to waste.

They may fall on dry, barren ground, yet another finds them and moves them onward. They may land on the edges of a concrete sidewalk, yet they can still keep growing. This wildcat place reminds me of the garden stories of my life. An important part of aging is making sure you have integrity as you look back, and can find beams of happiness in the dark times. Mine are truly wrapped up in gardening in all its myriad forms.

The Old Settler's Trail is a convoluted, up-and-down, twisty-turny trail. It creates major doubts in my mind whether "old settlers" used it given their limited resources and inappropriate footwear. The trail is full of rocks and roots waiting patiently to turn the ankles of this

Wildcat Mountain State Park

old hiker, and I'm glad I wore my high boots.

The trail runs through an incredibly deep, green forest, overarching and rustling softly on this warm day. There are grand sandstone outcroppings at various points on the trail. They are splendid! One appears to be a time-worn, eroded statue of an ancient sphinx. I wonder if it is the namesake of the mountain.

I finish the Old Settler's Trail, which is definitely a workout. I head to my car for the drive to the Hemlock Trailhead. It starts at a verdant and striking place of sandstone bluffs along the banks of the Kickapoo River. Remember not to get to close to the edges!

Parts of the Hemlock Trail are closed while I am here, resulting in a back-and-forth hike rather than a loop. My hike up to the peak of Hemlock Trail is tough, but the reward is absolutely stunning! The view is filled with rolling green hills of large pines and hardwoods off into the distance forever. I take a few moments at the peak overlook to remind myself of the reason for my Quest and all I am working to reclaim in my life as I turn sixty-five.

Being able to fully reclaim my gardener's status is important to me. It is a healing part of myself I freely share with others. It is my kind-hearted nature, which many see as a weakness to bully and exploit. That is decidedly not what it is! Being a kind person requires being a strong person.

Yesterday, at my part-time job at a local bookstore, I had a great conversation with a customer. A friend of hers is suffering from postpartum depression. I was able to show her some books, giving guidance and insight regarding this frequently overlooked part of being a new mom. I enjoyed planting seeds and sharing healing as I spoke with her.

I'll have to return to Wildcat Mountain to hike the Ice Cave Trail. It is a short one, but I am a worn-out "old settler" myself after doing these two rugged hikes on a sweltering day. The Ice Cave Trail sounds spectacular. It would be a wonderful feature to see in the winter when the small spring flowing through it is frozen. The description on the brochure/map makes me want to return, as it sounds immensely beautiful. On my Quest, I have found several parks I will return to again, hopefully with friends, this winter and next summer.

This evening, I sit alone in the gathering twilight of my garden in an area I created to be an intimate tête-à-tête, with the taunting presence of a second chair, with the tyranny of a second chair sitting empty. It is waiting to be filled with the warmth of a ruggedly handsome man, smiling back at me, lounging in the shade as we admire the sunset and birdsong. I close my eyes and imagine such a person filling up my second chair, and my life with love and dreams of future gardens.

Wildcat Mountain State Park

The Questions

1. What about this chapter resonated with you?
2. What is your favorite aspect of yourself?
3. How does this aspect help you find integrity in your life?

The Particulars

Sticker Required: Yes

Map on the State Park's Website: Yes, and it is detailed in color and topographic

Bathrooms for Day Hikers: Yes, but in the office

Office or Kiosk: Large, nice office with displays but can be closed depending on the day or season

Trail Markings: Well-marked with posted "You Are Here" maps

Seasonal Closures: None

Flooding Concerns: Perhaps along the lower areas near the Kickapoo River

Five Miles: Easy to get with no circles

Kohler-Andrae State Park
Sheboygan

5.62 miles
Highest Point: 647 ft
Lowest Point: 593 ft

June 22, 2022
Summer Solstice
Resilience and Sanctuary

This is the most emotional park for me and my favorite of all the parks. It is intensely bittersweet to come back today. One of the last times I was here, my mother was alive, and my child was a bright, dancing jewel, running along the edges of the waves, pretending to fly with the seagulls.

The sign for "V OK Waldo" brings back significant memories! It is the exit off Highway 23 to get to Kohler-Andrae. I remember breathing a huge sigh of relief when I saw it, knowing I would soon be in this blessed park. It is the only ubiquitous, green highway sign ever causing me to smile broadly and thoroughly. Once I see it, I know heaven is only a few miles away.

There is a wonderful, open state park office here. This is the first park where I allow myself to buy some merchandise. I purchase a t-shirt and a bandana. The ranger is a friendly young woman. When I tell her about doing my 45 x 5 = 65 Quest, she smiles enthusiastically and says, "Oh! What a super cool thing you are doing! You need to write about it. About all your experiences and all the things you like and don't like about the parks. It would make such a great book!" I have to agree with her. I think my coming-of-age Quest is a good story.

The road to this park has changed incredibly. When I first started coming here in the late 1980s, the two-lane highway across this part of Wisconsin was filled with marvelous rolling hills and delightful curves. My car would start to stall out, going up the mighty incline of the terminal moraine outside Fond du Lac. That road traveled through little towns like Glenbeulah and Greenbush, and by the Old Wade House, winding its way slowly and scenically to Lake Michigan.

Now, the beautiful, old highway is a soulless straight four-lane. Even the terminal moraine of the last great Ice Age has been flattened on the new highway. Back in the day, my ears would pop when I got to its summit! The pressure change was a heady rush and a part of the joy I felt knowing I was going to Kohler-Andrae. I feel a deep sense of sad nostalgia for the old road, and I am whole-heartedly missing that long ago and long gone sweet stretch of asphalt.

The first time I ever came to Kohler-Andrae was with my mom. She brought me here because I was suffering intensely from a broken heart. She hoped being by Lake Michigan and the enchanting, wide beach would help me feel less somber and defeated.

After that first visit, Kohler-Andrae became my sanctuary. In the 1980s, I would bring friends, and we would picnic and fall asleep on the beach. I was incredibly tan by the end of the first summer! We would stay here until 8 or 9 p.m., ensuring we were sober, and then drive home toward the setting sun. I spent the majority of my free time at this park that entire summer. I was healing my heart-broke

Kohler-Andrae State Park

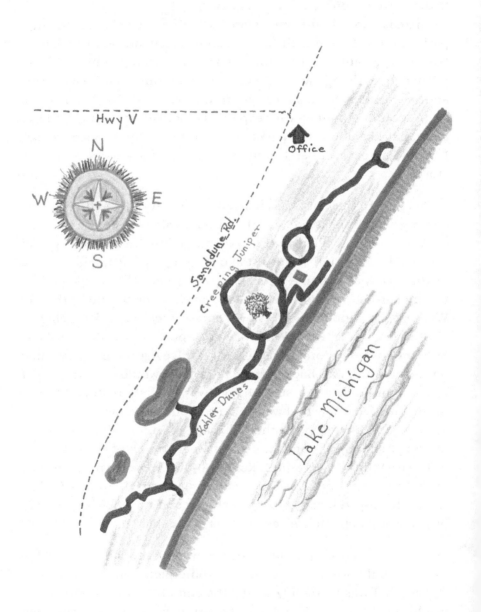

self and filling my soul with waves, sand, and wind.

The second summer of my near-constant K-A days, I brought a man here, the only one I ever did. He was a handsome pilot from California transplanted to Oshkosh to fly DC-3s. He had heard me talk about going to the beach and was incredulous there was any such thing in Wisconsin, prompting me to bring him to Kohler-Andrae. I have a dreamy, warm, late summer memory of him and me driving along the highway looking for "V OK Waldo."

Back then, the beach was at least 10 or 20 feet deeper, even more similar to an ocean beach. Giant beach cleaning machines regularly came to ensure it was flawless. It was before the zebra and quagga mussels came, state park funding was cut, and the alewives died in massive numbers.

I came to Kohler-Andrae for the last time as a young woman a few days before I moved to New Mexico to seek my fortune. I remember sitting here on the beach, soaking up the sanctuary of the place and grieving, knowing I wouldn't see it again for a considerable time. I resolved to, wherever I was, have this kind of sanctuary created somewhere for myself.

The duplex I rented in Albuquerque had a 10-by-10-foot walled garden. I created a sanctuary of entirely white flowers: roses, nicotiana, alyssum, petunias, and dianthus. I included several hummingbird feeders, wanting a touch of red to attract the countless ones living in New Mexico. The garden would, literally, glow in the moonlight! I would relax in it, gazing at the Sandia Mountains, dreaming of brighter days.

Years later, when I lived in Rocky Comfort, Missouri, my mother sent me a collection of things from Kohler-Andrae. It was soon after the birth of my child via an emergency C-section, and she wanted me to have pieces of this heavenly place. In the package, I found stems of dried beach grass, a seagull feather, a still-sticky pinecone, smooth lake pebbles, and a letter from my mom filled with love and care. I put them all in an old wooden box I had found at a flea market, something unique and precious to keep them safe—a box of sanctuary.

When I moved to Carrizozo, New Mexico, I created a sanctuary by constructing a labyrinth in my backyard, looking out over the open range. It was made out of large, gray stones I hauled in my pickup from a dry streambed a few miles away. I brought the main center stone of the labyrinth with me when I moved back to Wisconsin. In my garden now, the most common word people exclaim when they first glimpse it is *sanctuary*. It invariably makes me smile!

I park in the Sanderling Nature Center lot and start my hike with tears in my eyes. I'm not listening to any books today like I usually do when I'm hiking. I need to feel this place again, soak up all the memories, and simply be in the beauty of it. I start my mileage on the loop of the nearby Creeping Juniper Nature Trail, stopping at the oldest and largest dune pine. I know this tree remembers when I was here with my mom and my broken heart. I take a small branch from the ground to put with the feather, cone, grass, and stones I have of hers. I'm glad I have zipper bags in my backpack. I situate the branch in one and fill the other with warm beach sand.

I'm definitely being hit by "sneaker" waves of grief today. Grief has a way of surprising us, like the deadly waves sweeping unsuspecting beachgoers out into the ocean. A long processed and set aside sorrow can return in overwhelming ways, taking us back out to be "lost at sea." It is an unfortunate part of this coming-of-age time in one's life—the coming to terms with the loss of our parents and the strangeness of being an orphan.

I finish hiking the Creeping Juniper Nature Trail and circle back to the Sanderling Nature Center. There is a trail heading north called the Kohler Dunes Cordwalk. It leads to the beach, a picnic area, and parking lot number two.

The cool, sweet wind is welcome here today. It is a scorching day, with not a cloud in the sky, and I take advantage of trees as I go for shaded respite. It is a markedly different way of being here than during the time in my late 20s when having full-on, intense sunshine was the quintessential experience.

When I used to come here as a young woman, none of this was here. Only one solitary bench stood north of the Nature Center at the top of a large dune. It afforded me time to contemplate my life, my future, and my everything about the world. The cordwalk going up to the lone bench with its commanding overlook of the lake magically drew me to it. It was a place of hope for me, where I would sit for innumerable hours, dreaming of brighter days in my future.

That hope is noticeably challenging now as I approach sixty-five. It is difficult for me to wish for any of the things I did sitting on the bench many years ago. I dreamed of a new life, an excellent job, and a loving family. Some of those things I have had, and some of those things I have lost.

For me, this summer, it is the Quest. I try to focus significantly more on the near future than the distant one—one full of uncertainty, loss, aging, and death. I think it is a powerful lesson this Quest is teaching me. I need to be more present in the time I'm in instead of fantasizing about the future.

I have a sense of melancholy today. I will still dream of brighter days ahead. It's just not the same as it was when I was here in my youth. I have different things creating bright days for me and different expectations of the world and of the people in it. I don't mean to say I'm jaded. I mean to say I am more realistic, defined, and finite.

The trails are all corded boardwalks, which must've been a Herculean effort! It reminds me to renew my Friends of Kohler-Andrae State Park membership. I've been a member, off and on, since the first time I came here, and after today, I know I need to be one again.

I take the time to go to the observation deck at the top of the Sanderling. It is definitely worth a stop! I linger, filled with wonder, taking in the view before I descend to find a place in the shade for a snack. With my granola bar in hand, I remember when I first brought my child here. I had returned from New Mexico to visit family and decided to swing by my favorite sanctuary. We ran along the beach, smiling, laughing, and jumping in the waves.

After we moved to Madison, we came here again on one of our weekly summer adventures. We were enjoying the beach life when we noticed a young boy throwing rocks at the seagulls, encouraged to do so by his parents. Eventually, he hit one, knocking it stunned out of the sky and down onto the hot sand. Witnessing this, my child ran up the beach—snarling, with teeth glaring, at the boy—and picked up the wounded seagull. We carefully checked the bird, its squawking little body shaken and alarmed. We walked with it inland toward the trees and set it down in a safe place to recover from being stoned by the mean little boy with his mean little parents.

My child was exceptionally compassionate, even at an early age. I am glad I recall that day. I hadn't thought about it for too long. My happy memories were buried under the sadness of my grief about this place. I find I also have great joy to remember about Kohler-Andrae. Therefore, during the rest of my hike, I will think about the blissful times at this glorious beach.

I hike the southern part of the cordwalk down to parking lot five and pass an older woman and her 20-something daughter. Smiling at them, I barely dodge another sneaker wave of grief. It helps to actively be thinking about the positive emotions I have felt in this park.

As I reverse back to the Sanderling, I am too hot. They have a refreshing cold water fountain inside, and I top off my hydration pack. I fill my water bottle, drinking it down and refilling it again before I set off, feeling decidedly better. I hike the Creeping Juniper Nature Trail loop again, trying to get in my mileage and not let myself down. I have to do my complete Quest!

Eventually, with my feet in the water, I know why Kohler-Andrae became my sanctuary. This is what I imagine heaven is like—an endless, beautiful brown beach, the sand between my toes, the cool water lapping gently on my ankles, and walking for all eternity. To have an infinity of beach, sun, water, and time rolling out before me is surely the equivalent of the Elysian Fields.

Back at my car, my five miles done, I rinse off my sandy feet with the last of my backpack reservoir water. When I return, I will hike the Ancient Shores Trail, which circumnavigates the Friends Fishing Pond. It sounds exciting and would make a great hike on a damn hot day like today, especially followed by a swim in the ice-cream-headache cold waters of Lake Michigan.

I think about how when I started my hike today, my heart was filled with grief, recalling the times of having a broken heart and thinking of the death of the woman who introduced me to this magical place. Now, my heart is filled with joy! I know the next time I come here I will be lounging on the beach after a long walk through this heaven on earth. I will be gazing out at the inland ocean, slipping into a drowsy summer nap, and listening to the waves as I used to when I was younger.

I need to stop being a stranger to this park and make sure I come on a regular basis after my Quest is over. Next summer will be a beach summer of friends and picnics, getting drunk, and falling asleep on the sand once again. It will be reclaimed! Only this time, I'll be under a sunshade for the sake of my old skin and only getting a bit tipsy. Maybe, I'll have a romantic beach read and phenomenally stylish sunglasses doubling as readers.

As I drive away, I make eye contact with the older mom who's here with her daughter. We exchange knowing smiles across hearts and across time. I realize again, profoundly at this park, my Quest is about reclaiming—grief and love and sanctuary.

When I get home, I add the pine branch and a small jar of sand from the beach to the wooden box with my mother's gifts of nature and comfort. I include a note about today for my child to find in the future. It is filled with delight and remembrance.

Kohler-Andrae State Park

The Questions

1. What about this chapter resonated with you?
2. If you have lost a parent, how have you incorporated the grief and found a new normal? If you haven't yet lost a parent, how are you cultivating relationships that will help you when the time comes?
3. In what ways do you find or create sanctuary in your life?

The Particulars

Sticker Required: Yes

Map on the State Park's Website: Yes, and nicely detailed

Bathrooms for Day Hikers: Yes, in the office or at Sanderling Nature Center

Office or Kiosk: Nice office with displays but can be closed depending on the day or season

Trail Markings: Infrequently marked

Seasonal Closures: None

Flooding Concerns: None

Five Miles: Circles required

Straight Lake State Park
Luck

5.13 miles
Highest Point: 1,358 ft
Lowest Point: 1,241 ft

June 23, 2022
The Day Before

We need many things for healthy aging: hobbies, exercising, eating right. We need to maintain relationships with loving family and friends. I would offer it is equally important to let go of non-reciprocal relationships.

I treat my friends in a kind and caring manner. I celebrate their birthdays. I go to the funerals of their family members. I drive them to doctor's appointments and pick them up after their colonoscopies. I regularly let them know I value having them in my life and am honored by their friendship.

Tomorrow will be the first extended overnight trip I am doing by myself on my Quest. I wasn't supposed to be alone. In fact, I rented a cabin back in April to share with two friends. Disappointingly, over the last 24 hours, both of them said things to me about the trip—statements I would have, on no occasion, ever said to a friend: "If I don't get my way, I just won't go then," "I never get to go anywhere, so I should be able to do what I want instead," "I don't want to have to sit around and wait for you," and several more related pronouncements.

There is an entertaining term for similar people gaining popularity on TikTok: "main character syndrome." I understood these two people were "high maintenance" as far as friends go. Be that as it may, I liked their company, and I'd been good-natured about doing what they thought was enjoyable. I did favors for them: watering plants and bringing clothes in a fashion emergency. The favors they did for me were allowing me to be a walk-on, recurring character on their "shows."

Having to change gears and go on this trip by myself, I spent this evening creating a new playlist of late 1980s and early 1990s country western music with some Patsy Cline thrown in for good measure.

This is the music I started listening to back when I was healing from the broken heart of my Kohler-Andrae State Park days. The pop songs of the era had way too many memories of the lost big love, causing me to switch to a different genre altogether. Little did I know, at that young age, the power of a story to heal, especially the stories of lonesome heartbreak in these songs. Now, I find the music comforting in manifold ways. It brings back memories, wonderful and bittersweet, most pointedly of the me I was then.

I am reminding myself of the reason I'm going on this Quest. It's about doing something I love to do in celebration of turning sixty-five. If it means friends can't join me because they have issues with commitment and accountability or want to be the only star on their "programs," that's how I have to play it.

June 24, 2022
Aloneness and Dragonflies

I am preparing to drive to the cabin on Balsam Lake, where I'll be staying for a couple of days to hike Straight Lake and Interstate. I am feeling high levels of trepidation. It's not the trip I had hoped for or the one I planned, but it is the one I'm taking because I need to stay true to myself above all. It is one of the major lessons I am learning from aging. I don't desire to be the "main character" of my life, but I should at least receive actors' guild trade union wages.

Two friends were supposed to accompany me to this remote location, agreeing to support me on my Quest. Everything about the trip had been discussed ad nauseam before I booked the three-bedroom cabin. Both agreed to the idea and said they would be covering their share of the cost. They told me they were happy to hang out at the lakeside while I hiked. Neither is a hiker, but I counted them as friends and was glad they were excited about coming along. I had hoped we would spend the evenings cooking and drinking wine, enjoying time together as we had on getaways in the past.

Yesterday, one said they wanted to do something else instead of what we had planned months ago. Though it sounded like a fun adventure, I told her the last-minute idea wasn't feasible, especially since I had already paid for the cabin. She refused to change her mind, instead engaging in emotionally manipulative behavior. I was only a "recurring character" for her, after all. The second friend decided not to go if the first one wasn't. In the past I have let things slide to keep the peace, but as I turn 65, I realize keeping the peace within me is paramount.

Therefore, I am driving to a cabin alone, and my friendships with those two are unsalvageable. Another lesson I have learned in my aging is not to let anyone play games with me. Even though I learned how to do "girl drama" games in junior high school, I don't play them, especially not with my friends. I am a grown-ass woman! I say what I mean. I treat my friends with respect. I keep my promises. I wait for them, and I support them in their endeavors. If they contact me and say they need my help, I freely give it. And dammit, I deserve the same!

With five-plus hours on my new country western playlist, I make the five-and-a-half-hour trip to Balsam Lake, singing my heart out as I go. I end up hoarse by the time I arrive, but my heart feels lighter.

I find the cabin, and it is nicely appointed, quaint, modern, and clean. If I had known I would be here alone, I would've chosen a smaller and less expensive place. I'm excited about it and, frankly, proud of myself for not staying home after all that happened yesterday.

I get settled in and head out to hike Straight Lake. I park in the lot off 120th Street. There is no office here, but there's a nice kiosk with maps and pictures. A "You Are Here" sign is posted, which is my favorite. As soon as I open my car door to start getting my hiking accouterments, I realize I left my socks back at the cabin. Damn!

After the previous day I had, I am lucky I remembered to bring my head! I do have my ankle socks. Hopefully, they won't allow blisters. It's always something, isn't it? Having an alternative plan is a must for hikers and for anything related to aging. Woefully, this is the first park I've been to where there is a hoard of blackflies in search of my soul.

I orient myself with the signage of the three trails beginning here—one way for the Ice Age, one way for the Straight Lake, and one way for the Rainbow Lake. I take the Rainbow Lake Trail, which is listed as a challenging, one-mile loop. I am finding mosquitoes to be the biggest challenge of this trail! I imagine it's the time of day because I'm getting out here late. I find a verdant, healthy-looking forest with many old-growth trees shading young maples.

This loop ends close to my car. Heading toward the start of the Straight Lake Trail, I encounter numerous garter snakes slithering and painted turtles wandering. I resist picking up one of the turtles to view its bright Rorschach underside, knowing doing so would be traumatic for the turtle, even though it is fascinating to me. I watch them lumber in their prehistoric way off into the grass at the edge of the parking lot.

This park has a profusion of different types of dragonflies! I love their symbolism. They remind us to take advantage of opportunities coming our way. They are emblems of hope and new beginnings,

Straight Lake State Park

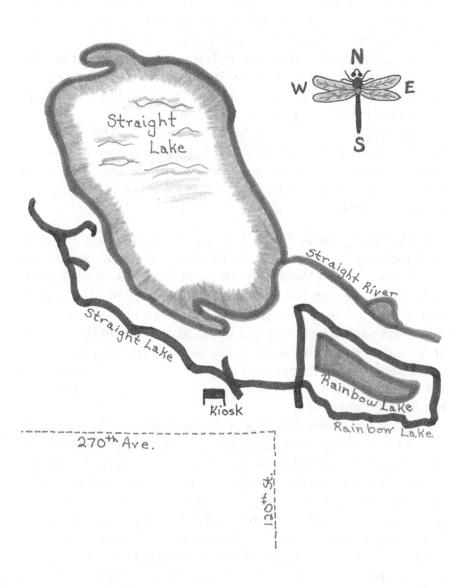

reminders to live each day to the fullest. Seeing them shining all around me in blues and blacks, purples and greens, warms my heart.

Recently, I read a study about dragonflies and the experience of time. Our concepts of it are apparently related to how quickly our surroundings change. Dragonflies can identify these changes 300 times a second but us only about 64. The researchers found that although time is both a construct and a constant, biology plays a part in how we perceive it. Absolutely phenomenal!

The Straight Lake Trail proceeds past the 10 available hike-in campsites. It's a great location if you are on the IAT. There are amazing views of the lake from the ridge the trail follows, but I hope it gets closer to the shoreline at some point.

The boat launch path off of the Straight Lake Trail brings me to a grassy shore on the water's edge. It is a splendid panorama with two brilliant, white trumpeter swans swimming on the quiet lake. There is a treed island in the middle, reminding me of the ones in the Lake District of England.

I hiked the Coast to Coast Walk across England in 2017 for my 60th birthday. It was something I had wanted to do since I first heard about it when I was in eighth grade. It was life-changing! Part of it wound through the exquisite Lake District outside Cumbria. One of the guys on the trip was a wild and beautiful man. He would put on his wetsuit and swim out to the lake islands when we would stop for the evening. It was incredible to watch him disappear in the water, soon to see him jump up on the island, smiling and waving. It is a sublime memory! In fact, I still use on every hike, the water bottle he bought for me.

After finishing the C2C, I was dropped off at a B&B near the Shambles in York. I had arranged to stay there the night before I was to fly home. He walked me to the door, squeezing my hand hard, looking deep into my eyes so others in our group might not notice the intensity of feeling. Then, he turned and walked back to the van. It was one of the most enchanting and poignant goodbyes in my life, right up there with the ending of the movie *Casablanca*.

Last summer, I was sipping the final pour from the small, unique, cork-stoppered bottle of elderberry port I bought while on the C2C. I drank it from an elegant, pink, cut crystal coupe glass, its shallow bowl decorated with leaves and flowers. I had found the glass at an estate sale of a wealthy woman of obviously refined taste. I could tell by the sheer amount of exceptional glassware she had enjoyed entertaining and parties with dazzling friends. I remember smiling to myself, thinking about when I bought the port. The man I met had sat beside me, explaining all the wonderful cheeses produced in Yorkshire. He was definitely a cheese connoisseur and was markedly excited about them. As the daughter of a Wisconsin cheesemaker, I was enchanted. We both chuckled, thinking about how he sounded like Wallace from the *Wallace and Gromit* animated film, where they flew to the moon and discovered it was truly made of cheese. The port tasted like the sun shining in an exotic land: bright rolling hills and a gorgeous Green Man sitting next to me, laughing in the warm summer air, joyous with the day. Wherever he is, I hope his life is full of wonder, beauty, and happiness. He deserves it, as he brought these things to mine.

I proclaimed to my child in March 2017, "I am going to, from now on until I die, fill my legs up with tattoos of all the breathtaking places I am going to hike."

They looked at me skeptically and said, "Okay, Mom," not knowing quite what to believe. When I was on the C2C and people who used to know me would ask about me, my child would say I was living my best life hiking across England. I was remarkably happy they thought this about me and what I was doing. The first hiking tattoo I have is from that hike. I only got up to three tattoos before the pandemic hit. Now I am on this Quest, and I have to come up with a tattoo for it, as it will be a major accomplishment when I am done.

I did get my five miles in, but I didn't end up hiking a trail I wanted to, the High Point Trail. I start out on it, but it was already after 6:30 p.m., and the mosquitoes were abhorrent, in fierce competition for my blood with the multitude of blackflies. It's decidedly not the time of day to be hiking out in this dark, still forest. Seeing all the turtles, snakes, dragonflies, and especially the swans, genuinely made my day.

Had I been able to do my original plan, I would have hiked this park on Sunday morning, but it was changed by "girl drama." How ridiculous I am still dealing with that. I am an old woman, for fuck's sake! I decided to hike Straight Lake today, allowing me to leave a day early from the cabin. The whole sense of safety is an issue for me in this isolated area, and I have to trust my gut.

It is evening, and I am sitting on the dock, back at the cabin on Balsam Lake, my feet dangling in the water. I forget how long it has been since I took the time to watch a languid summer sunset. I can't see them well from my house due to the trees. I resolve to find a picturesque spot near my home to watch them. I miss my relationship with the sky when I lived in New Mexico, where the sunsets were barnburners every night. It is something worth reclaiming!

June 25, 2022
The Day After

I slept well and got up late at my rented cabin on Balsam Lake. It stormed last night, and everything is puddled and wet, with more to come today. It is not a good day to hike at my next park, Interstate. Well, then, first things first: coffee brought from home.

During the height of the pandemic, I spoiled myself by ordering regular shipments of superb New Mexico Piñon coffee, and I haven't gone back. It is a dark roast with a touch of Mexican spiced chocolate. I put it in the coffee maker and turn it on. After a few minutes, nothing is happening. I momentarily start to panic, thinking maybe I won't have any coffee. I go back and check to make sure it isn't because the outlet's not working and wonder if I should, in the future, bring my own coffee pot to places. This one sits right next to a toaster; one is plugged in, and one isn't. After a switch of the plugs, coffee is brewing, and I am ridiculously happy! Definitely an ADHD morning.

It is a perfectly Scottish dreichy day. I turn on all the lights in the cabin in an effort to make it less gloomy. All the same, the view off the veranda is impressive. The lake is lovely as it wavers with the wind. It has taken on an unusual texture with the sparkling raindrops.

One of the best perks of working part-time at a bookstore is having access to fabulous newspapers. I brought several of them with me on this trip so I could linger over coffee and read. One of my favorite things to do when I was traveling in England, Ireland, and India was to read the newspaper every day. It's endlessly fascinating what ends up in them.

Newspapers in England had a similar bent to those in the United States—politics and world events with some human interest stories. I greatly enjoyed an article about Aidan Turner from the BBC show *Poldark*. He had been on location and dressed in costume when some women close to my age encountered him and asked if they could get a photograph. He ruefully declined as he couldn't allow them to take a photo of him dressed for the next season, it being a secret detail. The old British women cheekily told him he was welcome to take off his clothes. He grinned shyly, relenting to their humor, and went ahead and took a selfie with them.

The Dublin papers I read were full of political and environmental articles, with lovely stories about small Irish villages and things happening all over the country in the rural areas: markets, plays, fairs, races, etc.

Indian newspapers had the same political and small village mix but also included air quality reports and decidedly prominent sections about missing loved ones. There were endless pages of people who were lost. Information about them, where they were from, and how they disappeared was a vitally important use of newsprint, as is the obituary section of my daily newspaper.

It is not surprising I like to read obituaries. After all, I have a history of frequenting cemeteries and working with dying patients. I read an intriguing document in the Historical Museum of White Oaks, a dilapidated ghost town near where I lived in Carrizozo, New Mexico. The archive resembled a bookkeeping ledger, but rather than money, it was an accounting of the town's deaths for approximately 50 years, back in its heyday in the late 1800s. Too many women in childbirth, regrettably, filled its pages. An unlikely number of people were killed by lightning strikes, as well as those who met their demise by cattle, shot in misadventures, or attacked by mountain lions. A few died of natural causes such as heart attacks or strokes, but it was primarily accidents and disease and a startling number of children. A similar chronicle contains the death registry of Black River Falls, Wisconsin.

It was made into a book and is engaging reading if you're a history buff like me.

As we age, it is crucial to start thinking about our own obituaries. What should they include? Do we want to list the reason for our death as they did in those bygone days? How do we want our funerals to be? Having these things in place is an incredible gift we can give our loved ones left grieving when we die.

I have to say it's slightly lonely up here without the two women who were supposed to join me. Even though it's a wonderful spot, I feel like when I was in college going to a frat party alone because friends said they would meet me there, but they never showed up. I'm trying hard to fight this awkward feeling of wanting to go home. Damn it, I'm not a young woman anymore! I'm trying to do a Quest for myself to reaffirm and reclaim my life. I have to stay and hike at Interstate when the rain stops.

I spend some time surveying the materials about Polk County provided at the cabin. I find the Dancing Dragonfly Winery is on the way to Interstate from this location. How synchronistic! I must stop there. It would be decadent to arrive back home, tired from hiking, driving, and singing my lungs out, to crack open a bottle of wine from this outstanding area.

As I walk to the picture window with my cup of hot and spicy New Mexican coffee, I see a bald eagle lift powerfully from the lake's surface with a twisting fish in its talons. It soars off toward the trees behind the cabin. Even on a cloudy, rainy day, there is great beauty here. I spend the rest of the day writing, working on previous state park hikes. I had fallen behind on them, and having time devoted solely to the work is a rare indulgence.

It is my second evening at the cabin, and I'm sitting on the veranda, drinking a glass of wine. The sky is clearing, and the air is cool and dry. Tomorrow will be a good day for a hike! All around me, the redwing blackbirds' songs are acutely symbolic of high summer. I need to find myself one of the plush ones that sings when you touch its wing. Then, I can hear it in the dead of winter when I'm tired of bleak days and waiting for the spring to return. As I watch the sunset turn the clouds vivid crimson and gold, I think that when I am an old, old woman, I will need to be at a place like this with a sunset view.

Straight Lake State Park

The Questions

1. What about this chapter resonated with you?

2. Think of times you set boundaries regarding your friendships. What consequences have you dealt with as a result? How did it change your relationship with them and with yourself?

3. What goals have you set for yourself as you age?

The Particulars

Sticker Required: Yes

Map on the State Park's Website: Yes, and it is detailed in color

Bathrooms for Day Hikers: Vault toilets which may be closed depending on the day or season

Office or Kiosk: Kiosk with a map posted and information

Trail Markings: Infrequently marked

Seasonal Closures: None

Flooding Concerns: None

Five Miles: Circles required

Interstate State Park
St. Croix Falls

5.66 miles
Highest Point: 905 ft
Lowest Point: 551 ft

June 26, 2022
Spontaneity and Rugged Beauty

It's my last morning on Balsam Lake. I'm sitting looking out the window at the calm water, lingering with my dark piñon coffee and the remainder of my *New York Times*. The storm has gone through, and it will be a windier and cooler day with a high of about 70 degrees—perfect for hiking!

I am glad I am journaling these parks. I started a daily journal eight years ago, and it helps me make sense of my life. Someday, my child will read them and know their mother better, know more about my history, and know what it is like for me during this time in my life. It is why I decided to do the same for my Quest. I write and

I process and I hike. It is comparable to the Life Reviews I did with many hospice patients. The difference is I don't want to wait until I am dying to start thinking about what I need in my life and how I am going to look back on it with integrity. I would rather work on defining what is meaningful and important to me about my identity and purpose now.

I bid farewell to the cabin. I text my hiking safety buddy back home before heading toward Interstate. Listening to my new playlist of country western music on the drive reminds me of a man I once loved, Michelangelo. He was a train engineer, and I met him in the lounge car of the Southwest Chief on my first trip to New Mexico. These songs remind me of the extraordinary time he and I spent in Santa Fe and how wonderful and spontaneous our love for each other began.

I am on a roll with my driving and singing, and suddenly, I am here at the park! I'm not used to it. Most of my drives to get to state parks take a lot longer than 30 minutes. The beauty I see as I leave my car to do my prerequisite entry photo is outstanding. Two colorful ring-necked pheasants wander in the long, blue-green grass by the park sign.

The office is open, and another ruggedly handsome ranger is working there. I wonder if the DNR would hire me to work in one of these offices. The ranger tells me to stop at the Ice Age Trail Interpretive Center farther up the road. I'm going to check it out.

As I proceed to the center, I think about the concept of "ruggedly handsome." It is an odd term as there is no equivalent. Nobody says a woman is "ruggedly beautiful." In fact, if a woman's face has wrinkles and scars, maybe even a broken nose, from all the joys and pains, trials and accidents they've been through, people say things like "rode hard and put away wet."

I did an online search about this a while ago. The definition of "ruggedly handsome" is hardworking, a physical laborer, a warrior, weather-beaten, and tough. It is not necessarily traditionally handsome but a face marked by the endurance of hardship. The images I found were of Jason Momoa and Viggo Mortensen. I had to agree! When I searched for "ruggedly beautiful," I got photos of

Interstate State Park

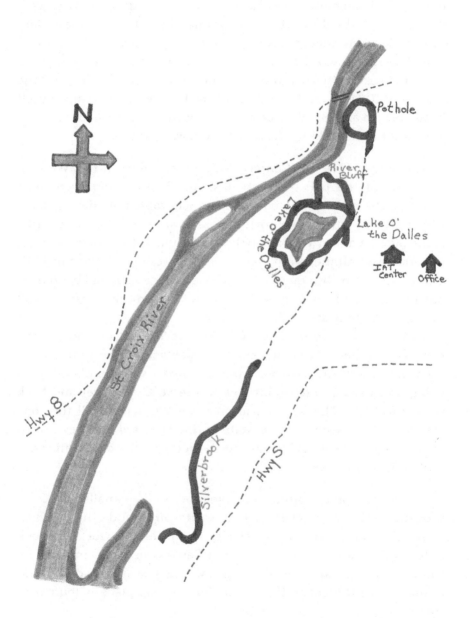

mountains, glaciers, and sea coasts. Is that what women are—like the earth in their severe and rare beauty? Striking and powerful, mighty and changing? I wish a search of images for "ruggedly beautiful" would show photos of women like Dolores Huerta and Aretha Franklin, Malala Yousafzai and Maggie Smith, Frida Kahlo and Maya Angelou. Albeit secreting and shielding my years, my face bears the scars of barbed wire, the lines of worry and of joy, and the creases of 100,000 smiles and counting. I resolve to describe myself in the future as "ruggedly beautiful" because I have made it to 65, and I am a hardworking, weather-beaten warrior.

Reaching the Ice Age Center, I find it incredible! At this Western Terminus of the IAT, there are displays, history, and even films about all the places affected by the unbelievable mile-deep glacier, which used to cover large portions of the state. I didn't realize this is the oldest park in Wisconsin. It was a cooperative effort between the state and Minnesota to set aside this wondrous place in 1895. There's also some fun merch. I purchase two Ice Age Trail bandanas, one for my friend Petra, as we have been slowly marking off the trail together as "thousand-mile wannabees."

I start off my five miles on the Pothole Trail. It's obviously the primary trail here for sightseers. It is spectacular! I stop to chat it up with a couple of handsome young climbers who are planning on going down the 200-foot cliff face to the St. Croix River and back up again. Wow! That's damn impressive! We discuss all the rock climbers I have seen at other state parks. They tell me they dream of climbing at Devil's Lake, but they both think the rock climbers at Willow River are crazy.

The entire trail is dotted with transitory wells—smaller potholes providing easy water access to the insects, birds, and other wildlife. Somehow, this place has a lost city in the jungle vibe. The rock outcroppings appear so precise and flawless as to be man-made. Unlike Straight Lake two days ago, where I heard absolutely no human noise the entire time I was hiking, this place is loud with traffic.

I come upon a pothole reminding me of a peculiar, erratic rock in the Wicklow Mountains in eastern Ireland, near Glendalough, or the

Glen of Two Lakes. Legend says it was the holy well of Saint Kevin. He was known for his miracles involving nature. He would sit on the large stone, and the well would miraculously fill with water for the animals to drink. Somehow, that boulder with a distinct pothole had ended up deposited there in the middle of a forest. The forces of nature are remarkable, indeed! During my hike in Ireland, our group stopped for a cold St. Kevin's Red Ale at the Wicklow Brewery after our jaunt through the area. It is a grand memory!

After finishing the Pothole Trail, I get in my car and head south to the start of the Lake O' the Dalles Trail. Hiking here, I'm reminded why I don't frequent Devil's Lake during the summer, especially on weekends. Today is a Sunday, and the trails are filled with shouting people, screaming children, and unruly dogs. My gosh! How much perfume do you need to wear when you're out hiking? The fragrance people are wearing overpowers all the lovely smells of this resplendent place—the smells of green growing things, dusty sandstone bluffs, and river water rolling by. The intense chemical scents exacerbate my respiratory disability, and I hurry away from the maddening crowds.

I am kind of turned around on these trails. I end up off the Lake O' the Dalles Trail, onto the River Bluff Trail, and subsequently, onto the Summit Rock Trail. There appear to be a lot of unofficial side trails, and it is easy to take a wrong turn due to inadequate signage. Nevertheless, it is marvelous. I am having a good wander on a fine day, and it's all part of the adventure.

Eventually, I make my way back onto the Lake O' the Dalles Trail and finish the loop. Then, to my car and farther south to the start of the Silverbrook Trail. If I walk this trail, I can finish my mileage easily and get ready for the lengthy trip home. On the Silverbrook, I hike out to the waterfall, passing by an old mine and the ruins of a mansion rumored to have been a house of ill repute in its glory days. This park is truly a multi-faceted and intriguing place!

My miles complete, I reluctantly leave this gorgeous forest. I take advantage of the bathrooms at the IAT Interpretive Center to change clothes for the drive. It will include a stop at the Dancing Dragonfly Winery to pick up a bottle to open when I get home. I am honestly enjoying all the dragonfly energy on this trip. They are truly the epitome of liminality, existing in a way lyrically magical. They shift from the water to the air, their lives shimmering and evanescent. Perhaps that is why I am acutely intrigued by them—their uncanny ability to be in two places at once, their sense of time so unlike my own. I find them intensely powerful and strangely comforting.

Arriving at the winery, I am surprised to see it out here in what looks like the middle of nowhere. It resembles some of the elegant wineries on the Leelanau Peninsula of Michigan, and I am happy I am taking the time to stop in for a quick tasting.

Finally home, I sit in my garden and enjoy the fabulous sound of a cork popping out of a wine bottle. I chose a girly, pink sparkling wine and am drinking it from a fancy Dancing Dragonfly Winery glass I couldn't pass up. As I use it now and in the future, it will be a tangible reminder of the fortitude and determination my Quest has taken.

Although the trip didn't pan out the way I had originally planned, I got in the hikes I needed for the two parks and experienced some exceptionally beautiful, different, and fun hiking today and at Straight Lake. Interstate State Park is definitely one I will return to in the future. I didn't even begin to explore all it has to offer, let alone the Minnesota side. And, so the Quest continues!

June 27, 2022
The Day After

Today, I was supposed to be driving home from Balsam Lake. The original plan was to be there with my friends from Friday to Monday. That way I could still get in both hikes in case severe weather issues arose. I have a full set of waterproofs, and a rainy day isn't a game changer, but hiking in a thunderstorm is another matter. Instead, I cut it short and came back Sunday. Therefore, I am spending today working in my garden, being squawked at by the robins who decided to build their nest right by my back door. Every time I come out, it's like a whole new world for them. I prefer crows because they are able to remember my face. Around four o'clock, I decide to go for a walk around my neighborhood.

Whenever I see someone in their front yard working on their gardens, I stop and ask them what they're doing. I appreciate it when others do so for me. We, gardeners, are understandably excited to talk to people about our plans. It gives me a chance to spread some good energy out into the world because I know being a gardener can be a lonely life. These brief social interactions are beneficial for our health and happiness. It is basic Midwest nice. We make eye contact with strangers, smile, and say hello as we go about our business out in the world. We gain inner strength and feel less isolated the more of these arbitrary, fleeting social encounters we experience. It is one of the reasons I enjoy my part-time retail job. I get to have short conversations with a variety of people when I am working. It may be a customer needing a good mystery recommendation, or one who loves newspapers as much as I do, or someone wanting advice on a sensitive topic and hoping for a self-help book.

On this walk, I have the pleasure of speaking with two different elder women. One is sitting in her yard alongside her equally elderly dog. She tells me she is weeding and working on planting some shrubbery and a few trees. I think she must be in her mid-eighties. She is astonishingly bright and happy to talk with me about all her plans and how the birds will come to these new plants. It is the hope of growing things that gardeners hold dear to our hearts.

The other woman I speak with looks to be a bit younger. She is sitting on the ground, digging holes. She explains the six dinner plate-sized holes surrounding a massive maple tree are to plant hostas. She relates she "is helping out the old woman who lives at the house." "That woman is in her 90s," she says, "and she can't dig the way I can." It makes me giggle a bit, and I compliment her, saying she is doing a superb job and the plants will be beautiful growing there.

She tells me she has "just turned 70, and when you turn 70, you can do whatever you want. If you want to spend the entire day digging holes in the ground, then that's what you get to do!" Her comment makes me smile all the way to my soul. She's definitely an inspiration to me for my next milestone birthday. Maybe I will have to come up with a Quest to find unique places to dig countless holes!

Interstate State Park

The Questions

1. What about this chapter resonated with you?
2. How do you define "ruggedly handsome" and "ruggedly beautiful" in relation to yourself?
3. What trips have you been on that didn't turn out the way you planned? How were you able to regroup and persevere?

The Particulars

Sticker Required: Yes

Map on the State Park's Website: Yes, and it is detailed in color

Bathrooms for Day Hikers: Yes, in the Ice Age Trail Interpretive Center, which may be closed depending on the day or season

Office or Kiosk: Office which can be closed depending on the day or season

Trail Markings: Not well-marked

Seasonal Closures: None

Flooding Concerns: Close to the river or creek in times of great rainfall

Five Miles: Easy to get with no circles

New Glarus Woods State Park
New Glarus

5.08 miles
Highest Point: 1,099 ft
Lowest Point: 656 ft

June 28, 2022
Aging and Birds

I love the sound of chirping birds in the morning while drinking coffee and reading the newspaper. My time spent with this daily ritual is exceptionally peaceful. In fact, there is a seldom-used word for this feeling, *seatherny*. It refers to the tranquil calm we feel as we listen to birdsong. When I add to it the tactile experience of a newspaper in my fingers, the sound of the pages turning, and the smell of the ink, I am serene.

For the last several years, my older brother has bought me a *Birds and Blooms* magazine subscription. He started getting it for me when I turned 60, and I was aghast! I would have loved to have had a subscription for an adventure, outdoor, or hiking magazine or an archaeology, history, or science magazine, but he gave me that one because "old people like birds." My brother is, as his son referred to him on a school report about what your parents do for a living, "a rockstar playing guitar god." Now that he is aging, he has started liking birds. He has bird feeders all around his yard, even orange, jam, and suet feeders. What the hell?!

I have two bird feeders, well, actually three. I have one stuck to the window where my cat can watch it. When I say that out loud, I can hear an old lady speaking! I have gone so far as to download the Merlin Bird ID app on my phone. It can listen to bird songs and identify them. Why is it that, as we age, we're extraordinarily intrigued by birds?

My leading theory is we slow down enough to appreciate their delightfulness. Doctors' offices usually have an aquarium where people can watch fish swim and remain calm while waiting for their appointments. Birds are similar. Watching birds eating and flying, singing and making nests is soothing. Maybe that's why we start liking birds. Now that I am retired, I am at a place where rushing around to get everything done is no longer my priority. If I take an extended moment to enjoy the blue jay on my fence or the downy woodpecker on my tree, I no longer have an inner voice chastising me to hurry and accomplish something.

Another theory I have about why older people like birds is, maybe, it is because they are the returned souls of our ancestors who come back to have a full life of flight and fancy. This became my idea as a result of a hike through a cemetery years ago. It was located within a foreboding Ozark forest and had been severely neglected. As I wandered through it, reading the stones, an unbelievable bluebird, the first one I'd ever seen, landed on a low branch right next to me and sang and sang and sang. I was mesmerized listening to it, enjoying its beauty. I had been trying to avoid a wave of grief from a recent loss, and the happy bird seemed to purposefully visit me to make my heart a little lighter.

On the subject of birds, I've been dealing with an Alfred Hitchcock-type situation for the last week or so. Robins have built a nest above the motion sensor light outside my back door. It's only about six

New Glarus Woods State Park

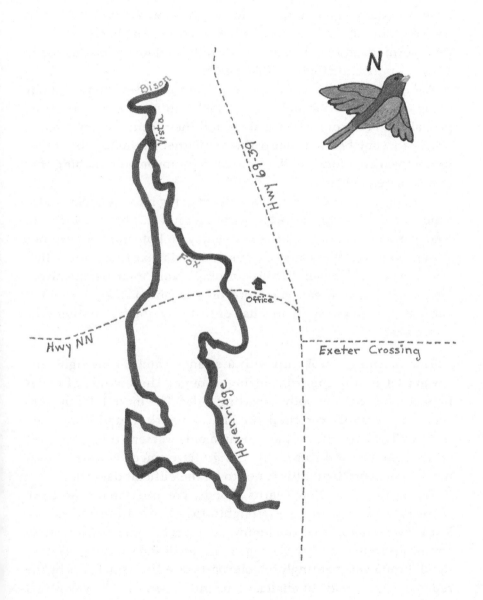

feet from the ground under the eaves of my house. Every time I walk outside, they dive-bomb me! They perch in my cherished ash tree and yell at me! I can't be out there, mulching and digging without having my head barraged with wings. They even attacked the neighbor who was watching my house when I was hiking at Straight Lake and Interstate State Parks a few days ago. The babies hatched this morning, and I cautiously peek out my door to look at them. They are pure and ethereal and beautiful.

Today, as I look at the nest, I don't want to upset the parents by going outside this morning. The attacks on me are based on the primal need to protect their babies and their future. In my visceral self, I can wholeheartedly empathize with them, thinking about how protective I am of my child. I would attack anyone or anything that ever threatened harm.

I am torn. A part of me wants to avoid going into my backyard for a month until the chicks are grown, but it's not feasible. I have fish to feed, gardening to do, and shade to enjoy on hot summer evenings with friends. I hate to cause them stress and make them think their wee ones are in danger. I realize, though, from their perspective, I am an existential threat. Therefore, on this fabulous day, instead of gardening, I am giving them a day of rest by going for another hike on my Quest.

This morning, I woke up with a strange catch in my right hip. I won't let it stop me from hiking, though. These kinds of aches happen now that my body is getting older. The more I do, the less they happen until a certain point. I have to work around it and keep moving. The opposite is apathy, which only worsens things with my joints, muscles, and spirit. One thing I have sincerely learned over my 64 years and 10 months is not to let the difficult days win.

Trying to get to New Glarus Woods, I'm frustrated. The drive there is supposed to be a straightforward one from my house. With several detours on the highways, it has become an excessively circuitous route. I end up driving on the small and winding Lily Rose Road through enchantingly bucolic parts of Wisconsin. I pass by the redolent green fields of alfalfa, corn, and mown hay. They contrast vividly with the reds of the barns and the silvers of the silos. Even though this Quest has actual goals, my feelings of frustration remind me how I must accept that the journey to get to them is as much, if not more, of the reason I'm doing it. I am reclaiming the joy of being here, alive in the world!

I arrive at New Glarus Woods to find the office closed. It's just a tiny building, but it would've been nice to be greeted by a friendly ranger. I proceed to the parking area and start off on the Havenridge Nature Trail. I am disappointed the fantastic guidebook for this trail is unavailable due to the closed office. If you're here and can get one when you come out to do this hike, it's worth it. The Havenridge is about four miles. I plan on branching out to the Bison Nature Trail to reach my mileage goal.

New Glarus Woods is a wonderful forest, alive and green and multi-storied. It's different from some of the places I've hiked, which were, tragically, full of dead ash trees and dying white pines. This forest sports black walnuts, shagbark hickories, basswoods, maples, and oaks. They look blissfully healthy.

Along this trail, I'm pleasantly surprised by all the owl pellets. There must be a dynamic population of night hunters here. There are also wild raspberries starting to pop. I take advantage of this woodland treat, a life-affirming joy in defiance of my aging hip.

I come to a Y on the trail. As I start to pull out my map, I see a "You Are Here" sign. I wish there were more of them in all the parks in the state. Another Y soon appears with no marker, and I decide to take the left-hand side. I end up at a dead end by a road. I'm not sure why it happened. It's not on my map. I backtrack to where I went off to the left and head to the right. On this trail, I come to a T intersection, and another "You Are Here" sign marks my way. Now, I know I'm on the correct trail, and I continue on the next half of the Havenridge.

Thinking I need a snack break, a bench magically appears about 3.5 miles into my hike! It's at the T of the Havenridge and the Vista Trails. After a brief respite, I continue to the end of the Vista Trail, where I hear a delightful sound from the New Glarus Brewing Company, a clock chime on the hour, and see the beginning of the Bison Nature Trail. I find it a dazzling and abundant prairie, and I hike to see the bison statue adorning this grassland.

There is a bounteous profusion of life on this trail: birds singing and tapping, insects buzzing, the warm air heady with pollen and monarchs. I have only seen a few of them this summer, and now, to see so many orange wings is genuinely heartening. This prairie full of coneflower, bee balm, phlox, and milkweed makes me astonishingly happy.

I continue hiking to the junction of the Havenridge Nature Trail and the Fox Trail. I follow the Fox back through the campground to reach my car. With my five miles logged, I change out of my boots into my sandals and head home. On the drive, as I wind around on the detours for Highway 69 and County Road PB, I realize my hip is no longer hurting. The pain of aging, be it emotional or societal or physical, for me anyway, is often alleviated by a good hike!

This evening, I fill my Dancing Dragonfly Winery glass with the last of the bottle I purchased on the way home from Interstate State Park. I sneak outside, attempting to avoid a scolding from the robins. I take the long way out to the far corner of my yard, and there, where they can't see me, I relax after my hike, trying not to disturb my feathered garden companions.

New Glarus Woods State Park

The Questions

1. What about this chapter resonated with you?
2. How have birds been a part of your life?
3. In what ways do you cope with the aches and pains of your aging body?

The Particulars

Sticker Required: Yes

Map on the State Park's Website: Yes, and it is detailed in color

Bathrooms for Day Hikers: Yes, in the office, but also by the playground

Office or Kiosk: Office which can be closed depending on the day or season

Trail Markings: Marked with "You Are Here" signs occasionally

Seasonal Closures: None

Flooding Concerns: None

Five Miles: Easy to get with no circles

Aztalan State Park
Lake Mills

5.05 miles
Highest Point: 893 ft
Lowest Point: 785 ft

July 3, 2022
Raspberries and Magic

On my drive to this park, there were numerous divine creatures hit by cars and left in carnage. As I stand here in the gravel parking lot of this ancient place, I am thinking about the people who used to live at Aztalan, the people who worshipped the Earth and the Sun. They would have never let the carcasses of deer rot away on the side of a highway.

All the damaged beauty, lying motionless on the roadways, is compounding the helplessness I feel today. Petra, my fantastic hiking buddy, was in a car accident, and I am genuinely concerned for her. As soon as I found out, I immediately contacted all our mutual friends. Seeing how my neighborhood community of women came together to make plans to help was heartening.

As a result, my thoughts on this park may end up more tangential and disjointed as I am struggling. I try to remind myself the tragic chaos of life has allowed me this day of grace, and I will endeavor to persevere.

I am wearing my shorty hiking boots again. I used them last at Harrington Beach State Park, where my feet got soaked. It's time to try them again, as they are comfortable and a bit cooler than my big ones. There should not be any wet trails to traverse as I have been waiting for this hot, dry summer day. There is a website to check the flood stage of the nearby Crawfish River. Over the last several weeks, I have been keeping an eye on it to determine the best time to come for a hike. I've been here in years prior, and the river was up past the rebuilt stockade, which cuts across the park, making the trails inaccessible.

As this is a historical site, a small museum is nearby. It is only open on Saturdays and Sundays until 4 p.m., making this a good day to come. It is right outside the park grounds, and I plan to circle back to see it after exploring the trails.

I am definitely glad I printed off the map of this park from the DNR's website. There is only a rough kiosk here, no park office, and no information to take with me.

The trails are primarily wide and mowed grass. None of them are named, which is appalling. They could have unique names from the original people. I am glad to have my little map with me to keep myself somewhat oriented as my mind drifts to thoughts of my friend. I start out hiking along the stockade toward the river. After reaching the Crawfish, I take a left on the trail running along the shoreline. There are a couple of sizable trees down covering the trail in several locations, the result of a recent windstorm. The mosquitoes have an active presence here in this thoroughly shaded area, but the trail is bountiful with raspberries, helping considerably to compensate for the bugs.

Continuing to hike up the hill to the area of the Marker Mounds, I cross the prairie by this magnificent row of behemoths, and it is a welcome respite. The area is resplendent with milkweed and white

Aztalan State Park

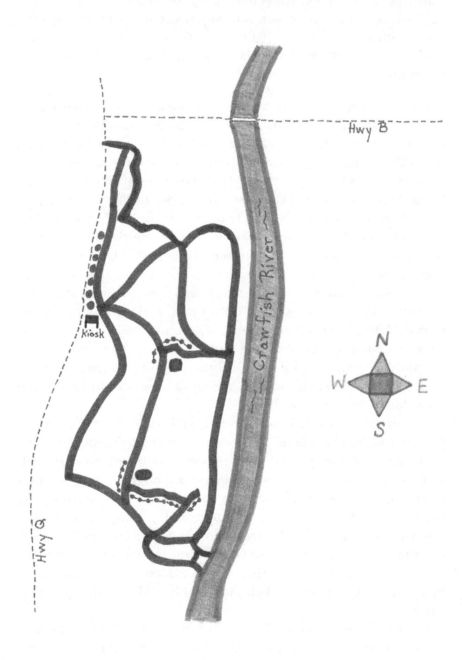

daisies. Even though it is much hotter in the sun, it is outstandingly beautiful and mosquito-free.

Along the other side of the stockade and back to the water's edge, I take the trail to the right this time. A massive, old oak is twisted in half and thrown to the ground. The chaos of a vortex is another reminder of the fragility of life.

There is a kind breeze going in this direction. It is rich with the slightly acrid fragrance of elderflowers and the pleasingly sweet scent of blooming milkweed. They create a high summer fragrance, making me smile. With brilliant sunshine and views of the river, it is a fine wander!

The park is accentuated by informational signs detailing the history of the place and its people. Through one of the signs, I find out Aztalan has a Cahokia connection! I am acutely fascinated by that ancient city. Cahokia, located near what is now St. Louis, Missouri, was a major hub of the great mound-building culture, with earthen pyramids dwarfing the ones at Aztalan and a celestial henge made from enormous tree trunks.

Reaching the end of the river trail, I circle off to walk the double-tiered mound. The view from the top of the largest one in the park is utterly splendid! The steps lead down to an open plaza, where archaeological digs have found this was a ritual mound for gathering, not for burial. The line of trees growing on the shore of the Crawfish River makes it a spectacular view.

Following the trail through the prairie back past the Marker Mounds to the edge of the park, I visit the historical society. It's five dollars to get in unless you're a senior citizen. I explain to the woman working there about my Quest to celebrate my 65th birthday at the end of August. She only charges me three dollars, the senior rate, and I donate the other two dollars to the museum.

There is scant information here about the Aztalan culture. Mostly, the museum buildings are about the remnants of the town of Aztalan, founded in the early 1800s by white settlers. However, there are a few marvelous examples of the works of the original people. They are protected in glass cases and were found on the site of what is now this state park. There are arrowheads, shell beads, copper earrings, and stone disks from a bygone spear-throwing game. The unreservedly most fantastic thing in the museum is the Shaking Tent Pendant! It is in a shadowbox frame hanging on the wall by one of the doors out of the main museum building. It is a carving of a shamanic ceremony the indigenous people of this magnificent place used to contact the Divine for answers to the questions of their lives. I imagine they were the questions all humans ask. Will I find love? Will this coming year be fortuitous? Will my children prosper? Will I die a noble death? It is a remarkable piece of sacred art.

I head back into the park and hike another circuit of the main trail, which runs by the river. The cool breeze and lack of mosquitoes on the right-hand side make it a fun trail to repeat, absorbing what it must've been like for the Native people who lived here. In this location, their abundance allowed them to pursue higher spiritual, communal, and personal needs. It allowed them to aspire to be creative, making jewelry, wonderfully ornate tools, and pottery that were as much form as function. When humans exist out of poverty and subsistence, there is room for the great expansion of culture to be reflected in the existence of art and architecture.

Perhaps they had the time and luxury I do to sit quietly at the end of a busy day and ponder the flow of the river, the arc of the trees, the songs of the birds, the stars in the heavens. It is a genuine gift to have the time to contemplate one's place in the world, to look back and think ahead, to examine emotions of love and loss.

This is the true purpose of my Quest. It is not to find but to reclaim. Letting myself, finally, just be myself. It is one of the supreme gifts of aging. I truly hope the wealth these original people had allowed them to do the same, even if only on a leisurely midsummer day.

Note: The website to check river levels in Wisconsin, https://water.weather.gov/ahps/region.php?state=wi.

Aztalan State Park

The Questions

1. What about this chapter resonated with you?
2. When your friends and loved ones are hurting, how do you cope with the sense of helplessness? What do you do to support them?
3. In what ways are you letting yourself be more authentic as you age?

The Particulars

Sticker Required: Yes

Map on the State Park's Website: Yes, and nicely detailed

Bathrooms for Day Hikers: Porta potty only

Office or Kiosk: Kiosk with no additional information

Trail Markings: Not well-marked

Seasonal Closures: None, but day-use only

Flooding Concerns: Trails may be closed due to high water in the river

Five Miles: Circles required

Yellowstone Lake State Park
Blanchardville

5.25 miles
Highest Point: 993 ft
Lowest Point: 570 ft

July 9, 2022
Purpose and Adventure

As I am traveling to Yellowstone Lake, the roadsides are bejeweled in high summer wildflowers: the frozen blue of chicory, the startling orange of lilies, and the lime-green umbels of burgeoning Queen Anne's lace. The rows of knee-high corn shine with different hues of green, from pale to dark to cyan, and shimmer in the gentle wind like waves across the ocean.

Yellowstone Lake has two, yes, two state park signs! This is the first time I have encountered such a thing. I stop to take my traditional entry selfie with the first sign, as the second one is a tad less impressive.

I exit my car to the sounds of songbirds; whistles and peeps and trills throughout the entire place. It's incredible! I chose an exceptional day to come here—80 degrees with a light breeze and abundant sunshine. There are only a few fluffy clouds in the intense blue expanse. Summer days in Wisconsin are like no other state I've ever lived.

The office is open, and there is lots of merch: t-shirts, patches, pins, books, etc., and a nice brochure/map. A communicative ranger is working, and we talk at length about my Quest and all the phenomenal state parks. From what I can gather, it seems visiting and/or hiking in all the state parks is something many people aspire to accomplish, but rarely all in one summer. Hiking a minimum of five miles in each one is not something he has heard of before. Perhaps it is because there aren't many who want to hike around and around in a small park to reach a mileage goal like I do. They don't know what they're missing!

Waving goodbye to the friendly ranger and jumping back in my car, I drive to the nearby parking lot at the beginning of the Oak Ridge Trail, where I am starting my hike today. The birdsong is remarkably thick and varied. It provides the park with the ambiance of a tropical jungle, an outstanding and beautiful cacophony.

A "You Are Here" sign is at the open triangular area where the Oak Ridge Trail and the Prairie Loop diverge. These trails are well-marked, wide grassy lanes. It's a lovely place to hike.

Walking through this musical forest reminds me of my desire as a 20-year-old to be an ethnobotanist. My first degree was in biology, but I ended up as a social worker. Said dream did not come together for me, but my Quest is about reclaiming. On that note, I want to reclaim my understanding of medicinal plants, their locations, and how to use them. I want to recapture knowledge I have not engaged with for many years. I recall a few: yarrow for colds and fevers, red clover for a sore throat, and mullein for a bad cough.

I finish the Oak Ridge Trail and start on the Prairie Loop. Both these trails have deer tracks leading off into the woodland. I picture an astounding amount of animals hiding in it during the day while I am out here hiking. This forest is full of hickories, their shaggy, gray bark splintering out in strange angles. It is a denser forest than many of the parks I have hiked in, where the ash trees were decimated.

Yellowstone Lake State Park

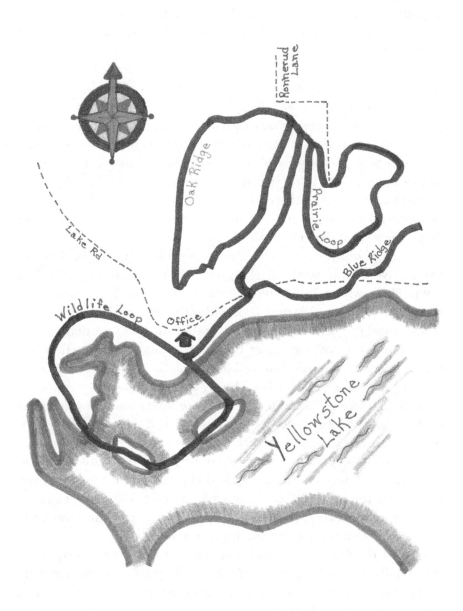

On the Prairie Loop, I encounter a quiet copse of pines with inches of dark brown needles on the ground. Virginia creeper traces its way across their fallen rough surface. These white pines are slowly dying because of the invasive species damaging our Wisconsin forests. My heart breaks for the trees as I take a long moment to stand witness to their slow demise. Farther on the Prairie Loop, through an enchanting open meadow of wildflowers, I spy a gravestone flanked by spruce trees about 20 feet off the trail. It honors a woman named Jane Corbett, who lived from 1925 to 1979. "Gone too soon," it says, and it is graced with a bouquet of faded plastic flowers. It makes me wonder who she was, why she's buried out here, and who still leaves her flowers. Maybe she isn't, and it is simply a marker commemorating her life. Either way, it is an incongruent, albeit charming, sight.

I finish the Prairie Loop and stop for a snack in a park shelter out of the earnest sun. After my break, I venture onto the Wildlife Loop, circling back past the park office. This trail takes me along the lake's edge by a waterfowl area. I stop and greet a delightful family out fishing for the afternoon. The children are all smiles and run alongside me for a while. They share my immense joy in this halcyon day! The trail is full of cattails in the marshy areas, chicory, and grapevines, everything growing all over the place in response to the plentiful sun and water. On the Wildlife Loop, the trees become a maze of willows and birch, with plenty of hazelnuts thrown in for good measure.

My Quest has surely given me a sense of purpose for this summer. After being rejected for a couple juried art shows, I felt aimless and unsure of what to do. My art has been my purpose through the pandemic and remains a daily part of it. Sometimes, an artist has to reclaim creativity, and my Quest is positively helping on that score. As we age, having a purpose is essential for maintaining hope and fighting the darkness of despair and loneliness.

Another of my foundational social work paradigms is the canon of Viktor Frankl. In his seminal book, *Man's Search for Meaning*, he delineates his tenets of Logotherapy or, by another name, Existential Therapy. Why are we here? What keeps us here? What gives our lives meaning and purpose? While working with clients during devastating times of their lives, his ideas assisted me in helping them find a reason to continue, a reason to hope for the future.

Having a purpose, whether abstract or personal, helps convert loneliness to aloneness. Being able to be alone is a description of love in a profound way. Aloneness gives us time to be true to the loving hearts of ourselves. It allows us to explore and confront all life has thrown at us and redefine it, giving it new meaning. It is a love, never lost, because it is given to the self. Life is not less than because of being alone if you are able to find sanctuary in your aloneness.

After finishing the Wildlife Loop, I start on the Blue Ridge Trail, the longest trail in the park. I hike until I reach a small low-water bridge over a babbling creek. What a magnificent trail this is! I will have to return and do the entire length, maybe in the early spring. Then, I could see the lake all the way around before it's blocked by deciduous trees. Today, however, I turn around at the bridge and retrace my steps because I know I will have my mileage by the time I get back to my car.

I have been looking forward to hiking at Yellowstone Lake. I had been here many years ago on one of our mother-child adventure trips. Every week in the summers, we would go on some adventure to somewhere new: to a park, a museum, a lake, or even to a different city to shop. I have a photograph I treasure of my little child, arms reaching to the sky, standing tall and proud on top of the enormous boulder next to the start of the Oak Ridge Trail. We were both immensely excited to be at this park together on that perfect summer day.

Thinking about the photograph reminds me of when I was pregnant. I was hiking along the edge of a sensational river in the Mark Twain National Forest on a day not unlike today. The sky was a brilliant blue, and the intense summer sun filled my body with a contented warmth. The broad but shallow river sparkled with sunlight as it flowed over the rocks scattered along its course. I stood on one of them to get a better view of the breathtaking scenery when I heard a strange cry—the call of an eagle. I remember squinting up at the sky and seeing seven bald eagles soaring above me. As I watched them circle above the stunning place, I felt a strange flutter inside my belly. I wasn't honestly sure I had felt it, and then, there it was again. The quickening happened in accordance with the flights of eagles! I charged myself at that moment to teach my child to be an adventurer, someone who trusted themselves to take on the challenges of this world with fortitude, integrity, and grace.

Thinking back to distant days and the first time I came to Yellowstone Lake; I feel my heart swell with pride. I know I kept the promise made on that golden day in the sight of eagles. I raised an adventurer and remain one myself.

Yellowstone Lake State Park

The Questions

1. What about this chapter resonated with you?
2. How have you been able to reclaim lost aspects of yourself as you age?
3. In what ways do you find purpose in your life? How have these changed over the years?

The Particulars

Sticker Required: Yes

Map on the State Park's Website: Yes, and it is detailed in color

Bathrooms for Day Hikers: Yes, but in the office

Office or Kiosk: Office which can be closed depending on the day or season

Trail Markings: Outstanding signage with frequent "You Are Here" maps posted

Seasonal Closures: None

Flooding Concerns: Some trails can flood due to fluctuating lake levels

Five Miles: Easy to get with no circles

High Cliff State Park
Sherwood

5.11 miles
Highest Point: 786 ft
Lowest Point: 660 ft

July 13, 2022
Navigation and Hummingbirds

I'm heading toward High Cliff, and my GPS says, "Continue on for 86 miles." A broad smile stretches across my face as I hear the directions on this gorgeous summer day. All the shades green has to offer surround me on the drive. Chartreuse, lime, emerald, and fern. Olive, juniper, shamrock, and moss. Mint, celadon, forest, and spring. I feel like I used to when I would return for a visit to Wisconsin during my years living in New Mexico. It is as if my eyes had been craving green, and now they are inundated and satiated by this day.

Driving along on the smooth stretch of newly laid pavement is like walking on the beach at Kohler-Andrae State Park. I want to continue doing it for the rest of forever, happy in my own self, full of joy about the summer. Road trips like this are a form of heaven to me.

I'm wearing my favorite bright blue hiking cap. I put a bee pin on it this Mother's Day in honor of my mother. I added a new bee pin to it yesterday. "Be kind," it says. Now, my hat reminds me of being loved and of being myself. The bee pins also remind me it is vitally important, as we age, to make oneself the priority and to share the world with true friends who make you feel more than, who lift you up, and who make time for you.

The office at High Cliff is open. Outside the door is a new, funky robot solar-powered check-in station. Inside, there's a friendly ranger and some incredible merch: hats, t-shirts, sweatshirts, maps, and nature information. I love their park shirts. They say, "Think Outside the Box" and have an outline of Wisconsin on them. I got a pink one from here a couple of years ago, and it is one of my favorites.

I enter the park and stop in the lot by the Pines Shelter. The map has an access trail from here to the Red Bird Trail. My perennial problem arises, dang it, as the trail on the map doesn't exist where it should be. I grow frustrated trying to find it. After wandering all over the area looking for it, I get back in my car and drive to the other end of the Red Bird Trail, hoping to find the start in the family campground. I find the trailhead, but no parking. I hate it when maps don't match with reality. It makes it overly difficult for the reality of my geographically challenged brain!

The closest parking to the south end of the Red Bird Trail is in the amphitheater lot. I walk back to camping spot number 40, the start of the trail, finally feeling like I can relax into my backpack. It's a nice campground, shady and quiet.

Starting my five miles on the Red Bird, I find it comes to a T fairly quickly. I take it north, to the right. A bit farther on is a stairway descending to the Lime Kiln Trail. I might hit it later. I've been on Lime Kiln many times before, but I'm trying to do something different today by hiking along the top of the escarpment. The views of Lake Winnebago from up here are spectacular!

High Cliff State Park

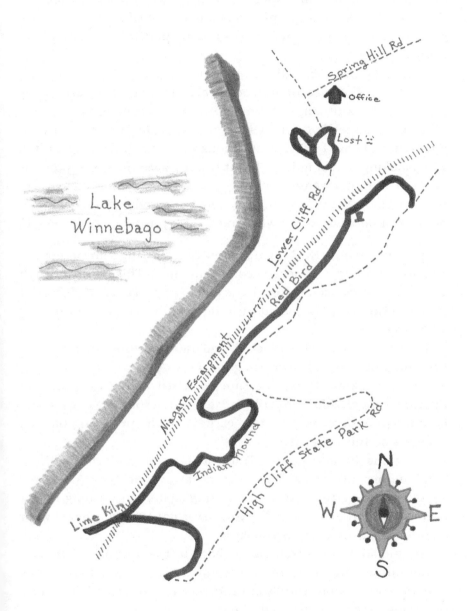

I grew up coming here in my late teens and early 20s and only ever did the Lime Kiln Trail. I spent frequent days dangling my feet off the edge of rock outcroppings and hanging out with friends. Maybe my getting lost here today is about finding parts of this park I have never experienced.

Seems like there is a hiking metaphor and an aging one in here somewhere. The idea of not being able to find the start of my journey and, eventually, locating it after much consternation. Hell, I'll look for something, and it's just not there, or I don't see it even if it is there. I have to search in various ways. It happens most often when looking for something, but it is not what I think it should be, not what I think I want. Eventually, I come across what I needed in the first place. Not just an analogy here but a Rolling Stones song to boot: "You can't always get what you want ... you get what you need."

I take a right onto the Indian Mound Trail, passing a linear mound, a panther mound, and several conical mounds. This is part of High Cliff I have never seen before. I was looking for that, after all, wasn't I? I am continually fascinated with the mound-building culture and adore the panthers!

My frustration with my lack of geographical functioning at the beginning of this endeavor has gone away. All my cares disappear when I am hiking. I take the time to forest bathe, with the sun filtering through this incredibly dense forest of young maples. There is minimal undergrowth in this earnest shade, providing blessed coolness on this balmy day.

Along the Indian Mound Trail, many spur trails head off in confounding directions. There are no arrows or "You Are Here" signs, and it's getting a little frustrating again, but nothing I can't overcome. I am of the mind if you never got lost, you never went anywhere outside your own backyard.

The Indian Mound Trail circles back to the Red Bird Trail, and I continue hiking along the escarpment. The rock outcroppings here take on an otherworldly appearance of an ancient civilization's buildings, long ago reclaimed by nature.

At the Red Bird Trail's north end is a monumental statue of Ho-Chunk Chief Red Bird. A sign relates he was a warrior and a leader during the Winnebago War. It was yet another example of the Ho-

Chunk people fighting back against invasion and exploitation by European settlers. The war was all over in less than a year, with Red Bird arrested and dying in prison a few months later. I take several minutes to gaze out at the lake from the statue's vantage point and visualize this place before, when it belonged to the original people. How beautiful it must've been then—clean and pure and sacred. I would have fought and died for it, too.

Hiking back on the Red Bird Trail, as I near the family campground, I take the steps down to the Lime Kiln Trail to ensure I have the mileage. The descent from the escarpment is enchanting! Numerous rock formations appear, again, resembling the ruins of bygone cities. There is an astonishing hush about the place.

High Cliff State Park is at the top of Lake Winnebago, and I grew up at the bottom. Well, I mean to say the other end. On the way home, I decide to stop in and spend some time with my brother, who still lives on the farm.

He and I are decidedly creative people. He is my older brother and still plays in a metal band a couple of times a month. He is currently putting together another album of his original work. Unlike our other siblings, he and I share an intense need to create. If we couldn't be creating, we would shrivel up and die. He's quite an inspiration to me because he's 67 and still out there slamming his guitar, breaking the rules, and expressing his talent.

On the wide front porch of the old blue farmhouse, he and I talk about everything under the sun—my favorite type of conversation. We sit on wonderful, dark green iron chairs, the vintage kind, which rock slightly because of circles of metal under the seats. He plays softly on one of his acoustic guitars as we discuss hiking, hollyhocks, and hummingbirds.

Along the sunny end of the porch is a trellis, heavy with trumpet vine. He tells me how he learned to charm the hummingbirds as they buzz around the orange flowers. He says he tried playing various types of musics—rock, blues, folk, classical, etc.—but they had no preference. However, when he started experimenting with changes in keys, they started to react. There were some keys they liked and some they intensely disliked, causing them to fly away. Their favorite, he says, is the key of "C." If hummingbirds are near when he is playing guitar on the porch, he plays in that key so as not to disturb their inquisitive beauty. As he tells me this, starting to play again, three hummers whir around his head before rejoining the others near the vine. My brother, the hummingbird whisperer!

Driving home with the setting sun, I am thinking about the many times I have gone to see my brother's bands over the years. As a young woman, I was his stalwart groupie, exceedingly proud to watch him play. After moving from Wisconsin, I rarely saw all the permutations of musicians he worked with. Now he is an old bird lover, and his current band includes some dear friends he has played with his entire life. I have seen this band several times and always find it bizarre. Not because of the music—I love me some headbanging rock and roll—but because of the people I see there. People recognize me as his sister, but I have no idea who they are. After all, we have changed greatly in 35 to 40 years.

Today, as my brother and I were talking, he mentioned a friend of his having recently visited. I said, "I remember him. I slept with his brother."

He responded, "I slept with his wife. Well, that was before they met and got married." We both laughed about our reminiscing. I guess, in our younger days, we knew how to charm and whisper other things, too!

High Cliff State Park

The Questions

1. What about this chapter resonated with you?
2. When you return to places you frequented when you were younger, what memories do you find there?
3. Remembering times when you have been lost, both figuratively and metaphorically, how were you able to find your way?

The Particulars

Sticker Required: Yes

Map on the State Park's Website: Yes, and it is detailed in color

Bathrooms for Day Hikers: Yes, in the office and other picnic areas

Office or Kiosk: Large, nice office with displays; can be closed depending on the day or season

Trail Markings: Infrequently marked

Seasonal Closures: None

Flooding Concerns: None

Five Miles: Easy to get with no circles

The Trip to Paradise
Cornell and Paradise, Michigan

13.42 miles
Highest Point: 816 ft
Lowest Point: 589 ft

July 17–July 20, 2022
Ghost Towns and Fresnel Lenses

July 17, 2022

I'm taking a break from my Quest hikes to do an Upper Peninsula adventure with my dear friend Diana and my new friend Chris.

On our first night in the UP, we will stay in a lovely, gambrel-roofed cabin outside Cornell, Michigan. We stop for last-minute necessities in the bustling city of Escanaba. If you don't know Elmer's County Market, you are missing out. His smiling face is one of a kind! A couple of six-packs of Yooper Ale are definitely on our shopping list. The last time Diana and I were here, we tried the beer and enjoyed it. We went to the Upper Hand Brewing Company to visit and buy some Yooper to take home with us. It was open, and we walked in but couldn't locate anyone. We joked about how we could wheel a handcart full of beer out of there, but our better angels prevailed. I sent a whimsical email to the brewery, telling them how much we liked their product and how we had stopped by as we passed through, debating our choices with the lack of adult supervision. They sent me stickers, coasters, and bottle openers, which I shared with Diana. It was their way of thanking us for being honest lovers of their beer.

The cabin is on the bank of a shallow section of the Escanaba River. The slow-moving, exceptionally clear water is full of delightful brown frogs and scrambling red-clawed crayfish. The quiet of the place is immense. I stand by the river for the longest time, reveling in it—the lack of noise so absolute as to cause my ears to strain to hear.

We talk and reminisce, making a nice dinner of lasagna and salad. Chris is an incredibly thoughtful person. The bottle of wine she brought is called "3 Girls," and we laugh together until the stars come out. We can see the arc of the Milky Way from this remote location, something I have sorely missed living in the city.

July 18, 2022

After a breakfast of dark coffee and fresh croissants, we pack a lunch and head out for an adventure. The temperature is expected to be in the high 90s, and we are off to the cool shores of Lake Michigan on the Garden Peninsula. Our destination is Fayette State Park. I read about it in my UP travel book, and it sounds like a great way to enjoy this amazing and sweltering day.

On the way, we make a side trip to see Kitch-iti-kipi, the great Mirror of Heaven. Diana and I have seen it before, but Chris has not. It is an outstanding freshwater spring, over 200 feet across and 40 feet deep, reflecting the world. It is eternally cool but never frozen. Everyone I have ever brought here is shocked to see it, phenomenal as it is and, yet, not commercialized. Only a Michigan State Park day pass is needed to get in, and the raft ride is free.

There is a short boardwalk to the unusual human-powered raft, which takes sightseers out to the middle of the spring and back. The raft has a partial glass bottom, and it's moved by the muscles of the riders turning a large wheel attached to a cable. As it slowly moves to the center, the roiling sand at the bottom is easy to see, as are the giant trout plumbing the water. It is a magical marvel of nature, over 10,000 gallons per minute bubbling up from the depths! Anytime I get close to Kitch-iti-kipi, I can't help but stop to experience it. The beauty of this clear, teal-colored pool never grows old.

Next, onto the ghosts of Fayette in the park encompassing its remains. It is a historical site of the once bustling 1880s town. Fayette's smelting furnace operation changed iron ore into pig iron bricks for transport to Escanaba for processing. This wonderful park includes a factory, a multi-story hotel, and houses of the three very stratified social groups. In all, there are 20 buildings at various stages of preservation.

The houses of the middle class, the shopkeepers and blacksmiths, the foremen and doctors, can all be toured. Livable and well-appointed, the few remaining houses all occupy one street of the old town. It was the liminal street located between the furnace and the furnace workers.

The house of the factory superintendent, who oversaw all the shipping, hiring, and leadership of the village, is a commanding spot on a high point near the shoreline of Lake Michigan. A broad, wraparound covered porch looks back toward the factory, off to the blue waters of the Big Bay de Noc, and across to the tremendous limestone bluffs.

The houses belonging to the working class—those who gave their lives to the heat, misery, and cacophony of the furnace—are gone. However, a re-creation of one of them is standing where many once stood. The squalid conditions the workers had to endure, the overcrowding, poverty, lack of sanitation, and frequent deaths from injury and disease are presented in stories inside this small cabin. More history is on view in the Visitor Center of the park.

My writer's mind starts to tell my friends a story about the women who lived here, a story of desperation, community, love, and exploitation between the various classes. Perhaps the women gossiped together while making bread, talking of babies and broken hearts. Maybe the shopkeeper's daughter fell in forbidden love with a handsome, gritty charcoal maker. Conceivably, the superintendent coerced sexual favors from the pretty young wives of the furnace workers, threatening to fire their husbands if they did not indulge his lust. The gaiety of children, unaware of their poverty, playing in the cool waves of the lake juxtaposed against the deaths that came too early to many of them. My friends agreed with me; this place has terrific stories to tell and would make a great TV series!

We hike to the bluffs to see them up close. They have the look of a smaller version of the famous ones of Dover—white and gleaming in the afternoon sun. As we get near, the whole area takes on the appearance of the ruins of an ancient city, like the rock formations of several Wisconsin State Parks. Here, eking out a living among the cracks in the bluffs, are some of the oldest living cedars in the entire Great Lakes region, their roots working to split the limestone for 1,400 years!

We drop our packs by the bluff, remove our hiking sandals, and sit on the ledge of the lake, our feet loving the forever-cold waters. The time here, next to generous and caring friends, talking, musing, and delighting in our summer freedom, will surely be one of my brightest memories in the coming winter months.

All three of us are interested in more of the history, so we don our gear and hike to the cemetery of this ghost town. What a grand spot to spend eternity on the shores of Lake Michigan, surrounded by the hush of a forest. The stones stand witness to the devastating diseases coursing through the workers over the years. Whole families were wiped out by the usual suspects of dysentery, pox, fever, and "the bloody flux." I think about the courage of those left behind and of a funeral I attended for a young boy taken too soon. I remember sitting in the church, watching his father as one of the pallbearers carrying his coffin. The look on his face, his teeth gritting hard with the burden of steadfastly bearing his son's body to its grave. A burden, righteously carried, a burden unlike any other. I predict the trauma in the father's left hand from grasping the coffin handle will last a lifetime. Perhaps in 20 to 30 years, his hand will ache, and he'll rub it absentmindedly. For a soft, brief moment, until he realizes why, he will find peace. Peace in the moment before he knows his hand still bears the wound of the day he carried his lost boy home. I wrote a poem about that day, and I remain honored to have been able to provide a modicum of solace to the boy's school friends. I include it at the end of this section.

All in all, our excursion at Fayette State Park was a good six-mile hike on an intensely sunny day made cooler by virtue of the majesty and wonder of Lake Michigan. We enjoy our last night at the Cornell cabin, with a comforting fire at the riverside, sitting in the twilight watching deer coming out of the forest to drink. It has been a special day.

Poem for a Grieving Father

It is my last gift.
The last gift I can give you, my son, my strength.

The strain in my arms.
The clench of my jaw.
The set of my brow.
My eyes locked forward, unblinking.
My son, my strength is yours.

With my strength, I bear us to new lands, my son.
Yours, a land of unfathomable mystery.
Mine, a land of unfathomable sorrow.

All my strength is yours, my son.
My final gift
As I carry your coffin away.

July 19, 2022

This morning has us packing up and heading to Paradise, a tiny hamlet on the outskirts of Upper Michigan's Tahquamenon Falls State Park. We rented a cabin on the shores of Lake Superior, not far from the center of town. It is a scenic three-hour drive from Cornell. After we arrive, we take time to settle into our new spot with its breathtaking view of the greatest of the Great Lakes.

Hiking gear at the ready, we are off to the state park for a late afternoon wander to view the Upper Falls. We stop in the Visitor Center to grab information and maps. There is merch of every description and a brewery right here in the park. We formulate a plan to return there after our hike.

The Upper Falls of the Tahquamenon River is loud and coppery, awe-inspiring and magnificent! Its unique color is the result of the influence of the forest: cedars and spruces and hemlocks. I feel a sense of sincere humbleness standing next to its powerful force. The short hike around it has multiple viewing platforms to take in the grandeur of the second-largest falls east of the Mississippi.

With our brief sojourn complete, we wander back to the Tahquamenon Falls Brewery. We each buy a cold pint in a special glass printed with their logo. A local brew on a hot day shared with friends after a fabulous outing is the best!

Back to the Paradise cabin for dinner and a conversational fire on the bluff above the lake. The three of us bond over wine and stories of men and memories of children. I feel exceedingly fortunate to have these two women as my friends—easy and reciprocal in our relationships with each other. They are true blessings in my life!

July 20, 2022

Our first morning in Paradise. It almost sounds like there should be half-naked firefighters serving us breakfast in bed in this scenario. Alas, instead, it is up early to hike again at Tahquamenon State Park. We begin at the Upper Falls, taking the Giant Pines Loop to reach the Wilderness Loop Trail, which will take us on a solid seven-mile route to and from the Lower Falls and allow us to have some time in the deep forest.

As we start out, the air is still, the shade is intense, and the ground is wet from a rain a few days prior. We stop to gaze at the largest white pine in the park. There is an informative sign nearby relating its immense size and age: 120 feet high, 5 feet in diameter, 15 feet in circumference, and 185 years old.

Stopping, albeit for an astonishing tree, is not a good idea. It let the hordes of mosquitoes following each of us catch up. Even with near-constant DEET reapplications, we decide to turn back after about a mile. By the time we decant from the mosquito-ruled hellscape of the dense forest, we all swear they have drunk a couple of pints of our blood! We regroup and drive to the Lower Falls, imagining the hike to them on the Wilderness Loop Trail would be gorgeous after a hard freeze killed all the insect vampires.

When I was here in the past, the only way to the island in the center of the Lower Falls was by boat. I am amazed to see a new, shiny bridge now spans the space. The area around the Lower Falls has been built up with boardwalks, making for much-needed accessibility. The new bridge leads to more boardwalks and trails on the island. We get in a good hike while listening to the thunder and rhythm of the cascading water all around us. The breeze here is keeping the ever-present mosquitoes at bay.

Happy from our experience at the Lower Falls, we return to our cabin for brunch and a quick nap as the early afternoon becomes cool and overcast.

With rest and food, we are ready for another adventure to the Great Lakes Shipwreck Museum. It is located outside Paradise on the grounds of the Whitefish Point Lighthouse, the oldest in operation on the lake. It is here where Lake Superior begins to meld with Lake Huron that many a poor sailor met his death in the icy, cold waves.

The museum consists of several buildings, all with tales of this place's unbelievable and calamitous history. The glorious glass Fresnel lenses used in lighthouses can be seen in many sizes. The one hung high in the main museum building is a Second Order. It is almost six feet in diameter and is not the largest size! There is a smaller Fourth Order lens, three feet in diameter, in a case for viewing up close. It is truly a divine work of art. To think these powerful lenses that guided the ships of the great lakes were once lit with the oil of sperm whales boggles my imagination.

Of course, before we leave the museum grounds, we have to watch the short film about the lamentable wreck of the famous SS *Edmund Fitzgerald*. At the end of the showing, the only dry eyes in the house belong to the woman working in the theater, who hands out tissues to the viewers as we leave.

On our drive back to our little cabin, we stop at the Paradise Grocery for more Yooper Ales to bring home. As we peruse the store, we are eyed with some suspicion by the local shoppers and employees. We are strangers, after all, with KN95 masks on and me with blue hair. I go to check out first. The woman working the register is aloof until I remark on her tattoo. I tell her I love it and show her mine. We each have a remarkably similar pair of birds on our right wrists! I ask the reason for hers and tell her the reason for mine. Both tattoos are about flying with someone we love with all our hearts. It is the perfect icebreaker! As we talk more of tattoos and small towns, my friends check out with their ales, and we wave a happy goodbye to the helpful staff. I have found, over the years, genuine curiosity about tattoos is the way to many a stranger's kinder side.

We spend the evening in peaceful camaraderie, packing and preparing for the drive home tomorrow, which will include a Quest stop for five miles at Governor Thompson State Park.

Governor Thompson State Park
Crivitz

5.18 miles
Highest Point: 990 ft
Lowest Point: 910 ft

July 21, 2022
Electricity and Blueberries

Dreamland Avenue. Moonshine Hill Road. Skyhawk Lane. Molly Four, Meadowlark, and Jack Pine. These are some of the wonderfully creative street names we pass on our way off Highway 141 to this park. My supportive friends Diana and Chris are totally on board with helping me with my Quest as we journey home from the Upper Peninsula of Michigan.

Diana and I try to take adventure trips together whenever possible—one year strolling through Barcelona and one year hiking in Ireland. This is the second time we have been UP'ing together. This time, we decided to invite Diana's friend Chris, who I am still getting to know and genuinely appreciate. On this trip to the UP and back, I am glad I am traveling with true friends! We do things together, like make coffee, build fires, cook, and are considerate of each other, our differences, and our challenges. We thank each other and take turns with ideas. It is the easy flow of reciprocal friends spending time together, the effortless flow of complete electrical circuits humming along side by side.

I consider friendships as comparable to the flow of electricity. All of us have our own electrical circuits. Think of it like the simple case of a lightbulb. Current flows until it reaches the bulb, and only a complete circuit will create light. A person with kind, generous, and loving energy operates like a full circuit. They constantly feed their own flow and ensure everything is working properly, with or without the added energy of others.

Some people's grids are high maintenance, demanding, and needy. They have to be in control of all the electrics with which they are involved. They aren't necessarily coming from a bad place; they are simply trying to shine without enough internal energy. For them to produce light, they have to take from others, and any disruption challenges the function of their incomplete network. An example would be those erstwhile companions from the Straight Lake chapter.

Of course, being around genuinely good friends is incredibly re-energizing. Even when you have a full circuit, energy levels do drop, given the circumstances in life. Though not fundamentally needy, recharging our grids with true friends is necessary to continue to produce light. These friends are caring, focused, protective, loyal, and steadfast. They can be counted on to do serious as well as fun things with you. You can talk about everything from long-lost loves to wild dreams to shameful incidents, from gruesome birth stories to battles with cancer to the deaths of loved ones. With this sharing, full circuits are enhanced.

The older I get, the less patience and tolerance I have for people with deficient grids. I want to spend my time, energy, and care on reciprocal, true friendships. If I give kindness and don't receive kindness, I feel sorry for the other person, but I don't want to devote my energy to them.

Governor Thompson State Park

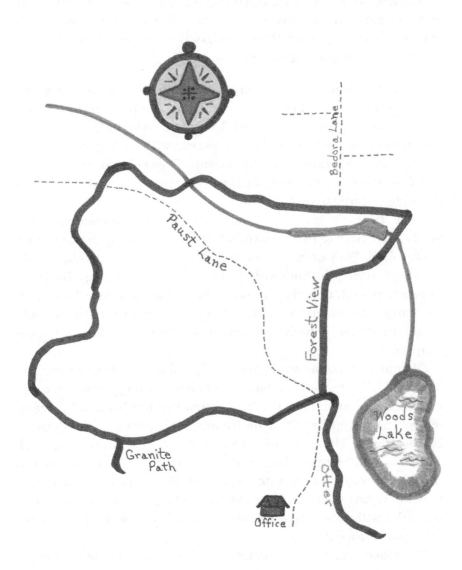

This park has a dazzling and fantastic park office! I think it is the grandest I have seen. The building is massive with multiple gables, and inside is an impressive stone fireplace. The bathrooms are flawless and posh, with multiple stalls. There's lots of merch of every kind and description, as well as two fountains to fill our water bottles.

After a quick lunch by the beach of Woods Lake, we begin on the Forest View Trail. The trail starts in the parking area, crosses the street, and joins with the Pine View Trail to the left for a wander through a pine plantation. The environment here is markedly different from the Tahquamenon area. There are no mosquitoes, and the forest is dry with a hot, steady wind. Given the choice: hot and dry or mosquitoes? Hot and dry always wins!

The Forest View Trail winds through a plethora of different tree populations, from white pines to balsams to maples to oaks. There are otherworldly stands of birch, sentinels against today's striking blue sky. Hazelnuts abound, as do bracken ferns and garter snakes. The Forest View Trail is on remarkably shallow soil, with granite bedrock peeking through on virtually every step. This must be an almost primeval forest in the spring. When wet, I believe the plentiful moss would become plush as it creeps over the exposed boulders along the trail.

Diana finds a few blueberries, though most have already been claimed by birds, deer, and bears. We three hikers savor the cobalt pearls of exquisite blueberry flavor with our faces to the sunshine.

Out of curiosity, we take the Granite Path to the left off the Forest View Trail. It takes us to a spectacular, pre-Cambrian granite outcropping right at the surface. The stone is covered with dry moss and lichen, again making me think of how lush it must be here when there is sufficient rain. The trail to this rocky vista is adorned with wintergreen on both sides. What a delightful little plant! Its sharp fragrance invariably reminds me of northern Wisconsin.

Forest View Trail is the longest trail in the park, and with our side trails and wanderings, it gives us 4.61 miles. We bust out the last bit of distance on the Otter Loop before heading back to the car. Number 24 is in the books!

Back at home, I sit on my deck this mid-summer evening, enjoying the gentle breeze, the setting sun, the cicada hum, and the quiet purr of my cat, who positions herself as close as possible to the inside of the nearby screen door. One of the sure blessings of this Quest is the firm understanding I have to be my own best friend first. Followed then by true friends who support me through thick and thin, as I do for them.

Governor Thompson State Park

The Questions

1. What about this chapter resonated with you?
2. How do your friendships increase or decrease your personal energy?
3. What do you find to be most challenging about being your own best friend?

The Particulars

Sticker Required: Yes

Map on the State Park's Website: Yes, and it is detailed in color

Bathrooms for Day Hikers: Yes, in the office and by the beach area

Office or Kiosk: Large, posh office with displays, may be closed depending on the day or season

Trail Markings: Infrequently marked

Seasonal Closures: None

Flooding Concerns: None

Five Miles: Easy to get with no circles

Wyalusing State Park
Bagley

5.11 miles
Highest Point: 1,186 ft
Lowest Point: 794 ft

July 24, 2022
Small Towns and Odd Jobs

I listen to my country western music playlist while driving to Wyalusing. It includes a song that was my favorite when I first moved to Albuquerque in my early 30s—a song about time. Since I have been thinking a great deal lately about wasting time and spending time and killing time, this track seems very appropriate for my Quest today.

All my life, I've had difficulty telling time, especially on a digital clock. Maybe, it's because I learned to tell time on one of those old wooden music box teaching clocks. Maybe, it's the neurodiversity. Anyway, this and a lack of quality future planning on my part led me to approach my life without a definitive plan.

I have lived like a leaf in a stream, floating wherever the current takes me. Sometimes I was stuck in an eddy, which can be annoyingly uncomfortable, but mostly I flowed along on my way to the great ocean, enjoying doing a multitude of things in my life and trying to keep an open mind.

Every year, when I was employed as a school social worker, I would get to talk to groups of middle and high school students for Career Day, telling them what I did for my job. Inevitably, the question asked was, "How did you become a social worker?" I would tell them about all the jobs I've had in my life, living in four different states:

- Cheese factory worker
- Pizza maker
- Donut fryer
- Lingerie model
- Fabric store clerk
- Greenhouse worker
- Floral designer
- Chemical research and development technician
- Medical lab technician
- Hospital social worker
- Hospice social worker
- Bereavement counselor
- Geri-psych unit manager
- School social worker

The students were perennially shocked by how many jobs I'd had, erroneously thinking they needed to decide on one direction before they graduated and then stay with it. It normalized for them that there are many ways to live a life and that it is perfectly fine to not follow a linear path. Now, not wanting ever to be bored even though I am retired, I claim as my jobs: artist, gardener, writer, and bookstore clerk.

The overarching premise of my life has been developing connections and grounding myself wherever I was, whatever I was

Wyalusing State Park

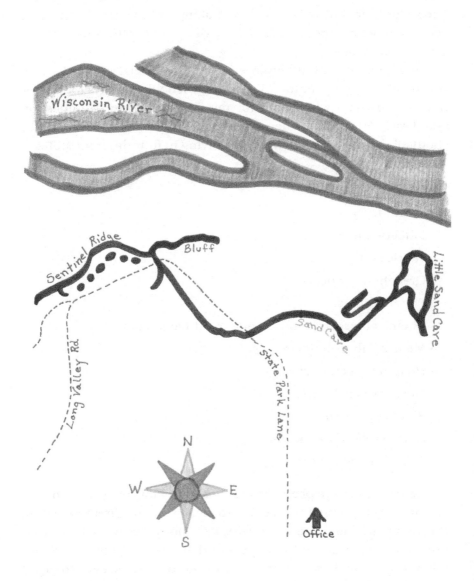

doing. Maybe that is my definitive plan: being where I am, creating sanctuary, enjoying good friends, and searching for beauty. Perhaps, not the best plan, but not the worst one either. It is a fundamental task of aging: reflecting on your past, befriending it, and traveling forward with it in a healing way.

On the drive west to the Mississippi, the roadsides are covered with the periwinkle blue of chicory and the white umbels of Queen Anne's lace. Acres of cornfields, undulating in the breeze, are starting to tassel.

If you end up taking County Highway P, be prepared with an excellent kick-ass highway song before you start driving on it. It is an outstandingly fun road with big hills, wide curves, and a 55 mph speed limit! It makes me wish I still had my sweet little Ninja 250 motorcycle.

Entering the park, I find a wonderful, open building surrounded by one of the loveliest gardens I have seen outside of a state park office. The majority of them have small native plant gardens, but Wyalusing's is phenomenal. There is no merch, but it has lots of maps and information. The older woman ranger is excited to hear about my Quest. She fills me in on trailhead locations, closed trails, and the best ones to hike. She provides me with sound advice on this sweltering day to not go all the way down to the river. She warns hiking back up when it's over 96 degrees is not the safest idea.

I start my mileage on the Sand Cave Trail, heading to the Little Sand Cave Loop. Hiking into the shade of the forest, I take off my sunglasses and am enchanted by the beauty of this magnificent green place on this high summer day. My wonky hip is a little sore today. It's probably due to all the hiking in the Upper Peninsula of Michigan this past week, followed by ninja gardening yesterday. I felled a small tree with my chainsaw and spent hours hauling and distributing three yards of cedar mulch. I will take it a little easier, which isn't a bad thing since it's such a warm and extremely humid day, and I am an old woman, after all!

The bugs are pretty nonexistent, but so is the flow of water, as there hasn't been a downpour here in many weeks. What is probably a stunning waterfall when there's been regular rain is now a slight flow over many layers of cascading rocks, making for an easy step across to continue on the trail.

As I hike on Little Sand Cave Loop, I see its namesake. It has a delightful trickling waterfall draining down on smooth-edged rocks. I imagine when it's raining heavily here, the place is running with water, and the sound is glorious. Many parts of the trail look like they could become slippery on those kind of days.

Hiking back along the loop, I take a spur to the Big Sand Cave. Again, only a small trickle of water is cascading down the carbonate-sandstone cliffs, but the colors! Emerald green and yellow ochre— truly beautiful! At the pebble base where the waterfall hits the ground, there is a scattering of stones, an enchanting shade of turquoise green. I wonder if they have copper in them and if they're coming out of the cliffs as this waterfall runs.

Due to the heat of the day, after wriggling my fingers in the falling water and splashing some on my face, I decide to take respite in the cool shade of this microclimate. I let my mind wander to the idea of time: spending, wasting, fleeting.

Most workdays, I hit the snooze button on my alarm clock, which gives me an extra four minutes before it goes off again. I think about four minutes in the liminal space between asleep and awake. It isn't long, but I often have vivid dreams in this brief interval, dreams of entire lifetimes. I think, too, about what the last four minutes of my life will be like. How dissimilar they will be from the soft, quick sleep my cheerful clock reminds me is over.

Time stretches out, expands, and shrinks, depending on what's happening in life. Being older, do I waste more time now? I feel like I do. Sometimes, I chastise myself for not being productive enough after a life of working way too much. I wasn't necessarily effectual in every single minute, but I seemed to be able to accomplish a great deal on any given day. I have to remind myself that spending an hour reading or 20 minutes solving a sudoku puzzle is beneficial time. Spending what seems like just a few minutes, but it's actually hours on an art project, is not wasting time. It is time well spent! Be gone, chastising voice; you are no longer relevant.

I finish the cave trails and take a seat at a picnic table near their trailhead outside the Paul Lawrence Interpretive Center. My blue hiking hat is soaking wet and dripping. Its moisture-wicking fabric is no longer wicking moisture. It is extraordinarily humid and heavy and hot with a coming storm. I take time to drink the rest of my water bottle and fill it and my hydration pack from the nearby fountain. Jumping in my car and cranking the AC, I drive over to connect with the Sentinel Ridge and Bluff Trails.

The overlook of the confluence of the Wisconsin and Mississippi Rivers must be brilliant on a sunny day. It is strikingly lovely even on this cloudy, soon-to-rain afternoon. After hiking the short Bluff Trail, I head off down a long length of stairs onto the Sentinel Ridge Trail.

The forest here is close and still. All over on these hills above the rivers are conical and linear mounds. The lives of the original people who lived here were probably filled with plenty—the rivers and forests brimming with food and the views off the cliff stirring their souls as they do mine.

Increasing humidity and the nearness of rumbling thunder prompt me to exit the trail into the Green Cloud Picnic Area and return to my car to finish my five. As much as I adore thunder and lightning, I don't want to get caught in a rolling storm in a dense forest.

This has been by far the wettest I've gotten during this hiking Quest. I have hiked in the rain and not been this soaked. It's oppressively humid, and there's absolutely no wind. I'm looking forward to hopping in the shower when I get home, even though I feel like I have taken a shower already in my clothes and backpack! I'm glad I keep a set of dry things in my car to change into when I'm done with a hike, especially when there are hours of traveling back to Madison.

Driving home on the fabulous County Highway P, I pass the Dew Drop Inn. I always appreciate a good play on words! It is an older, gambrel-roofed, blue building with an expansive deck overlooking the nearly endless horizon of cornfields. The parking lot contains several ATVs. There are folks outside, talking and laughing and drinking. I wonder about this isolated farming culture and reminisce about being part of a similar situation when I was young. I used to truly enjoy all the small-town fireman's picnics and mud runs, the cute farm boys and beer tents. I feel a pang of loneliness, missing the sense of camaraderie found in the rural Wisconsin gatherings of neighbors and friends.

I sit outside this evening, enjoying the power of the storm. All the hair on my body stands on end, full of static electricity! The lightning brightens the sky remarkably, as if dawn has come. The thunder booms in vast waves of resonant sound. No wonder I appreciate the word *ceraunophilia*, which means to love thunder and lightning and to find them intensely beautiful.

I bring to mind the salient words of a Shakespeare sonnet. I had memorized them for a special occasion years ago: "Love's not Time's fool." If I truly intend to spend these last years of my life in wisdom, to spend those last four minutes with a light heart, then I need to devote time to loving myself and the people I care about. I need to let everything else sort itself out and stop worrying about being productive.

Sonnet 116

"Love's not Time's fool, though rosy lips and cheeks
Within his bending sickle's compass come;
Love alters not with his brief hours and weeks,
But bears it out even to the edge of doom.
If this be error and upon me prov'd,
I never writ, nor no man ever lov'd."

—William Shakespeare

Wyalusing State Park

The Questions

1. What about this chapter resonated with you?
2. Make a list of all the jobs you have had in your life. Which were the best and the worst?
3. How has your relationship with time changed as you've gotten older?

The Particulars

Sticker Required: Yes

Map on the State Park's Website: Yes, and nicely detailed

Bathrooms for Day Hikers: Yes, in the office and at picnic areas

Office or Kiosk: Office which can be closed depending on the day or season

Trail Markings: Infrequently marked

Seasonal Closures: None

Flooding Concerns: Trails may be difficult during wet times of the year

Five Miles: Easy to get with no circles

Lake Wissota State Park
Chippewa Falls

5.22 miles
Highest Point: 1,000 ft
Lowest Point: 904 ft

July 31, 2022
Dementia and Ageism

My good friend Britt is with me, and I am giddy and excited to be hiking with her! She is a teacher and lifelong adventurer with tremendous stories. I booked us a hotel room for a two parks in two days trip to Chippewa Falls. We have been trying to carve out a couple of weekends this summer for her to join me, including this one and, hopefully, one to Rib Mountain State Park in early August. The drive today is full of everything under the sun conversation, making the time and the distance fly by.

Lake Wissota has a grand sign and a deluxe office, a clue to it having considerably more visitors. I wish they all had fabulous entrances, as each park I have hiked has its own unique beauty.

Britt and I take a moment to talk with the older woman ranger who thinks my Quest is amazing. I ask her about trail information, as I was unable to find any on the DNR's website. She pulls out a multi-page list of trails and their descriptions from a file rarely shared with visitors due to a lack of funds for printing costs. Again, I cannot understand why our glorious Wisconsin State Parks are not fully funded.

I tell her I am honored by her kindness and generosity in giving me a copy. She smiles and remarks my Quest is probably why I don't look anywhere close to sixty-five. I feel happy and validated, and my hikes are exceptionally better when I can chat with a friendly ranger!

I have always had the "looks younger than she is" thing. I used to hate it when I was in my mid-20s, and people would ask me what year I was going to finish high school. However, it became a boon as I got older, especially regarding dating younger men. While physical looks are a sign of age, I believe temperament is a substantially better indicator. I think what keeps me seemingly younger is a combination of being open, curious, outgoing, and involved with current ideas. Nothing ages a person faster than closemindedness, bigotry, and the "isms."

With the entry photo and office visit complete, we stop at a table by the Lake Wissota Overlook, giving us a stunning view of the water. A nearby educational sign sports a topographic relief map and historical details about the park. It is a prime spot for a pre-hike picnic. Britt is an accomplished vegetarian cook, and she did not disappoint today with her terrific recipe for tofu wraps. They are the perfect meal after our three-hour drive and before our five-mile hike. I am dearly gifted to have friends who can put on a good picnic!

We start out from the Overlook to the beginning of the Lake Trail. It follows a ridge above the shoreline, and with the day brilliant and the sky cloud-strewn, the views are spectacular. The constant breeze off the water makes mosquitoes nonexistent. There are effigy

Lake Wissota State Park

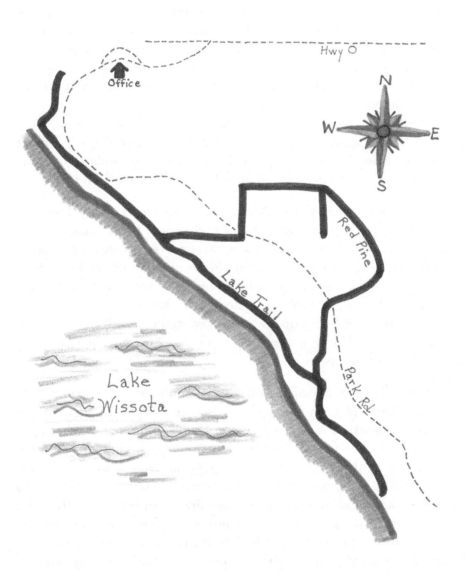

mounds along this trail. I am acutely moved to see them, feeling the history and ancientness of the places where they exist.

There is a spot along the Lake Trail where you can descend a stairway to the water's edge to take in the scenery of the mighty Chippewa River, slowed by a dam to form this lake. We spend several minutes here enjoying the gift of this day. Proceeding on the trail until its end near the beach area, we again take time for the view. My soul is drinking in this enchanting place!

I think you can learn a great deal about a person when you're hiking with them. Even if you know them well, there is always something new to experience about who they are, their history, and their dreams. It has to do with the slow motion of walking through the forest with someone, the hush and the beauty and the connection. Conversations can range from anywhere to everywhere, making it a wonderful thing. To share inner thoughts in a tranquil, content place is an excellent recipe to strengthen a friendship.

As we hike, we start talking about the many trials of working in K–12 schools, dealing with all the behavioral and mental health concerns of countless children, families, and staff. This has me thinking about the people with marked levels of despair I supported as a social worker. As I age, the need to actively confront my own feelings in this regard is one of the main reasons I love to hike.

When we are out with nature, she wraps us up in her greens and her blues, her browns and her reds. Even in the dark winter, she surrounds us in her whites and grays. Embraced by all these colors, it is difficult to feel despair. It is difficult to imagine not wanting to be in this immense, wide world. In nature, color and wildness bring resilience. It is the same for us.

Our bodies are made to be in nature. Listening to the sounds— the rustling of leaves, the chaotic symphony of birdsong, the aching creek of trees in the wind as they bend and sway. Experiencing the smells—the warm, dusty scent of sunshine on a sandstone bluff, the heady perfume of petrichor, the tang of a wintergreen leaf. Yes, even the smell of dead alewives on a Lake Michigan shore. To feel the roughness of a shagbark hickory, the caress of moving water, a humid breeze on outstretched hands, the sense of electricity from an impending storm. These sensory experiences are what our souls truly need. If only every grade of our schooling would emulate the meaning of Kindergarten: children spending time in the garden of nature.

The more removed from nature we are, the easier it is to succumb to despair. As I hike beside my friend in this marvelous park, I mourn for the people in the world who will never be in a place of green and blue, brown and red, but only in concrete and shadow.

We continue our hike on the Red Pine Trail through a managed pine plantation, here since the 1950s. It brings us back around to the Lake Trail after some confusing moments. I have come to believe it is not a quality hike without getting a tad lost, but perhaps it is the geographically challenged part of my brain talking. As we arrive back at my car, another five-plus miles at park number 26, I know I will return to Lake Wissota again. My curiosity about this park is piqued by the trail information given to me by the kind ranger. It is astonishingly picturesque here, with miles more I want to explore.

The room I booked for us at the Cobblestone Hotel is decent, not too expensive, and right in the heart of Chippewa Falls. Everything we need is within easy walking distance, including a scenic park on the river.

We clean up and change out of our hiking clothes. Britt does research into some vegetarian restaurants close by. She decides on the Blue Marble Pub, a place with wood-fired pizza and sandwiches as well as local beers on tap. It has an inviting outdoor patio for us to sit and enjoy the warm evening air. What an excellent choice!

On the walk over, we enjoy the interesting neighborhoods and eclectic houses. We locate seats at one of the pub's umbrella tables close to their little herb garden just as our waitress comes out to greet us. She is a striking and beautiful woman with lavish green hair and several lip piercings. I wonder if it is difficult for her in this small town, and I hope she has found other alternative people to create her tribe.

When she returns with our sandwiches and pints of Leinenkugel's, I strike up a conversation with her regarding her multiple tattoos. I am endlessly curious about the art others choose to permanently share with the world. She tells me stories of her four daughters, symbolized on her skin, and how she is raising them to be strong, independent women. What a gift she is giving to the future!

After our sensational meal, Britt and I decide to wander over to Riverfront Park before returning to the hotel. The last few songs of a Sunday concert in the obviously new bandshell are being played by a hip cover group. There are many families and food carts and flower gardens. We walk to the shore, find a sizeable swinging bench, and take the time to share stories, to be, to swing. This has been a positively fine day, and tomorrow, another hike.

Back in our hotel room and settling into sleep, I ponder tattoos and am reminded of the elderly patients I worked with who suffered from dementia and Alzheimer's disease. I was lucky enough to have been trained in Validation Therapy by its developer, Naomi Feil. It is an insightful way to interact and communicate with patients who have lost their ability to recall. It helped me discover remarkable connections with those who seemed lost inside themselves.

Our bodies remember things. They save memories as our brains do. When brains deteriorate, and the pathways are lost, the body can still find them. Knowing this is why I have tattoos, so my body will remember important times and loved ones in my life.

I have countless stories of people whose bodies revealed vivid memories their brains could no longer summon. One is of a man who refused to converse and would sit in his hospital room, hitting his thigh hard with his fist. Using my Validation Therapy skills, I was able to ascertain why. He revealed he had lost all his memories—couldn't find them anywhere—but there were ones so vitally important he had to hold on to them no matter the personal cost. They were the memories of his son, the son who he used to perch on his thigh and tell stories, give hugs, and share love. He hit his thigh repeatedly so as not to forget his boy.

Another is of a woman who lived with one of her daughters. The advanced state of her Alzheimer's had left her only able to rock back and forth, endlessly counting on her fingers. Through a series of interventions with these therapeutic techniques, I learned what her fingers remembered. Her daughter sat in awe of her mother's stories about the eight children she did not want to forget as she counted them off over and over. Each finger held her memories of them, their families, and their lives.

Our bodies remember things: good and bad, divine and traumatic. And therefore, I actively store the sublime ones I want to keep in case my brain is no longer able to locate them.

Lake Wissota State Park

The Questions
1. What about this chapter resonated with you?
2. What do you think keeps you feeling young? What makes you feel old?
3. In thinking about body memory, where have you stored important memories?

The Particulars
Sticker Required: Yes
Map on the State Park's Website: Yes, and nicely detailed
Bathrooms for Day Hikers: Yes, but in the office
Office or Kiosk: Office which can be closed depending on the day or season
Trail Markings: Infrequently marked
Seasonal Closures: None
Flooding Concerns: Possibly in very high water times
Five Miles: Easy to get with no circles

Brunet Island State Park
Cornell

5.31 miles
Highest Point: 1,015 ft
Lowest Point: 971 ft

August 1, 2022
Integrity and Despair

Today is the halfway point between the Summer Solstice and the Autumnal Equinox. I feel the waning of summer. It is a liminal day, a threshold day, no longer one but not yet the other, a transition day at this, my 27th park.

Britt and I are up early for a hotel breakfast and cups of much-needed coffee after our night in Chippewa Falls. We pack up our belongings and hit the road to Brunet Island. The closer we get to the park, the closer to the road the trees become, invariably a good omen.

I stop to get the customary entry photo of my smiling face by the state park sign. Out from behind it walks a doe with two sparkling spotted fawns—cute and delicate creatures.

The park office is small but pleasant. There's a nice bathroom, and even though there is no merch, there is a great deal of information. It occupies what looks like an old 1950s ranch-style house. There is a young woman ranger busily typing on a computer. It would be quite boring in the small space with few visitors unless you were working on a good project. I speculate she is getting her master's degree online in forestry or finance, but maybe she is simply logging hours on Sims 4.

I ask her more about the trails. The Nordic Trail, she relates, while the longest in the park, is exceptionally buggy this time of year. My mind hearkens back to the bloodlust of Kinnickinnic and Tahquamenon, deciding to do the loops on the island instead. Brunet Island sits between the Chippewa and the Fisher Rivers. The breeze from their convergence will surely keep the mosquitoes away.

We get back into the car to drive to the start of the Jean Brunet Nature Trail Loop. This trail has a happy, little bridge flanked by soft, balsam firs. It reminds me of a crossing a fairytale princess might encounter while lost in an enchanted forest. Several small ponds embellish the landscape. I am intrigued to know if otters and beavers live in them. They look to be superb places to play as a water mammal, plus it fits with my whole aesthetic of this place as a fantasy land.

After completing the loop, we head off onto the Pine Trail. It takes us to the boat landing, where an extravagantly huge, woody station wagon is parked. What a fabulous old car! Britt and I laugh, thinking of our similar childhood family station wagon memories: no seatbelts, loud V-8 engines, and falling asleep after endless summer drives spent rolling around in the back with siblings.

The trails at this park are few on the island proper. We connect to the Spruce Trail, which winds past a somewhat incongruent ballfield. It looks odd to see a flat open meadow in this profoundly forested area, and I wonder if the ghosts of past players will emerge from behind the trees. In contrast, several deer wander out of the forest to nibble the tender grass.

Brunet Island State Park

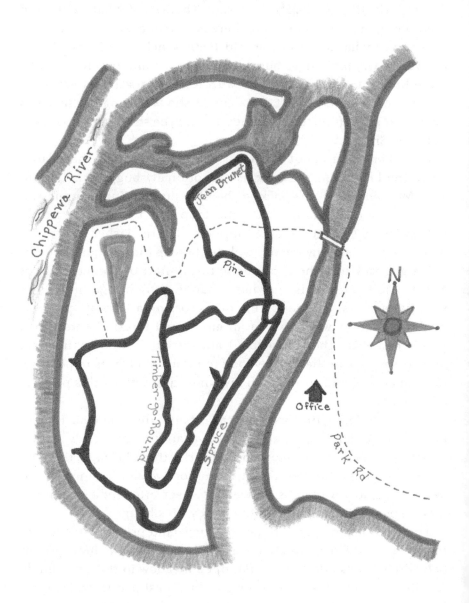

The beach area, with its expansive views of the stunning Chippewa River, offers us the sight of an old iron structure from the industrial age looming nostalgically on the far shore. It is a massive conveyor for moving trees to be cut into lumber back in the boom times of this part of Wisconsin. Fake coyotes are propped in the sand near the shore, meant to scare real geese away. They are worse for wear, their bottlebrush tails threadbare; the geese unimpressed and unafraid.

We wander up a grassy bank to a rustic log pavilion. Built by the CCC, its impressive fireplace has a plaque above the mantle reading, "Where Friends and Nature Meet." This is a fitting motto for our hikes today and yesterday. I feel honored to learn more about my friend and her life. It is incredible, all the things and jobs and places people can experience.

To get in my mileage, we spend some time walking on the road to the south and to the north camping areas, all the while gazing out at the spectacular waterfront. We cut back into the forest on the Timber Trail. Supremely quiet and primordial, it is a dreamscape of grazing deer wandering close enough to touch, undisturbed by our presence. In these woods, there is no understory to speak of, only tufts of fountain-like grass. It makes the forest floor seem to flow like water, adding to the otherworldly quality of the place.

Britt has a quick wit and a fantastic sense of humor! It is one of her most endearing qualities. As we hike on the Timber Trail, taking repeated wrong turns on the Pine Trail, we end up going in circles. She quips we are on a timber-go-round, and we laugh like free, silly children.

My mind wanders back to the importance of being in nature and its effect on our brains as human beings. With the collective despair of COVID, it is even more imperative we have opportunities to be in nature, and it is vitally important as we age. Even when we are elderly and frail, being outside where we can see water and sky, trees and prairie reminds us that we are not alone; nature is with us. She reminds us the cycles of birth and life and death are normal and holy.

The societal grief of the pandemic has us all mourning lost time. Our lives were upended—weddings canceled, funerals left unattended, our important days not marked, not celebrated. It seems strange to think about grieving the loss of time; nonetheless, it is a true occurrence. It can be grieving the loss of an anticipated future, a past no longer to be reclaimed, or a present not comfortable and positive. There is the added grief of having not been able to create memories with loved ones we had to isolate from or who died before their time.

This is why I have mentioned, in some of my musings, how I will hold memories of my hikes in these parks close to me for the coming long, dark winter. It is because I have known, and will continue to know, a sense of despair hiding in the corners of my life. Yes, I still get out and hike in the winter, but it has become increasingly difficult as I've gotten older. My body is more sensitive to the cold, and the idea of falling on a slippery patch of ice is not one I wish to entertain. Having the memories of these fun summer hikes in my brain will certainly help me during my frozen outings when I am wrapped up in thick, heavy layers—metal cleats on my boots— rather than dressed for the heat in short sleeves and thin polyester.

With the five miles obtained, we hop off the timber-go-round onto the Pine Trail and head to the car. On the drive home, Britt plays a comical podcast about the insatiable allure of Girl Scout cookies. Having been a Girl Scout leader back in the day, I can completely relate. Find the dealers. Secure the product. It feels delightful to laugh and drive, sharing the end of this liminal day with a good friend. Stay in the shadows, despair! You are not welcome here.

Brunet Island State Park

The Questions

1. What about this chapter resonated with you?
2. How has the pandemic affected your life?
3. In what ways has the experience of being in nature helped your emotional well-being?

The Particulars

Sticker Required: Yes

Map on the State Park's Website: Yes, and nicely detailed

Bathrooms for Day Hikers: Yes, but in the office

Office or Kiosk: Office which can be closed depending on the day or season

Trail Markings: Well-marked

Seasonal Closures: None

Flooding Concerns: Perhaps in times of high water

Five Miles: Circles required

Copper Culture State Park
Oconto

5.07 miles
Highest Point: 624 ft
Lowest Point: 355 ft

August 5–August 14, 2022
The Days Before

August 5, 2022

I tested positive for COVID yesterday and am at urgent care today. I thought with my age and respiratory issues, it would be good for me to get on top of this early with medications. I am fully vaccinated, boosted, and wear a mask in indoor public places, but I still caught it.

As the nurse is checking my temperature and blood pressure, she asks me a question I have never been asked before by a medical professional or anyone, for that matter. "Do you have a sense of impending doom?"

It is a thought-provoking question, given my Quest. I don't have what she is asking. I don't have extreme anxiety or intense feelings of fear related to the COVID diagnosis. However, as I have written previously, with turning 65 in a few weeks, I am experiencing end-of-life, existential thoughts, not in an overwhelming way, not in a clinical way, simply in a coming-of-age way.

August 6, 2022

All I can do today is lay around and be sick. I'm not doing or accomplishing. I'm not creating or adventuring. I'm defined by the healing of my body. Waiting around to get well is a hell of a lot better than waiting around to die. As a hospital social worker, I worked with many patients for whom this was the case—elders who couldn't understand why "Jesus wouldn't take them" because they were waiting to leave. They weren't terminal; they had lost all purpose and desire to live.

I've done a lot of my social work practice around the issues of suicide and suicide prevention. I believe few people sincerely want to die; instead, they see it as a way to end the suffering they are experiencing, be it emotional or physical. However, I have worked in hospice with enough patients at the end of their lifetimes to make me a firm believer in assisted suicide. I think it should be a fundamental right we have as human beings to end our lives with dignity on our terms instead of lingering in acute pain as the last days and hours pass.

When I was in my early 30s, I went to a meeting of the Hemlock Society in Albuquerque, New Mexico. The Society is one of several organizations seeking to legalize physician-assisted suicide. A young evangelical zealot stood up to protest the whole concept, yelling loudly and spouting scripture at the approximately 100 people who gathered to hear the presenter. A tall, elegant man slowly rose to his feet and pointed a thin finger at the younger man. He began to share how he watched helplessly as his beloved wife of over 70 years slowly died in excruciating pain. How he longed to give her the gift of release, the way they had done for their aged dog many years ago. He was soft-spoken, his raspy voice not able to express all the grief he felt, but he dug deep and shouted at the younger man, "When you are my age and have lived my experience, then you will have the right to say something about choosing to die. Now, you need to shut up and sit down!" The auditorium went utterly silent. The zealot sat down. The wise elder cautiously retook his seat, and the rest of us applauded him for his strength and his truth.

As I rest for another day, feeling fatigued and sickly, I am heartened by the check-ins from my friends, asking how I am faring and offering to bring me things I might need. Sometimes, it can be difficult to ask for help, and it's wonderful when friends reach out.

In the early evening, I feel like I need to go into my garden and feed my fish. I haven't fed them since yesterday morning, and they are hungry. I sit on the swing hanging in my garden, the same one from my front porch in Rocky Comfort, Missouri. It is by my pond, and I'm listening to my bare feet shuffling back and forth as I gently push it. There is the soft sound of the gurgling waterfall, the loud hum of cicadas, and the sharp cries of blue jays. I think it's 96 degrees right now, even though it's close to eight o'clock at night. I close my eyes and absorb the sounds, the textures, and the movements of the air, of my hips on the swing, of my toes rocking slowly. I save them in my mind and in those parts of my body so I will remember this day.

I know there will be days ahead when my memory of this hot August night, made hotter still by the COVID fever, will be a blessing of a memory—not in a cold Wisconsin winter, but in the cold winter of my aging self. It is how lifetimes are described, as the seasons of the year. Autumn is my time now, being almost sixty-five. Winter will be more like 85, and this memory is for then.

August 8, 2022

I find as I get older, I am embracing chaos far more than I did when I was younger. I could not make sense of the world if it were not in some way ordered and predictable in my youth. Now, it is easier to view chaos as the ruling force of our planet. Chaos reigns, but if you pay close attention, you can still find order and beauty in its divine pattern.

Looking for beauty in times of darkness and despair is something I learned from my grandmother, Elizabeth. She was 12 years old when her only sibling died of Spanish flu in the last big pandemic. Her life was one of poverty and chaos and grief, creativity and joy and love. It was in beauty she found solace during her extraordinary times. She taught me it is there to be found, even in absolute devastation.

August 12, 2022

COVID symptoms continue to zap my strength, but I am slowly improving. I sit here, looking out my front window, fatigued and unable to do much of anything. I am reminded I have to realistically think about only having 5 to 10 years left of my life. The Quest has helped me in keeping existential dread at bay. Today, overcast and rainy as it is, and struggling to breathe, I feel it. I know I need to prepare. I don't want my child to have to deal with my leftover weird collection of stuff. I want them to have a clear plan of what to do after I die. My dad gave this gift to our family, and it was, in retrospect, a wonderful blessing. I want to pay it forward and need to better organize my affairs.

August 14, 2022

I think the main effects of COVID are finally behind me. My lungs are somewhat compromised, but I'm hopeful in the next couple of weeks, I will be able to hit some of my big hikes. Before getting this virus, thinking about doing the Balanced Rock Trail at Devil's Lake State Park was no problem. Now, I feel it's going to be two or three weeks more before my lungs are capable of heading up that strenuous trail again.

August 16, 2022
Chaos and Bees

It feels spectacular to be heading to my next park. On my way out of Madison, I make the wide curved turn off Highway 18 onto I-90, heading toward the 151 North exit and experience something strangely surreal. There in front of me, on the back of a dark blue flatbed truck, is a gigantic, celadon green Chinese dragon. It has a bright yellow neck and a lavender snout and is sporting an enchanting smile. What a wonderful welcome back to hiking after having COVID—a smiling dragon looking at me as I continue on my

Quest!

This is my first hike post-COVID and only my second one in August. Being sick set me back in my endeavors. It is a state park outside my Quest parameters as it is run by Oconto County, but looks to be an easy hike. The DNR's website offers no maps or trail descriptions, only a note to be sure to go before Labor Day.

When I was sick at home these last weeks, I spent some time making a new playlist of big band music to listen to during my drives. It is one of my favorite genres. Back in high school, while everyone else was heavily into disco, I was going to the Oshkosh Public Library and checking out LPs of all the big band greats: Benny, Tommy, Glenn, Artie, the Count, and the Duke. Using the height of available tech for the time, I made mix tapes of all my favorites. There was something special about the cracks, pops, and skips on those worn-out 33 1/3 records. I felt a definite affinity to the 1940s, the time period in which those bands existed. Understanding the music and culture of that decade became invaluable when I was working with WWII vets.

I have used several different psychological frameworks in my social work practice over the years. Erik Erikson's eight stages of psychosocial development have served me well. As I said in an earlier chapter, the final stage starting at 65, is Integrity versus Despair. It is a time to look back on our lives, taking stock of all we have been and all we have done—our triumphs and our regrets. Being able to see our lives as meaningful, fulfilling, and contributing to humankind gives a sense of integrity to our contemplation. Despair, on the other hand, is a reflection of selfishness, wasted time, and unanswered questions.

In this year of turning 65, I have done a good deal of thinking about my life, of processing and considering as I have hiked alone through the forests. Knowing I helped even a handful of people find healing provides me with a sincere sense of integrity about how I have lived my life.

Today, I am remembering one of those people. I used to know his real name, but he preferred his fabulous moniker, Bones. He was a commanding person. There was a sense of jocularity about him but also a sense of intense despair. When I knew him, he was 86

Copper Culture State Park

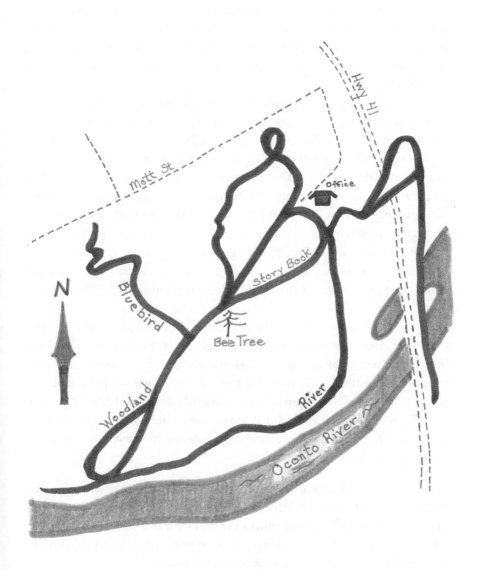

years old, sharing with me how he had survived the attack on Pearl Harbor. He had awoken with an upset stomach and decided to go topside for some fresh air and a cigarette. The first bomb hit his ship, destroying the crew's sleeping quarters, where he would have been if not for the bout of seasickness. He carried the survivor's guilt with him all those years. We spent many hours together working through the painful grief and unimaginable horror he experienced when he was only 18 years old.

At the Geri-Psych program where I worked, the staff and elders would have our lunches together around a big table. One day, as I sat down next to Bones, he put his glass right on the edge of the table after taking a drink from it. Being the mother of a toddler at the time and constantly watching for that very thing, I instinctively grabbed his glass and moved it closer to the inside. It is just what moms do, not wanting it to be knocked off accidentally. He looked at me with the face of a fierce warrior and said, "I know what you just did. And I know why you did it. But at my age, I get to put my glass wherever the hell I want to put it, and you do not get to move it." It took me aback, and I apologized profusely. He smiled and said, "Okay, we're good."

He taught me how to be around elders that day, and every day I knew him. Because someone is old, it doesn't mean you treat them like a child or take away their autonomy and their self-determination. Because someone is old, it doesn't mean they have dealt with all the trauma of their lives. Those were valuable lessons I learned from working with Bones, and I have since used them with many clients in my practice. I only hope someone knows to treat me the same when I get to be in my eighties.

There is no park office here at Copper Culture, but there is a quaint little museum. It is in a 1920s red brick farmhouse decorated with Xs and diamonds made out of blond brick. The museum is staffed with volunteers, and today, there is a knowledgeable and friendly woman at the desk who gives me a map and a brochure.

We talk of Aztalan State Park and Missouri's Cahokia Mounds State Historic Site and of copper smelting. She asks me why I stopped in, and I tell her about my Quest. She is full of excitement about it. This makes me feel pretty damn good, even though my breath is still a little hard to pull.

She tells me about the history of this park and how it is the site of one of the oldest cemeteries in the Americas. In the 1950s, after many years of looting, archaeologists excavated the site, and the people buried here long ago were taken away to reside in the Milwaukee Public Museum.

It breaks my heart to think about the families who cared for them and gently returned their bodies to the earth with sacred objects and divine ceremony. How could they have known their loved ones would be dug out of the ground and deposited on a shelf, somewhere far away from where they were placed in love and grief, in longing and memory? She informs me the Menominee Tribe has been in talks with the Milwaukee Public Museum to have the remains returned to their descendants, to return them to the place where they belong.

They were the people who lived before Cahokia and Aztalan, before the great mound-building culture. They were the Copper Culture, and they created and dreamed and lived here more than 6,000 years ago! They were here 2,000 years before the Pharaoh Khufu decided to construct the Great Pyramid of Giza. I am in awe!

I bid adieu to the museum volunteer and walk back to my car to grab my hiking poles. Normally, I wouldn't use them on a flat terrain, but in my first recovery hike, I decide to bring them along.

I start my five miles on the River Trail, and it's full of the wonder of summer. Goldenrod is blooming all around. I spot a huge golden-yellow spider weaving between stalks of tall grass. Golden frogs are hopping on the trail, a yellow-green so bright they appear gilded as the filtered sunlight sparkles off their backs.

The Oconto River has a strong flow to it, flashing in the sunshine. Its amber water flows swiftly past the trail. Close to the edge, it is remarkably clear, all the way to its brown, sandy bottom. This park, similar to Aztalan State Park, is best to visit during a dry time of year. Otherwise, you'd miss being able to walk on this trail. There is evidence it floods frequently.

My heart is genuinely happy to be out hiking again! Even though it will take multiple loops to get my mileage here, it is a near-perfect summer day in the low 80s, with a nice breeze, dry air, and no bugs. It would be delightful to live close to this park, to come on a pretty day and wander by the river. There are plenty of great picnic tables and shade trees, and the forest is multi-storied and healthy. It is a beautiful spot!

Where the three short trails of the park, the River, the Woodland, and the Bluebird converge, there is an astounding and fantastical sight. It is a monumental white pine, one having a somewhat tortured appearance rather than a tall, symmetrical one. It harbors a delightful surprise—bees!

The rich fragrance in the air surrounding this tree with its wild honeybee hive inside is transcendent. It is a marvelous, resonating smell of pine sap mixed with a slight sweetness of wildflower honey, complemented by the delicious hum of thousands of workers. I give it respect and deference, keeping my distance, all the while overwhelmed by the desire to peek inside. I start off on the Bluebird Trail before I do something I would very likely regret. It begins by the honey tree and moves through an abundant, healthy prairie full of Queen Anne's lace, bee balm, and the ubiquitous goldenrod.

I finally get my miles at Copper Culture through a series of loops on the trails, including the Woodland and the Storybook, and by crossing the highway through a tunnel. The arched entrances are decorated with artistic renderings of hiking people, and it leads to the South Trail and an interesting bridge over the Oconto River. I have hiked in circles, but I feel fantastic. I am not looking forward to the long drive home, but it's all part of the journey, all part of the Quest.

I am grateful to have recovered from COVID, unlike too many millions who did not. I feel humbled to be on this Quest and living my day today, enjoying the bright sky and the warm sun, the flowing water and the drone of bees. I am honored to have the time to reflect and remember, yet saddened by the absence of countless lives in this world, taken by an invisible enemy. I hope they will all be remembered and grieved, with love and longing, like the Copper Culture ancestors were.

Copper Culture State Park

The Questions

1. What about this chapter resonated with you?
2. In processing your life's experiences, what are some of your triumphs and some of your defeats?
3. What have you learned from the elders you have known in your life that helps you as you age?

The Particulars

Sticker Required: No

Map on the State Park's Website: No maps

Bathrooms for Day Hikers: Yes, in the museum and by the picnic area

Office or Kiosk: Kiosk and a museum

Trail Markings: Not well-marked

Seasonal Closures: Museum is only open between Memorial Day and Labor Day

Flooding Concerns: During high water levels of the Oconto River

Five Miles: Circles required

Note: Every year, in late November, I purchase a Christmas ornament commemorating something significant that happened during the year, something I want to remember. For example, for the year I hiked the C2C, I bought myself a small mercury glass pair of hiking boots. In looking to commemorate my hikes in the state parks this summer, I was hoping to find a wonderful ornament shaped like the state of Wisconsin. The only one I could find was blue with a football and a tankard of beer on it. It absolutely did not represent what I wanted for my 45 x 5 = 65 Quest. I did find one in mercury glass with two bees climbing on a honeycomb. It perfectly relates to the pins on my favorite blue hat and returning after COVID to hike with wild honeybees.

Mirror Lake State Park
Baraboo

5.30 miles
Highest Point: 795 ft
Lowest Point: 720 ft

August 21, 2022
Dating and Jazz

Traveling today, I am enjoying my swing music playlist. When I listen to this music, the images of the WWII veterans I worked with become vivid in my mind. I must have stored all those memories like a string of pearls. That way, I could find them whenever I was in the mood or wanting to sing, sing, sing.

I am reflecting on my time as a medical social worker as I make my way to Mirror Lake. I call to mind an 82-year-old man who was admitted to the hospital. He had to be restrained at night because he became exceptionally agitated and violent in his sleep. In working with him, I found out why. It was all the images. They had cost him his marriage and his family and stolen his sleep for over 60 years. The images he had desperately tried to purge with too much alcohol over too many years. They were the images of the unspeakable brutality he had experienced as a 19-year-old medic in France during WWII. The entire time we were talking, he kept commenting about how I was incredibly beautiful. How, if he were 50 years younger, he would SO ask me on a date! If that had been the case, I might have taken him up on it. He was a ruggedly handsome man even still. I asked him if he would be able to use my beauty to help him in his nightmares, to imagine me guiding him away from those terrible memories to a place of safety. He quipped, "Would it be okay if I pictured you naked?"

I laughed and replied, "As long as it is only while you are dreaming."

The next day, as he was being discharged, he walked up to me and grabbed my hand tightly. "Thank you, beautiful lady," he said. "I did see you there with me. You helped me walk away from the tank full of carnage and blood. I haven't slept so soundly in years!"

I leaned into him and whispered, "Was I naked?"

"No," he beamed. "You were like a holy angel of light. Thank you." Remembering him, I think of the gift he gave me on the day he left the hospital, the gift of being able to look back on my life with integrity. I was able to be a gardener planting a seed, the seed of a peaceful night's rest for a tortured soul. I was able to teach another to search for beauty in traumatic times.

Arriving at the park, I find a small, open office with friendly rangers. There is no merch, but there are maps and interesting literature about the park's history. I'm glad I saved Mirror Lake until this point in my Quest, not doing all the parks close to my house right at the beginning. It's only about an hour away, and with me still recovering from the effects of COVID, it is my choice for today. I plan on taking it easy doing my mileage here. This is not a race, after all. It is a Quest. I start off on the wide and grassy Pioneer Trail, which begins near the park office by the Smokey the Bear sign.

When I lived in the remote town of Carrizozo, New Mexico, my child attended Capitan Elementary School. As a cub, Smokey was found in 1950 badly burned by the Capitan Mountain Gap fire and

Mirror Lake State Park

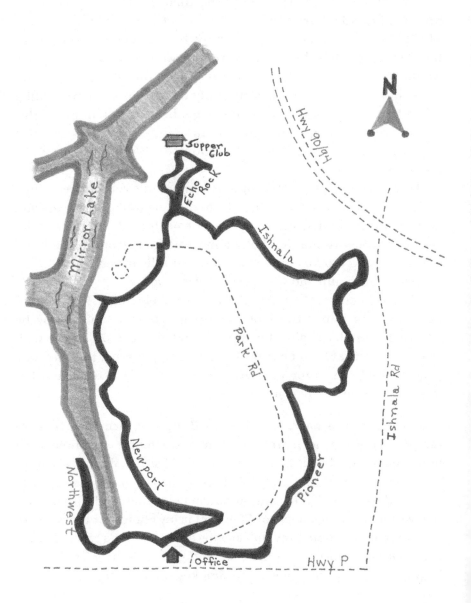

became the living symbol of the government's forest fire prevention campaign. As a result, there was a Smokey the Bear mascot at every school function, parade, community fiesta, etc., anywhere in Lincoln County. Smokey gave hugs to the little kids and high fives to the adults. I used to get silly excited, sharing my child's wonder and joy in seeing a big walking bear with a hat! It was similar to a sighting of Santa during those early years of our lives together.

I am acutely appreciative of the well-marked trails here at Mirror Lake. There are frequent "You Are Here" signs and wooden posts with accompanying symbols for the various trails. The symbol for the Pioneer Trail is a Conestoga wagon.

Chicory is everywhere. Little purple asters are starting to come out as well. There was a good rain here a day or two ago, and the sandy soil is still damp, allowing for a myriad of mushrooms everywhere. The forest of white pines, balsam firs, oaks, and birch is thriving, and there are even ripening hazelnuts safe inside their green, frilly jackets.

I come to a T intersection where the Pioneer heads off to the right, and the Ishnala Trail heads to the left. I'll take the Ishnala and see where it leads me. I find it strange that the trail symbol for the Ishnala is a teepee. The Ho-Chunk people, whose land this was and whose language named this trail, created wigwams as their traditional homes. Maybe it has to do with the concrete teepee outside the Ishnala Supper Club. I do find satisfaction in what the word *Ishnala* means, "stand alone." For me, this is how my life has been these last several years. I do not crave solitude, but it has been thrust upon me so best to embrace it.

I spent way longer than was healthy walking around with an albatross around my neck in an effort to not be alone. I didn't realize the weight I was carrying and the energy I was wasting until I stopped, until the divorce. Before I was married, I had intermittently spent time as a single, unpartnered person. Nonetheless, there were occasions when I had multiple boyfriends: ones who knew how to fix cars, ones who liked to go out and party, ones who liked to stay home. There were farm boys and bass players, concrete finishers and funeral directors, firemen and cowboys. I ended up referring to them all as "baby" when I answered the phone because I wasn't always sure which one it was, their voices sounding similar. This was well before cell phones could identify the caller. My dad went so far as to jokingly give me a tongue-in-cheek book about dating too much.

After the divorce and before the pandemic, I started dating again. Something about having to put on my readers to browse dating apps is positively comical to me! There are some general norms about dating as an older person I don't abide by, one of which is letting it develop as a friendship first. Everyone I have ever been good friends with, I knew right away we would be friends. It wasn't something I had to try and figure out. A limited number of years are built into the equation of dating after sixty. It takes away the desire to waste time on "developing" when I know early on if they would be right for me. I don't need to have someone; I want to have someone. There's a big difference.

Another thing I find perplexing is the idea of the "warts and all" at the initial meeting. I understand to have a relationship, you need to be accepting of the other person's flaws and foibles, but why on the first date? For all the dates I have been on, I have fixed my hair and makeup, worn my best fashion. All the men I met were fairly decent. I can't say they were completely unattractive.

At times, though, it became difficult for me to tease out if the way they presented themselves was a social work issue or something else entirely. Is the ripped and pilly old sweater you chose for a first date actually the only thing you have to wear? Or is it because you relied on your ex-wife to pick out all your clothes and ensure you were dressed appropriately for the occasion? Is the fact you haven't showered for several days an issue of accessibility to hygiene products or a mental health issue involving a lack of self-care? I find it genuinely curious they would introduce themselves in such a manner.

I may find it regrettable your ex was a psycho-bitch from hell, but it is not first-date conversation fodder. If you're compelled to talk excessively about her with a new woman, at the very least, do yourself a favor and spend more time alone. If you feel the need to mansplain for over an hour to a grown-ass woman you just met, I don't know what generation you are in, but it's not mine. I understand "warts," but when you first meet a possible romantic interest, putting your best foot forward is a minimum. Why go on a date if you are not at least somewhat excited to get to know a new person?

It is said older men want to date younger women because older women have higher expectations. That is wrong on multiple levels, not the least of which is because it maligns younger women. Often, when we are younger, we have no clue about "warts" until we are past the point of no return. After 60, we know there will be flaws; we just don't want them front and center on the first couple of dates. Let's face it. As we get older, we should have higher expectations for ourselves and others in our relationships. It goes for men, too. None of us should settle as we might have when we were younger. I am not saying I am god's gift, but I am a pretty good catch: intelligent, active, and not bad-looking, either. And, hey, I can even shower and dress myself! I can talk about something besides my ex and take care of my own business.

What did all the pre-pandemic dating teach me? I learned I don't need a placeholder man like I did in my younger days. I can pay for my car to be fixed. I can go out or stay in by myself. I want someone who is loving and playful, silly and slightly dark. I want someone who will be the Gomez to my Morticia. Growing up, they were my favorite TV couple. They never criticized; they only respected. Gomez applauded when his querida was better at something than he was. She supported her bubala's wild eccentricities, never tiring of his passions. Their union was full of joy at the wonder of life.

I have to say my enthusiasm for my Quest feels like it's waning today. The weeks of being sick with COVID have taken a toll on me. I will keep putting myself through the paces, doing my five miles, and hopefully, getting my excitement back again by the end of my time here at Mirror Lake.

There is a Y intersection where the Ishnala crosses and continues on the other side of a highway. I decide not to do that part and take the left trail. I want to be in the forest rather than getting too close to civilization; thus, I am avoiding roads as much as possible. This branch of the Ishnala Trail follows a quiet ravine, abruptly taking a steep turn downhill. It has me thinking about my somewhat disjointed hiking plan today.

I drove to Mirror Lake listening to swing music, and now my mind is filled with thoughts of jazz. Swing is, after all, a style of jazz, albeit more arranged and danceable. First-rate jazz is full of improvisation, of navigating around a central melody—finding all the available musical angles. I decide I am on an improvisational hike, wandering and finding whatever the day may bring. Yes, this sounds much better than calling it disjointed!

Jazz is about ending up where you're going, dealing with what comes along, and existing in the moment. Certainly, my Quest has taught me this is how my life is as I age. It's not a planned, harmonious piece. It is creative, spontaneous, and expressive, albeit at times discordant and haphazard. The goal simply is to be 65 and try to live more good days than bad.

I follow the ravine past fabulous rock outcroppings, which come closer and closer to the trail. At one point, the trail curves and weaves tight between them and opens up by a small stream. It is fronted by a bench with the insightful statement, "Enjoy the moment." It certainly is a breathtaking spot right here on this day. Thanks, Marty, for your bench. I needed this message today.

The trail passes under a rust-brown metal bridge arching over the ravine, leading me to a paved trail. Taking a left on this short spur, I end up in the Ishnala Supper Club parking lot. It looks to be a wonderful spot for a brandy old-fashioned on a summer afternoon. In fact, they boast theirs is the best ever tasted! I'll have to save that for another day, instead rejoining the paved trail to see where it takes me. After a short distance, I come to another T. One way leads to more of the Ishnala Trail on the other side of the highway, and the other leads back into the forest. Forest is my choice today. I'm not sure where it's going to take me, but hey, jazz!

It delivers me up across the bridge I recently viewed from underneath. What a lovely view of the ravine from the top of this span. Crossing the bridge, I start off on the Echo Rock Trail. Its symbol is a side view of a rock outcropping. It is paved and provides a nice path for people with mobility issues, all the way from the supper club to the bridge and beyond.

The Echo Rock Trail follows the lake shore to a boat launch area. This is where the action is! There's a place to rent boats, get bait, and buy lots of fun Mirror Lake merch: t-shirts, hoodies, and more, all with a brilliant park logo. After a quick selfie with the lake in the background, I continue on my way past this happening spot. On to the Lakeview Trail, I go! This is a splendid trail, well-marked with a fish. It leads me to a swimming beach, busy with people splashing on this warm, late summer Sunday.

I catch the Newport Trail heading in the direction of my car. Its symbol is a paddle-wheeled boat. I mightily appreciate these unique trail marker designs! They provide a sense of comfort to someone like me who has a tendency to meander and get slightly lost. I wish more of the parks were as well-marked. It actually is an accessibility issue, come to think of it.

The Newport Trail brings me back to the park office, but I still have about a half mile to go to reach my five. I head off on the Northwest Trail, which is marked by a compass and begins at the far end of the parking area. As I hike, I find myself in a harmonious and healthy forest. To the right of the trail is Mirror Lake, tranquil and glistening in the sunshine. It takes me to a small overlook with a grand view across the narrow lake toward the beach area. I am happy I needed some mileage on this marvelous trail.

As is my wont to do, I am constantly on the lookout for interesting, incongruent things. Here on the Northwest, I spy on the ground a Swedish Fish, its bright pink-red juxtaposed against the warm green of the trail. I have found many delightful things in my hiking days: a plastic alien, a toy Dalmatian, a fabric rainbow with a pot of gold, rings of keys, and multiple beads. I am similar to a magpie picking up all these peculiar items. My all-time favorite was a blue and gray striped baby sock, still warm from the tiny foot it had recently embraced.

I return the red candy fish to the ground and retrace my steps. I'll have my mileage done by the time I get back to my car. This is a wonderful park! I will definitely come back here, bring some friends, hike more of the trails, and maybe even rent a boat. On my next visit, I will leave time for an old-fashioned at the Ishnala Supper Club when the day is done.

I find as I sit in my car, unlacing my hiking boots, I have regained much enthusiasm for this Quest. It really is a spontaneous, somewhat crazy adventure to go on as an official "senior citizen."

Through it, I have confirmed to myself the journey is the important thing, and a bit of improvisation helps find and create the beauty in life. I will continue to indulge my inner crow, looking for unusual, shiny things. Perhaps, after the Quest, when I rejoin those dating apps, I will find the shiniest of all things: love.

On my way home, I stop at a local hardware store to purchase a bag of river gravel for my dry creek bed garden project. I was getting ready to load it when an elderly man walking by offered to put it in my car. He was obviously 15-20 years older than me but still willing to use his strength to help a stranger. I am grateful to him for increasing my joy in this day and for reminding me there are good men in the world. Now, I simply have to find one closer to my own age.

Mirror Lake State Park

The Questions

1. What about this chapter resonated with you?
2. What do you/would you find challenging about dating at your age?
3. What interesting things have you found on a walk?

The Particulars

Sticker Required: Yes

Map on the State Park's Website: Yes, and it is detailed in color

Bathrooms for Day Hikers: Yes, in the office and by the boat launch area

Office or Kiosk: Office which can be closed depending on the day or season

Trail Markings: Outstanding; trails marked by frequent signs containing symbols

Seasonal Closures: None

Flooding Concerns: Trails may be wet, but no flooding issues

Five Miles: Easy to get with no circles

Peninsula State Park
Fish Creek

5.15 miles
Highest Point: 699 ft
Lowest Point: 433 ft

August 25, 2022
The Day Before

I knew I wanted to hike somewhere incredible on my birthday, so I planned this trip to Rock Island State Park. It was right at the beginning of when I started this Quest back in early April. I will be making stops at Peninsula and Newport, but Rock Island is the main destination. I chose these parks for my birthday hikes because they are the most complicated trip of all my journeys on this whole adventure.

I made the decision to rent a place and go by myself, making it an experience outside my comfort zone. As we age, it is good to challenge ourselves to new and complex situations. I wanted a wonderful, spacious cabin right on the water. That way, if it rained the whole time, at least I could look out at the bay through floor-to-ceiling windows. I chose an upscale place in Gills Rock, near the very tip-top of Door County.

I selected this location because it was close enough to catch the ferry to Washington Island and then drive to catch the ferry to Rock Island. I needed to be able to hike five miles with enough time to make the return trip to Door County.

Back in May, I was telling Diana about my plans. She said, "Well, I'm going to go with you!" She purposely invited herself, and I am honored and humbled by her friendship. It reiterates to me as I age to surround myself with people who support me in the ways I support them.

It seems like long ago, years ago, ages ago, when I made these plans. Is it because so many hikes have happened since? Or is it because I have changed as a result of this Quest? I think it is a bit of both. I'm feeling happy, excited, and fulfilled. It's finally getting to be my big milestone birthday. This extravagant trip I planned is happening, and sunny skies are predicted!

August 26, 2022
Aeries and Lost Cities

Now, this is what I call a state park office! Two friendly rangers are working behind a substantial counter with lots of information and maps for visitors. It even has a fabulous two-stall women's bathroom. There is a small alcove dedicated to a gift shop full of fun merch. I splurge and get a Peninsula neon green, moisture-wicking hiking shirt and a pint glass with a marvelous painting of the Niagara Escarpment.

Diana and I start off on the Eagle Trail. It is a trail punctuated by rugged terrain, high cliffs, and fantastic views of the bay. On this trail, there is the ever-present bustle of waves complementing the peacefulness of white cedars. Immense and beautiful, they take my breath away. Their gloriously convoluted roots are ubiquitous on this trail, and I am reminded, once again, of how much I love my LEKI hiking poles. The Eagle Trail is gorgeous but tricky, resplendent with intricate tangles and erratic dolomitic limestone rocks made slippery from yesterday's rain. It is an advanced and difficult trail, full of steep climbs and sharp descents.

As we finish the Eagle Trail, it is time to ascend the stairs to the top of the 60-foot-tall Eagle Tower. The view from the top is magnificent! On this clear blue dazzler of a day, we can see for miles across the waters of sacred Lake Michigan as it curves into the Nicolet and Green Bays. There are numerous small islands off Peninsula, and the tower affords us a stunning vision of the one called, for obvious reasons, Horseshoe.

To leave the aerie, rather than taking the stairs, we use the 850-foot long, fully accessible ramp. It is an outstanding engineering feat, wonderful for those with mobility concerns. The ramp takes us for a tour of the tree canopy as it slowly touches down to the earth once more.

Ascending and descending this tower, like the other towers I have done on my Quest, brings to mind the scourge of ageism. Why? Because it goes against the common misconception that old people can't do strenuous things. To espouse ageism is the proverbial shooting of oneself in the foot! We need to actively confront what we have internalized about aging. It has to be a work in progress. It takes continued diligence to silence the negative voice in our heads, which reinforces the subtle forms of it we've learned over the years. We must educate ourselves and call it out when we see it. This is especially important when dealing with medical providers who all too often minimize symptoms in elders and attribute them to "you're just getting older." We must be fierce when addressing these myths about aging. When they say it is normal for us to feel depressed or lonely, or to experience undo pain, we need to have the words to counteract their ageism. It helps to be prepared with what to say before you go for an appointment.

The perception of youth being the ideal is rampant in our society. It can be found in the ads for "anti-aging" products, looking good "for your age," not being able to "teach old dogs new tricks." Those stereotypes can get into our psyches as the years add up and cause us to view ourselves as less than. They can adversely affect our physical well-being and our ability to recover from the inevitable

Peninsula State Park

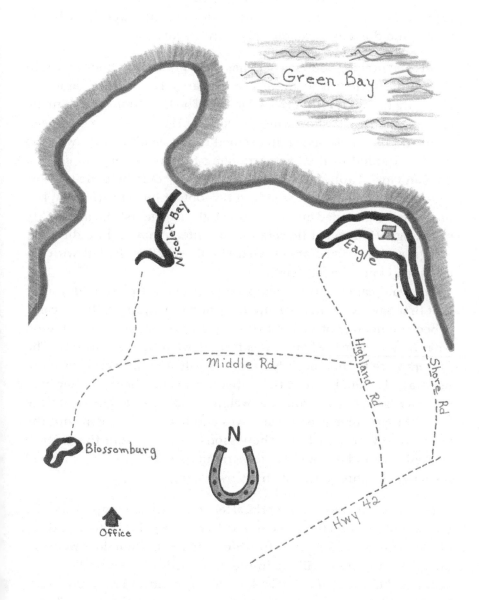

setbacks. Even if it is in the form of benevolent ageism, such as being overly protective or using pet names, it is still ageism! We must purposefully reframe the narrative by using words signifying not weakness but power. Not grumpy, but badass. Not helpless, but capable. Not doddering but resilient. Not sweetie, but call me by my name. And don't ever call me spry. I am mighty!

All this thinking about ageism has me reminiscing about Thorvald Thorvaldsen. He was a stranger in a strange land with a name like his living in Albuquerque, New Mexico. The first time I met him, he entered the flower shop where I worked. He was a bent and aged man, and no one in the shop seemed to notice him to ask what he needed. I stood in the back arranging flowers, seeing his light of grief and love. I approached him to ask how I could help. He took his cane and tapped me on the side of my foot, not in a hurtful way, but one which demanded attention, one fighting against the invisibility of old age. He needed flowers for his wife. I showed him different things, and we talked about what she liked. When he left with his bouquet, I know he felt seen.

Thorvald came into the shop every week on the same day after that first day. He would walk up to me and tap my foot with his cane. It became his way of saying I was a good person, and I understood what he was doing, what he was feeling, what he was carrying. The flowers were for his recently deceased wife and his weekly visits to her grave. He taught me to never dismiss an elder because they have mobility issues, bent from the weight of life. He taught me to see beyond their current physical selves and instead see them with the vision of my heart. I think the lessons I gained from the elders I worked with and the ones I had as friends over the years have helped me have a brighter outlook on my own aging.

Not too far into the park after the office complex is the Blossomburg Cemetery. Diana and I both like the history and art of old cemeteries, and after finishing the ramp excursion, we're off on a drive to find it. Hiking in the graveyard, I am enthralled once again by the solace of being laid to rest in an old and tranquil forest. It is the third cemetery I have hiked this summer: the one at Tower Hill State Park, the one during the Upper Peninsula of Michigan adventure, and the one here today. The Blossomburg is full of lighthouse keepers, historians, settlers, and farmers. They rest with the sounds of the forceful winds from across Green Bay.

Our introspective wander among the old stones complete, I still lack half a mile to reach my goal. We get back in the car and drive to the Nicolet Bay Trail to complete my five miles. We finish the hike with views of the beach and the striking lake—another park done. Now, our minds begin to drift to plans for the rest of our day.

There is a cool, still evening in store, and acquiring firewood is on our agenda. On the way out of the park, we come upon an incredible wood shed. It provides firewood for the park campers and is an elaborate operation. We purchase a wagonload to take with us. Three sweet, hardworking preteen boys haul it to our car and load it into the back. We have a pleasant conversation with them about the end of summer and back to school, what grades they are going into, and what their dreams are for their new year. Having worked in middle schools for almost half my time as a school social worker, I validate their concerns about how difficult those grades can be. Diana compliments them on their strength and kindness. We are both planting seeds!

This is not the trip I had planned. I had thought of doing these three parks alone. The trip I had planned was one of owning my aloneness and attempting to dispel my loneliness. However, this trip reaffirms that I have dear friends who support me. My heart is made whole and happy as a result. I am delighted Diana invited herself along.

We make our way to the Gills Rock cabin, and it is everything it was advertised to be. It is right on the bay with sensational sunset views. We sit in oversized wooden chairs by the water's edge, drinking wine, laughing as good friends do, and remembering our day. There is a substantial firepit for us to burn the wood we bought in the park. After dinner, a grand conflagration is on brand for us as we firm up plans for the rest of the trip.

Tonight, I will dream about the convoluted and technical hike on the Eagle Trail, requiring each and every step to be precise and well-placed to be able to reach the "lost city" of dolomite close to the bay.

It is one of my favorite hikes on the Quest! Peninsula is an incredible park. I will surely return to it again and again.

I am blissful! This is park number 30. When I first started my Quest back in April, I had no idea how much I would learn about Wisconsin, about myself, and about how I want to spend the next 10–15 years of my life. What a gift this Quest has been! I am coming to terms with my aging self and this liminal time of my life. How could I have ever known my silly idea would end up being remarkably healing and life-affirming? Spending the day watching my steps and meticulously placing my feet has an intense level of heartfelt meaning for me as I prepare to turn sixty-five.

Peninsula State Park

The Questions
1. What about this chapter resonated with you?
2. What have you internalized about the stereotypes about aging?
3. How can you confront those stereotypes in yourself and society?

The Particulars
Sticker Required: Yes

Map on the State Park's Website: Yes, and it is detailed in color

Bathrooms for Day Hikers: Yes, in the office and other areas of high tourist traffic

Office or Kiosk: Office which can be closed depending on the day or season

Trail Markings: Infrequently marked

Seasonal Closures: None

Flooding Concerns: Trails may be wet, but no flooding issues

Five Miles: Easy to get with no circles

Rock Island State Park
Rock Island

6.59 miles
Highest Point: 696 ft
Lowest Point: 434 ft

August 27, 2022
Time and Experience

With its large kitchen, nautical coffee mugs, and expansive windows looking out at Green Bay, our vacation rental in Gills Rock is perfect for catching the ferry. It's only a seven-minute drive, and Diana and I are here in line to catch the 8:00 a.m. to Washington Island. Then, we're on to the 10:00 a.m. ferry to Rock Island.

As we wait in the queue, I see a free-standing white office to buy tickets. The older man inside is no-nonsense and holds no quarter for repetitive questions about things clearly posted. I am glad I take the time to read about the tickets as I stand in line, unlike several people in front of me. It results in me being in his good graces and, therefore, getting polite conversation and insider information. I buy tickets for both ways to both islands.

The ferry from Door County to Washington Island is packed with cars and ATVs. Apparently, there is a festival happening there today. The line behind us for subsequent ferries is lengthy, making me pleased we started this day off early. I guess I should have checked on it beforehand, but I wanted to do this hike for my milestone birthday, and I would have come regardless of any events. The 30-minute voyage begins, and the water is smooth, gray-blue, and sparkling. The buoys and piers are crowded with shiny black cormorants. I could not have asked for better weather!

I have never been to Washington Island, and I am pleasantly surprised by all the agriculture. I had assumed it would be more commercialized like many towns in Door County. Yes, there is a small shopping district, but it appears to be more focused on the locals, with its anchor being a nice grocery store. There are several tourist places, especially near the docks with all the fancy boats, but we are on a mission to reach the Rock Island ferry. The 20-minute drive across Washington Island is easy and beautiful. I will have to come back here in the future for more sightseeing.

We find the parking lot for the Rock Island ferry with no troubles. This ferry is walk-on only with no cars or bikes. We gather our hiking gear and head toward the dock. There is an interesting restaurant right near it, but it is closed this early in the morning. A stop at the Jackson Point Soup Company after the hike becomes our plan.

The ferry is a short 10-minute ride staffed by kind and earnest crew members. As we pull up to the shore, we are greeted by a lovely woman with a hardy shout. "Welcome to Rock Island!" I am exceptionally excited to be here!

We hang back, taking a few photos and my mandatory entry selfie by the grand park sign. I am waiting to see in what direction on the trail the majority of people from the ferry are headed. Most go to the left, human nature being to go clockwise when confronted with a circle. We head off to the right with the overnight campers to escape the sizable crowd.

The Thordarson Loop Trail circumnavigates the island. We walk past the camp host's cabin, feeling envious of their position. How incredible to spend the summer on Rock Island, caring for campers,

Rock Island State Park

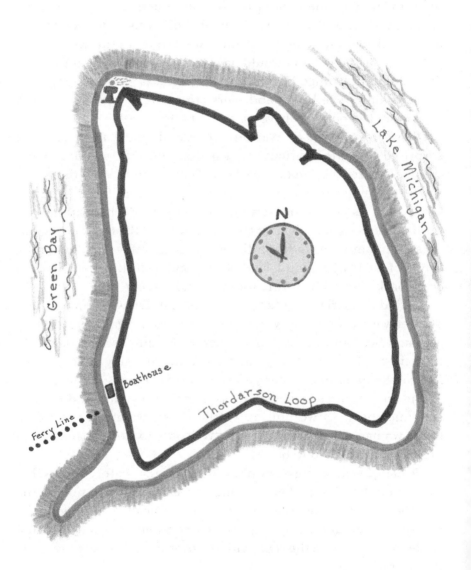

enjoying the solitude, and stargazing. The campsites along the trail are simply amazing! Some are right on the rocky limestone beach. Ah, to fall asleep under the silence of cedars—the waves gently crashing.

Kingfishers, with their strange clicking calls, dart along the shoreline as we hike. The trail is sandy in spots, rocky in others, and often crisscrossed with the gnarled roots of old trees. The forest is healthy and mixed with cedars and hemlocks, maples and beeches. Due to recent rain and the spray from the lake, the undergrowth is rich with a plethora of mushrooms: shelf, boletus, and coral.

Three cemeteries are on spur trails off the Thordarson Loop, including one with Chester Thordarson's grave. He was the steward of this phenomenal island until it came to be owned by the state. Surrounded by small fences, each has only a few stones, many marking those who died too young, as infants and children. I breathe a sigh of remembrance for them and of thanks for myself, being able to live to this age. One of the cemeteries has a stone for the first lighthouse keeper, David Corbin, who served from 1837 to his death in 1852. He was named for the crows and ravens, like me. There are rumors of his lonely soul still haunting the island.

As we go, I keep thinking to myself, as I had on the Coast to Coast Walk across England, I could spend eternity hiking here on this splendid day, chatting and laughing with my dear friend. It is truly a heaven-on-earth kind of day. Today is one of those perfect summer days, a day for which the word *halcyon* was created to describe. I feel immeasurably lucky I possess the gift of unstructured time on such a day. I have the luxury of being in a halcyon world, and I am full of awe and joy.

We make our way, hiking along the loop to the Pottawatomie Lighthouse. Entry is free, but donations are greatly appreciated. Rock Island tees and sweatshirts, patches and books are sold here. Shoes must be left in the entryway if you want to tour the lighthouse. It feels good to take off my hiking boots and patter around on the soft, worn smooth, wooden floors in my stocking feet. A knowledgeable, kind, and friendly elderly couple are volunteers at the lighthouse. They spend several months here, even sleeping in one of the lightkeeper's rooms. What a sweet gig!

She is barefoot, and he has shoes with paper booties covering them. She is full of interesting facts about the families who lived here and the history of this place. I am glad we take the tour with her rather than exploring independently, as did most other visitors. Waiting in line to climb the steep stairway into the lantern room, we have a great conversation with the husband. Nearby, there is a display case with different sizes of Fresnel lenses. We talk about our trip to the Great Lakes Shipwreck Museum near Paradise, Michigan, and all the spectacular lenses they had on display. He tells us this lighthouse has a grand Fourth Order lens. Our turn to ascend the stairs comes, and we wind our way up to the top. The view from the lighthouse tower is incredible out over the vivid blue of the great inland sea of Lake Michigan.

As we are getting ready to leave the lighthouse, I ask the gracious volunteer why the face clock hanging on the wall by the merchandise display has a sign under it, stating, "This is the Actual Time." She explains at this tip-top point of Rock Island, digital clocks on cell phones skip back and forth. Diana and I look at ours per the woman's instructions, and even though we are standing shoulder to shoulder in the lighthouse entryway, the clock on my phone is on Eastern Standard Time, and Diana's is on Central!

As we begin the last third of the loop, I grow quiet, pondering the capriciousness of time, fickle in the hours it gives us. And of time's constant companion, death, that took the lives of children a century ago on this wild island, yet lets me be here hiking as I turn sixty-five.

I enjoy reading books and watching shows about traveling in time. How miraculous it would be! I once knew someone who was able to achieve a return in time. As an elder with advanced dementia, she did not exist in my time but in her own personal location on the space-time continuum. She was not a feeble old woman alone in a hospital room. She was lively and fashionable, sitting in the dazzling lobby of a stylish, upscale hotel in New York City in 1963. She was waiting for her daughter to arrive, her heart bursting with joy and anticipation. That was where she stayed, always, waiting for the splendid day with her child to begin. Working with her genuinely hit me. If I ended up with a similar fate, a fate where I was in a different time forever, I would want it to be like hers, a place of love, happiness, and adventure.

It makes me think of what I have come to term "Quintessential Moments." They are the brief respites from the flow of time where we feel like we can live forever, ecstatic in those astonishing minutes. Fleeting moments where we feel we could die just then and be perfectly at peace to have lived in this great world. I have several, and reflecting on them helps me feel the sense of integrity we all need to experience as we reach this age. I am exceedingly fortunate to have these and appreciably more such memories:

- Walking up a seemingly endless flight of steps on a sublimely sunny day in Monterosso, Italy, with my gorgeous child by my side. Reaching the top and gazing out at the intense turquoise of the Ligurian Sea below, watched over by a giant statue of Neptune.

- Seeing the Pat Metheny Band at the Paolo Soleri Amphitheater in Santa Fe, New Mexico. It was open to the clear, star-filled sky on a full moon night. I was caressing my latest fling as we sat entranced by the flowing sounds of wonderful jazz.

- Riding on a Kawasaki Ninja 750 motorcycle, my arms wrapped tight around my big love's leather-clad torso as we sped down country roads through the warm summer twilight.

- Swinging with my divine newborn baby on the deep green front porch of my house in Rocky Comfort, Missouri. Both of us were peaceful with the gentle movement. I remember feeling time disappear, knowing nothing was going to change my world.

I still have that porch swing all these years and distances later. I hang it in my backyard in the summer and swing on it every chance I get, taking time to cherish my quintessential moments. Knowing I had these sensational adventures provides me with comforting solace. Thinking about these moments in our lives is an integral part of one's Life Review.

Coming upon the Hilltop Gate snaps me out of my reverie. It is the remnant of a wide-reaching fence once used to enclose a garden back in Chester Thordarson's day. Only the gate remains now, surrounded by chain link to protect its strange and precarious balance. It consists of three giant tree trunks positioned in an arch fitted with dangling, rectangular flower boxes. It is a folly in the truest sense, created for purely aesthetic pleasure rather than function.

We finish the Thordarson Loop with a tour of the blue limestone Boathouse. Rock Island seems an unlikely place for a marvelous homage to Icelandic culture until you take the time to read the history displays. Chester called this building his "Jewel House of Art and Nature." Displayed around the interior are extensive photos of all the buildings and gardens back in their heyday, as well as drawings of Chester's creative and fantastical electrical inventions. His work on transformers and energy grids made his fortune. It is an enchanting space filled with treasure reminiscent of a Viking hall. The gigantic light fixture in the center is truly remarkable. It is made of rams' horns and wood and colored glass. The original wooden furniture roped off for protection is exquisite, heavily carved, and elegant. My ancient friend, Thorvald Thorvaldsen, would have surely loved this place!

The most extraordinary feature of the boathouse is the Poetic Edda fireplace. Constructed of colored stone, it is the centerpiece of this grand open room. Yes, this could indeed be a hall in Valhalla! Incised runes in the metal header of the fireplace were taken from the Icelandic Eddas. The poem given by the Norse God Odin reads, "Fire is one of the best things for the sons of men and so is the sign of the Sun if a man manages to keep health and live virtuously." Above this runic quote, carved in wood and set in stone, is yet another quote, this one from a collection of Elizabethan poetry by Richard Hill. "Be wise in mirth, and seeke delight, the same doe not abuse, In honest mirth, a happie joy we ought not to refuse." The quotes convey the nature of this day: enjoy the fire and the sun, and be happy and healthy on this unique and awe-inspiring island!

We walk to the dock to catch our ferry, taking a moment to marvel at the outstanding arches on the water level of the Boathouse. The vibrations and echoes of the lapping waves are mesmerizing within its stone façade. I imagine the eyes of Chester Thordarson were the same icy blue as the Lake Michigan water beneath this architectural wonder.

It is a choppy ride back to Washington Island, the water kicking up in the late afternoon. The restaurant I mentioned earlier? It is now open! We sit outside by the water's edge, drinking Vacationland IPA and reflecting on the day's expedition. We enjoy this place greatly, and we each buy a pint glass etched in black with images of the two islands and the logo of our hosts.

On our drive across Washington Island to the ferry taking us back to Door County, we stop at Mann's Grocery Store for a six-pack of the Door County Brewing Company's beer to enjoy back at the Gills Rock cabin. There is definitely something about a local brew, especially when traveling.

Due to the festival going on today, it seems an endless wait to get back to the mainland. Glad to be in line and planning how we would work out the details if we didn't make it off the island before the ferry stopped running, we decide to "live virtuously" and in "honest mirth," being patient and trusting of the process. However, several impatient, entitled, and angry jerks keep cutting the line, driving in the left lane against traffic coming off the ferry. We can't help but have a sense of *schadenfreude* to see the ferry staff turn many of them away to the back of the queue.

The evening at the cabin consists of a roaring fire by the lakeside, IPAs, good food, and loving friendship. It was a halcyon day indeed—one I would not mind being stuck in forever if my individual temporal nexus ever so dictated.

Rock Island State Park

The Questions

1. What about this chapter resonated with you?
2. Make a list of the quintessential moments in your life. How does remembering them help you find meaning and peace as you age?
3. In what ways do you endeavor to "live virtuously" and to find "honest mirth"?

The Particulars

Sticker Required: Yes

Map on the State Park's Website: Yes, and nicely detailed

Bathrooms for Day Hikers: Yes, in outbuildings by the boathouse

Office or Kiosk: No park office or kiosk, but some information in the boathouse

Trail Markings: Infrequently marked

Seasonal Closures: Requires two ferries, which run from Memorial Day to Labor Day

https://wisferry.com/rock-island

Flooding Concerns: None

Five Miles: Easy to get with no circles

Newport State Park
Ellison Bay

5.43 miles
Highest Point: 684 ft
Lowest Point: 565 ft

August 28, 2022
Milestones and Dark Sky

We are packing up this morning at the Gills Rock cabin. After drinking coffee from the cheery white mugs with blue ship wheels emblazoned on them, Diana and I vow to return to this lovely place on future trips to Door County.

On our way home, we visit Newport. After a stop for a park sign selfie and a visit to the office for maps, historical information, and friendly ranger banter, we park close to the beach of Lake Michigan. We are greeted by outstanding late summer weather and the murmur of eternal waves.

Parking Lot Three works well as an easy access point to the junction of several trailheads: the Fern, the Lynd Point, and the Europe Bay. The Fern Trail is accessible for those with mobility, hearing, and visual concerns. I am heartened to see these in more and more state parks. We start off on the Europe Bay Trail, as it leads to the Lynd Point Trail Loop for our first miles of the day.

The Lynd Point Trail Loop winds along the lakeshore, touched by wonderful breezes and crashing waves. The shade of lanky cedars filters the sunlight. They must be hundreds of years old. I am now officially an old woman, but I must seem like a toddler to them— my brief life compared to theirs so hectic in its folly. Their lives are steadfast and measured, purposeful and enduring. What we do have in common are the lives we support: them, the birds, the insects, and the fungi; me, the hearts I've helped heal along the way, the child I adore, and the friends and family I treasure.

The sound of the water kerplunking deep within the cliffs below, breaking up the rocks, is a constant reminder even what appears permanent is perpetually changing. In our human lives, aging is a similar evolution. We must become comfortable with change and uncertainty while holding steadfast as we are battered by all life throws our way.

Many spur trails branch from the Lynd, offering closer views of the lake, each revealing some newfound delight, from a beach of smooth limestone pebbles to broken erratics to sandstone layers wearing away with every wave.

I am incredibly impressed with this trail. It flows through an abundance of different and varied kinds of forest, even through what I can best describe as a mysterious and spooky one—its floor resplendent in lycopene and weighted with moss. The trail continues its wander, hugging close to rugged 10- to 15-foot cliffs, the ancient shoreline of a considerably deeper and primordial Lake Michigan.

As we finish the Lynd Point Trail Loop, we find the junction again and take the Europe Bay Trail Loop back to our car for a short drive to the start of the Hotz Trail Loop. The gate at the beginning of this trail is a fabulous surprise! It is made of stacked fieldstone and cement, and one look tells me a person with an artistic eye created it. The shapes and colors of the rocks are set in a superb balance of texture, size, and color. The gate is a remnant of bygone days when

Newport State Park

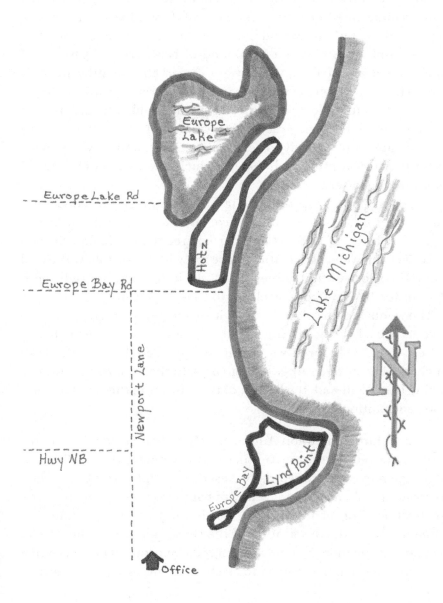

a man named Ferdinand Hotz owned this area of Newport. The historical literature I picked up at the park office describes him as an affluent man and a lover of trees. I imagine him sitting peacefully under a majestic white pine, smelling a wildflower like his namesake, Ferdinand the Bull. We would have been fast and fabulous friends!

The similarities between Ferdinand of Newport and Chester of Rock Island are striking. Both were remarkably wealthy in their time. They used their riches to preserve and protect natural places, allowing for our collective future. Decidedly unlike the billionaires during our time—their greed destroying whole ecosystems. They accumulate money purely to accumulate things and power. A mega yacht or a forest protected? I know which one I would choose if I ever won the lottery.

The Hotz Trail Loop rolls along on the tops of hardened sand dunes existing between Europe Lake and Lake Michigan. It brings us to the shores of the vast and perfect, reedy and shallow Europe Lake, its calm waters an inviting place for wildlife. We follow the trail along the shore until it comes to a T, deciding to take a right onto the Europe Bay Trail to walk closer to Lake Michigan.

The woodland on this isthmus is lush and dense and fragrant. We hike past backpack camping site 16 and see a spur labeled "Beach Access Trail." Of course, we take it! We proceed down to the Lake Michigan beach, and rather than go back to the trail, we kick off our hiking boots and walk the last bit of the journey in the soft sand and cool, enchanting waves.

I am a third-generation American. My father was born here; his mother moved here from Germany as a young girl. The German language has excellent words to describe complex emotions, such as *schadenfreude*, meaning a feeling of happiness over someone else's misfortune. One of my favorite words my German grandmother Anna used was the description of the sensation of specialness you feel on your birthday: *extrawursttagsgefühl*. She knew I appreciated a good birthday party and liked to celebrate mine and those of others as well.

Today is a significant milestone birthday for me. It's got me thinking of other milestone birthdays I've been lucky enough to have in my life:

- When I was 25, I went out dancing with my work buddies and met my big love.

- When I was 30, my sister took me skydiving, giving me a completely different viewpoint of the world.

- When I was 35, I complained to my great-uncle I was feeling old. He was close to 100 at the time. Handing me a silver dollar from 1957, he instructed me to keep it until I was his age, and then I would feel really, really old! I still have the coin, keeping it close until I can, hopefully, follow his loving direction.

- When I was 41, at the turn of the century, how strange I thought it was to have lived to the year 2000. I used to think it was impossible to ever get to that age! Then, all of a sudden, there I was on the 5000-year-old lava flow outside Carrizozo, New Mexico. I was watching a total eclipse of the moon, holding my child's little hand, and thinking about how my life seemed outstandingly different from what I could have ever thought possible.

- When I was 60, I hiked the Coast to Coast Walk across England, reclaiming the joy of being a hiker and experiencing the quintessential moment of seeing the North Sea after the Irish Sea.

- When turning 65, I am on this life-affirming Quest.

Milestone birthdays can be unique for different people. One of my dad's big milestones was when he turned the same age as his father had been when he died. It was a complex and emotional year for him. For my mom, the ones in which she first gave birth and gave birth for the last time were poignantly remembered. The celebrations for first birthdays harken back to a time when many children died before reaching that milestone. There are quinceañeras, bar mitzvahs, and golden birthdays. Turning 18 or 21 marks our formal transition to legal adulthood. Some people don't even think about birthdays. They hide from them or dismiss them or trivialize them. Women are taught to lie about them, not claiming the years we have been blessed to live.

For me, they are a time to pause and reflect on where I was, where I am, and where I wish to be in my life. On my birthdays, I like to spend time contemplating. I let myself remember all the regrets and the losses along with all the joys and triumphs I have had getting to this point in my lifetime. I reflect on how my life is: I am alive, I am loved, and it is enough right now in the present. I look to the future, thinking about goals I haven't obtained yet, and I let my mind drift in dreams and plans for adventures. I allow space to recognize things will change and there will be hard times ahead. I have capable, resilient, and beautiful things I can take forward with me. Those things have made me strong and powerful in my life. Remembering the countless people who never get to reach various milestone birthdays, I don't take them for granted.

The drive back to Madison from Door County is a truly pleasant one. We stop in Ellison Bay at the Kick Ash Coffee Company, a fascinating store in an abandoned mid-century modern church with an incredible arched ceiling. It is full of pastries and gifts. I buy some of their Dark Sky Roast coffee. It has a picture of the Milky Way on the label with information about Newport and its dark sky designation. We also stop at the taproom of Island Orchard for a flight of hard ciders. My favorite flavor is their apple lavender. I buy a bottle to bring home and have on a future day when I need to remember this weekend, the weekend I turned sixty-five.

Newport State Park

The Questions

1. What about this chapter resonated with you?
2. What types of things have you done on past milestone birthdays?
3. In reflecting on your life, what stands out to you about your past? Your present? Your future?

The Particulars

Sticker Required: Yes

Map on the State Park's Website: Yes, and it is detailed in color

Bathrooms for Day Hikers: Yes, but in the office

Office or Kiosk: Office which can be closed depending on the day or season

Trail Markings: Infrequently marked

Seasonal Closures: None

Flooding Concerns: Trails may be wet, but no flooding issues

Five Miles: Easy to get with no circles

Big Bay State Park
La Pointe

5.42 miles
Highest Point: 800 ft
Lowest Point: 551 ft

September 1, 2022
The Day Before

Petra has a cabin outside Washburn and is gracious enough to have it be our base as she accompanies me on two of my Quest hikes. The drive up is long but uneventful. Good weather and good company make the trip enjoyable.

After unloading and organizing, we head off to a concert at a distinctive, nearby venue. I have heard about it, and as we arrive, I am rightly impressed. The Lake Superior Big Top Chautauqua, located in Bayfield, is a local organization presenting concerts and events in its 900-seat canvas tent located at the base of the Mt. Ashwabay Ski and Recreation Area. Tonight's performers are the house band, the

Blue Canvas Orchestra. The show features songs written by John Prine and Nanci Griffith. I am quickly mesmerized by the dynamic abilities of the band members and the intimacy of the setting.

An older band member steps to the mic and sings a song, bringing the audience and himself to tears. His resonate voice is commanding on this early September night as he tells a story of aging, loneliness, and invisibility. His poignant performance is dear to the hearts of many in attendance. I am in awe of this place and the musicians, and once again, I am happy I made this Quest for myself. Otherwise, I would not have been able to share in this splendid evening of live music, full of emotion and autumn twilight.

After the concert, we return to the cabin for planning and much-needed rest in anticipation of our trip to Big Bay tomorrow. As I settle down for sleep, I think back to how my life was 15 years ago when I turned 50. I hosted a delightful party in my garden, complete with catered hors d'oeuvres, swing music, and a dance floor. I had purchased a beautiful, swirly turquoise skirt with threads of gold running through it for the occasion, even splurging on matching shoes. It was a wonderful evening, and my friends and I danced with our beaus in the moonlight. I wish I had taken more photographs or that my ex would've thought to do so, knowing how important it was to me—*extrawursttagsgefühl* and all.

My life has changed dramatically in the last 15 years. When I turned 50, I was running myself ragged, working 50–60 hours a week, parenting a teenager, and navigating around a disgruntled man-child. In the years following, I had to give up the job I loved due to the severe retaliation I suffered as a result of standing up for the civil rights of children. I became an orphan, a strange experience at any age. My child went to university and launched well into the great, marvelous world. I gave up trying to please and got a divorce. At 65, I am living alone, working part-time, and enjoying an incredible relationship with my dear child. In some ways, I am where I thought I would be; in others, I am not.

I don't know where I will be in 15 years, if I'll even still be when I am eighty. My child will be 41 years old by then, the age I was at the turn of the century. My father always used to tell me he didn't feel old until one of his children had a birthday, and then he knew he was aging because his kids were too.

Part of this Quest is reclaiming, redefining, and re-energizing my life. In my next 15, if chaos and time allow them, I hope to be able to look back with the same mix of bittersweet emotions I remember from my last 15 years.

September 2, 2022
Awe and Catamarans

We wake up early for an excellent breakfast of dark piñon coffee, avocado on toasted sourdough, and fresh tomatoes from Petra's garden. Sitting on the deck of her remote cabin, embraced by red and white pines, we make plans for our trip to Bayfield to catch the ferry to Madeline Island.

The ferry stop is a tight operation, with staff carrying credit card readers to cars for ticket purchases. Nearby, there is a white octagonal gazebo full of information about the island, as well as maps of Big Bay. The ferry crossing is astounding! The enigmatic waters of Lake Superior are turbulent today. The sky is a radiant blue with high, wispy clouds—harbingers of cooler weather to come.

In less than half an hour, we are back on the road, making the short drive to the park office. There is a bit of merch and a truly friendly ranger. In talking with her, I find out the trail I planned to hike, the Lagoon Ridge Trail, is closed due to beaver activity. I am excited to hear they are thriving even though the rangers find them a slight nuisance.

We park in the double parking lot near the campground and settle in for a spot of lunch. Petra is a professional-level picnicker! We feast on her tasty homemade farro salad and zucchini bread, an outstanding meal before a five-mile hike.

It is decidedly windy; the sky is becoming slightly overcast. The sun and shadow on the gently undulating forest are hypnotizing. Temperatures are dropping from a high of 87 today to a high of 62 tomorrow. I am thankful for this beautiful day on this beautiful island. Mooningwanekaaning is its original Anishinaabe name in homage to the golden woodpeckers who make it their home.

We start off hiking south on the Woods Trail. After only a short distance, we encounter a ghostly clump of Indian pipes. They are all around us in this part of the forest! The oddest of parasites, they live off the chlorophyll of the surrounding trees and thrive on their symbiotic relationship with the fungi on the roots. They are a striking, incongruent white in the verdant green of this dark, damp landscape.

As we reach the shore, we connect with the Point Trail. Hiking on it, we hear a low, hollow vibration, our footsteps echoing downward through the shallow soil. I marvel at the red pines and hemlocks clinging to the edges of the cliffs, knowing there are cavernous fissures in the ground below us.

The sound of the waves is dynamic and forceful as they crash against the red rock faces jutting out into the water. Grief can be like Lake Superior, a fathomless expanse of memories, revealing itself in waves. We can be caught unaware as they pull us under, sucking the breath right out of our lungs. It does get easier to climb out and dry off the more times it happens. It is a learning process, the accepting of a new way of being after a loss.

I am rightly humbled that the pursuit of my Quest has brought me to this phenomenal island. Listening to the resonance of the waves on this largest freshwater lake in the world is truly a quintessential experience! I stand here in awe of this place. The harmony of the birds and the wind, the smell of pines and mushrooms, the infinity of greens and blues, browns and reds, the textures of rocks and trees beneath my feet and fingertips. Moments of awe stop time, letting us simply be present, be human.

The sense of awe I find any time I am in nature, especially here now by Lake Superior, makes my problems fade, and my concerns become minor, easy obstacles to overcome. When I take the time to be, to experience a sense of awe, I return to my daily life with renewed creativity, freedom, self-determination, and compassion. Awe-inspiring things can be found everywhere. I think of it like beauty in this regard. You have to actively look for it, actively seek it out. It is the Navajo idea of "walking in beauty." Beauty exists before us, below us, above us, all around us. Awe is the same. Making the time to experience awe creates a ritual space, a chance to connect with the Divine. It was Walt Whitman who wrote about our souls being the electricity flowing through our bodies. When we experience

Big Bay State Park

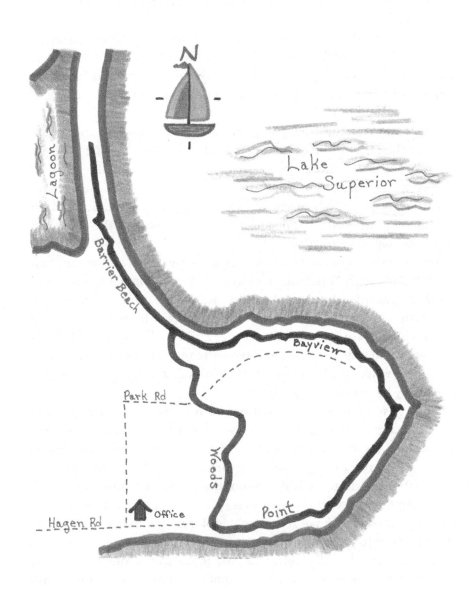

great beauty in nature, the electricity sings with awe, and we are genuinely in touch with our true essence.

The Point Trail takes us to the connection with the Bayview Trail close to the Point Picnic Area. There are families, swimmers, and brazen jumpers climbing on the sheer red cliffs at this dazzling part of the trail. The lake looks incredibly inviting in a calm cove of cerulean blue water, a clear sight line down to the bedrock.

As I have found several times on my Quest, there is a bench here with an earnest message. This one, located in the shade of pines with a view of the vast inland ocean, reads, "For Alex West. Who taught us to live large, love fiercely, and leap without fear. Jun 19, 2006–Feb 4, 2022." He was not quite 16 when he died. As I sit quietly on his bench, my heart is sincerely moved by these words. I must remember to follow them to continue to fully realize and truly honor the gift of time I have been given.

Leaving the stunning point, we continue along the shore via the Bayview Trail. There are mushrooms everywhere! The forest is moisture-laden here, and the fungi's strange shapes and muted colors glisten in the dappled shade. This trail takes us to its junction with the Lagoon Ridge Trail. Those dang industrious beavers have given me a reason to return in the future to hike what looks to be an incredible area. The Boardwalk Trail also begins here and is sure to offer its own delights.

We pause for a brief respite before continuing to the boardwalk, also called the Barrier Beach Trail. Looking out at the boats off the Big Bay beach, Petra muses she wants to find a good-looking man with a catamaran. I am not exactly sure what a catamaran is, but we laugh together, visualizing her life on such a vessel with such a man.

Walking on the mobility-accessible Boardwalk Trail, Petra declares, "We could walk on this until we are in our 80s." I counter with our need, at that age, to have a driver take us to this far up north park. Her great problem-solving mind exclaims, "The handsome catamaran man!"

The vegetation on either side of the boardwalk is fragile and otherworldly: blueberries and wintergreen, huckleberries and dwarf junipers, and the delicate frilly lichen known as reindeer moss. On one side of the trail is the lake. On the other is the lagoon—a reedy and shallow, downright beaver heaven.

We wander on through the Big Bay Sand Spit and Bog Natural Area. The boardwalk ends here, but the trail is wide, and the views are gorgeous. It is hard to believe this is still Wisconsin! I am curious if pitcher plants grow here in abundance in wetter times of the year. Soon, we reach the state park boundary and turn around for the hike back.

The return trip is a chance to experience this diverse and scenic trail from another perspective. As we walk, we hear a curious percussion on the pines. We are blessed to see the namesake bird of the island, a golden woodpecker, or in modern terms, a northern flicker. Its inner wings flash yellow-orange as it flies off in search of better drumming.

Reaching the Big Bay beach once again, the hiking boots come off for essential wading time in the cool, clear water. I pick two beautiful, striped stones from under the waves to remind me of this day as we finish the five miles.

On the drive back to the ferry, we take the long way, turning onto Old Fort Road. At its end, we find the La Pointe Indian Cemetery. Many of the graves are marked by unusual little houses. The informational sign explains the Ojibwe belief regarding the four-day journey to the afterlife. The houses are meant to protect the spirits of the beloved and the food left within for their travels. I leave a black and white striped, lake-polished stone on the cemetery fence next to other multi-colored rocks. They have been placed there along with numerous coins, from newly minted to darkly patinaed.

Catching the 4:30 p.m. ferry back to Bayfield, we find the lake less rough than it was this morning. What started as overcast and wildly windy became a glorious day of clear skies and warm late summer sun, taking us from hiking boots to bare feet in the ever-frigid Superior waters.

Arriving at Petra's cabin, we make a quick change of clothes. The prehistoric calls of pileated woodpeckers fighting in the red pines serenade us as we head back to the car on our way to main street Washburn. We enjoy a wood-fired pizza at DaLou's Bistro and a cold beer at The Snug.

After filling our water jugs from the artesian well at Thompson's West End Park campground, we decide on a ramble of the Washburn Lakefront Parkway. It winds along the Lake Superior beach and among the bluffs, highlighted by delightful bridges and informational signs. It gives us an opportunity to revel in the last visages of setting sunlight before we return to the cabin for a glass of wine and the necessary tick checks.

Being here at this secluded place, I am again reminded of the capriciousness of time. There are stolen moments and borrowed ones. Sometimes, it is killed. Sometimes, it is wasted. Often, it is lost, but it is always coveted. We make attempts to turn it back. It slows down and speeds up. We have no sense of it. Immortal and yet fleeting, it is the spending of it that makes it precious. The only part we can control of time is how we choose to give it.

Big Bay State Park

The Questions

1. What about this chapter resonated with you?
2. When you think about the losses in your life, how has grief returned in unexpected ways or unexpected times?
3. Where have you experienced a sense of awe and wonder? What did it feel like?

The Particulars

Sticker Required: Yes

Map on the State Park's Website: Yes, and nicely detailed

Bathrooms for Day Hikers: Yes, in the office and near the parking lot

Office or Kiosk: Office which can be closed depending on the day or season

Trail Markings: Infrequently marked

Seasonal Closures: Requires ferry which runs from June to January

https://madferry.com/ferry-schedule

Flooding Concerns: Trails may be wet, but no flooding issues

Five Miles: Easy to get with no circles

Copper Falls State Park
Mellen

6.05 miles
Highest Point: 1,230 ft
Lowest Point: 942 ft

September 4, 2022
CCC and Trees

Temperatures were in the 50s last night, and I need to dress quickly this morning. Hot coffee is a comforting blessing on this crisp northern Wisconsin day. After a breakfast of garden tomatoes and a terrific bread we bought yesterday from Café Coco's in Washburn, we get busy packing our belongings and closing up the cabin. The drive home includes a stop at Copper Falls.

The park office has a clean bathroom and a quality map. I am glad I brought the trail descriptions I printed off from the DNR website as a complement. We stop at the lot past the North Camp Area, as it is the central location for the trails to the falls. There is a fabulous concession structure built by the Civilian Conservation Corps at the start of the Doughboys Nature Trail. It has tons of merch and snacks for hungry visitors.

Log kiosks outside the building detail the features built by the CCC: trails and steps, bridges and a tower. The history of the camp is presented here as well. There is a wonderful photograph of the 165 young men of Company D-692. They were only here from 1935 to 1937, but they must have labored sunup to sundown in those years to leave such a grand mark on this park.

I find the history of the CCC fascinating. How different our country would have been without this program to quell the revolution rumbling to the surface during the Great Depression. With the unemployment rate for men at over 25 percent, the CCC took the ones most likely to commit violent crimes out of the general population. By giving those over three million unmarried, disconnected 18- to 25-year-olds a job, food, and housing, the government was able to create lasting changes to our park systems. They taught the men trades and reduced crime in the cities by almost 50 percent. Thinking of those tough times and remembering the stories told to me by elders who lived through them, I stand in admiration of the CCC's legacy.

We start the five miles on the Doughboys Nature Trail, which winds through the park's most scenic areas. The Bad River flows beside us, with remarkable overlooks at every turn. The trail brings us to a friendly ranger marking dying ash trees. We share stories of the giants—my garden, home to two 60-year-old ash trees treated against emerald ash borers for over a decade, and Petra's front yard graced by a strikingly tall white pine. He can tell we are honest dendrophiles, and he shares with us the locations of some notable trees within the park. The largest white pine in this forest is on the Doughboys Nature Trail, close to the CCC bench on the right-hand side. The decision was made to not cut it down in 1916 due to how difficult it would have been to remove. On an area by the Tyler Fork Cascades is a stand of old-growth red and white pines with burn scars from an 1896 fire. We make promises to find them and give them all manner of due respect as we wave goodbye to the ranger.

BETSY KORBINYR

Copper Falls State Park

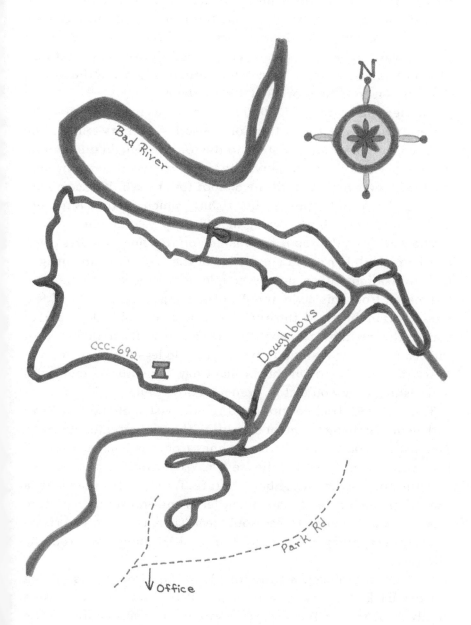

We follow the Doughboys down to the river's edge to get a better view of the Devil's Gate, an area of black lava on either side of the river. I wish the beautiful places in nature were not referred to with the word *Devil*. Wisconsin has too many Devils: island, lake, backbone, punch bowl, doorway, river, and this gate. The Native peoples gave these places spiritual and descriptive identifications. The settlers named them after evil incarnate. I hope, in the future, they can return to their original designations.

Our next trail is the CCC 692 Trail. It takes us to the Observation Tower. A woman at the bottom of the series of stairs tells us she counted, and there are 239 steps to the top. We remain undaunted! Are we spry? No, we are mighty! The trail takes us on steps through the forest, ever higher, until the 65-foot tower itself. We see a man coming down and smile at his t-shirt, which reads, "Naps are underrated," both of us knowing we will sleep well tonight.

The view from the top is astonishing on this fine, cloudless blue day. Petra, with her broad knowledge of the area, ends up engaged in conversation with a nearby couple about the numerous sites to be seen from this aerie: the Penokee Range, some of the oldest mountains in the world; the Apostles, a 21-island archipelago; and of course, the phenomenal expanse of Lake Superior. I stand in awe of the beauty, feeling grateful to my 65-year-old legs taking me up the tower to such a view. On this brilliant day, I am storing memories and wishing time would stop, even for a little while.

The CCC 692 Trail continues to remote vistas of the Bad River with hemlocks hanging on for dear life to the eroding embankments. This park encompasses the beach lines from the ancient shore of Lake Superior at the end of the Ice Age. What a unique area this is!

Returning to the Doughboys Nature Trail, we are met with a shaded microclimate of maidenhair ferns and equisetum. I picture this is how a Cambrian forest would feel. There is even a surprising little spring running by the edge of the trail, trickling down from the hillside.

We finish the mileage with another loop of the Doughboys, ending our day back at the concession stand. Petra says we must have a locally made treat, a Tetzner's Dairy vanilla ice cream sandwich. She is right; they are the best ever! We plan to return to Copper Falls the next time we are at her cabin to hike the far-afield trails like Takesson and Red Granite Falls.

On the drive back, we pass through quaint towns along Highway 13, each with its own claim to fame. Glidden, the black bear capital of the world, and Park Falls, the ruffed grouse capital, to name a few. Park Falls is also the home of the St. Croix Rods, purported to be "the best rods on earth." We can't help but get the silly giggles about that one, our bodies and brains weary after our travels.

The miles and hours stretch on in the dimming sunlight. A memory hits me in a quiet moment, like a sneaker wave, not of grief but of comfort, almost joy. It is a memory about lost memories, about an elder I worked with during my time as a hospice social worker. Something about my presence in her room one day validated her internal experience. Something about the way I looked or the way I stood, or my general countenance reminded her of long ago. She suddenly brightened and became animated and told me all about a day she spent with someone like me, sharing the recollection she was able to find before she slipped back under the mirrored surface of advanced Alzheimer's.

Thinking of her, I hope if I ever lose my cognizance, I will find a friendly face as she did in mine. A face to bring the memory of this day back to me, this day hiking at Copper Falls with my playful friend. I include here the poem I wrote about her:

To a Stranger from Lillian, Dying

She looked up at me, smiling.
Her face illuminated with recognition and love.
"It seems like it's been so long since I've seen you."
And I wondered who she saw when she looked at my face.
Her mother.
Her daughter.
Her friend.
And she told me,
reminded me,
of a day when we played in the summer sun
in short cotton dresses,
blue like the sky.

She looked up at me, smiling.
Her face illuminated with love and grace.
"Seems so long since I've seen you, so long, too long."

September 5, 2022
The Day After

It is morning, and I am unloading my car. I got home quite late yesterday and was exhausted after the long drive home from Copper Falls.

The red dust of the Lake Superior shorelines covers my white car. Soil kicked up on it, driving on dirt roads to my friend's cabin, the Big Top Chautauqua, and the other places we went while we were up north. I know I have to wash it off, but I think I'll wait a few days. It makes me smile to see it, reminding me of a wonderful trip.

As I unload, I grab my hiking poles. There is a sensation I get in my hands, permeating my entire body when I touch them. I can feel the power of the energy and nature from the places I've been and the happiness I felt in those places when I touch the handles of my hiking poles.

Even more than my hiking boots, even more than my backpack, the poles are dear to me. The boots are about the physical movements: putting them on, lacing them tight, striding forward. The backpack, covered in patches of places I've been, is about organization and planning. The feel of putting it on my back, more of a gross motor sensation. The hiking poles have something about them. They have been imbued with a feeling of magic. I think when I am a very old woman—if I'm lucky enough to be—the poles will become one of my few and highly prized possessions. They are talismans for me of adventure and confidence and joy.

Copper Falls State Park

The Questions

1. What about this chapter resonated with you?
2. When visiting Wisconsin's State Parks or the national parks, what structures built by the Civilian Conservation Corps have you encountered?
3. In considering those affected by dementia or Alzheimer's disease, how does this challenge how you think about your own aging?

The Particulars

Sticker Required: Yes

Map on the State Park's Website: Yes, and it is detailed in color

Bathrooms for Day Hikers: Yes, in the office and the concession building

Office or Kiosk: Office which can be closed depending on the day or season

Trail Markings: Infrequently marked

Seasonal Closures: None

Flooding Concerns: Trails may be wet but no flooding issues

Five Miles: Easy to get with no circles

Council Grounds State Park
Merrill

5.41 miles
Highest Point: 1,303 ft
Lowest Point: 1,073 ft

September 7, 2022
Harassment and Water

This is park number 35! I knew I would get to this point on my Quest but also doubted it, especially after the bout of COVID. It is gratifying to be on the road headed toward Council Grounds. The journey to the park is slower than I anticipated due to all the road construction on I-90. When I reach the fresh pieces of new asphalt, it is a fabulous drive! The roadsides are decorated with early autumn flowers: goldenrod, white asters, and nascent red sumac. Outside of Wausau, interesting and quizzical covered fields grow ginseng in the shade of thousands of feet of black mesh.

The park office has a friendly, happy ranger and lots of stickers, sweatshirts, and t-shirts. Their logo is marvelous and one of the best I have seen on my Quest. It is a black X with a bird and a hiking boot, fire and waves, each in a separate section.

I start off my five miles on what I think is the Northwest Trail, but I find out as I proceed, I am actually on the Brown Trail. The Brown keeps going north out of the park, which I don't want to do. I stop, turn around, and figure out with my GPS where I am and where I need to go. I walk back toward the entrance and search until I find the small sign for the Northwest Trail.

All this wandering has me feeling uncomfortable and reminds me of what happened yesterday, which caused a similar sense of unease. I was at the grocery store checking out in the 15 items or less lane when an older man came up right behind me, in my personal space, almost touching me. I stepped in front of my cart, creating some distance between us. As I unloaded my things onto the conveyor belt, I glanced quickly at him to see if he was backing up at all. He wasn't. Instead, he was giving me the "Hey, baby. You want to be with me?" look, one I have seen my entire life. He had the horrible beard that men of a certain age think hides wrinkles and a weak chin: the gray-white, grizzly, unkempt goatee. Where's my invisibility of aging when I need it? I am glad I am here in this peaceful forest today, taking a brief respite from awkward social situations.

The Northwest Trail starts as a narrow slip through a forest of white pines and maples. It is evenly adorned with wonderful Leopold benches. They were obviously hand-built by people who genuinely love this park. I take brief advantage of them as I hike, sitting in many of them for a moment to enjoy the views. The trail leads me out of the forest to a gloriously sunny hill surrounded by a broad, awe-inspiring meadow. It is picture perfect on this clear sky day. I stop for a snack at a sizeable circle made up of those outstanding benches. I eat slowly, taking the time to breathe, to soak up the sun, to be.

As I sit, contemplating this prairie, I remind myself to drink more water to lighten my load. When hiking, packing water is the heaviest thing, and thinking about this brings to mind a good lesson for my

Council Grounds State Park

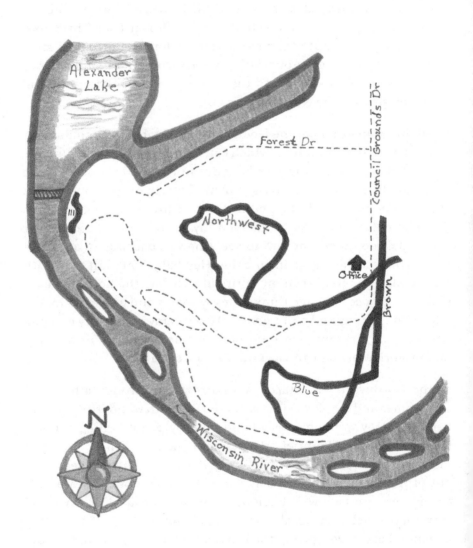

aging self: don't carry anyone else's "water." By this, I mean don't take on the needs, the traumas, the responsibilities of other people for them. Of course, I will absolutely carry the "water" of the ones I love if and when they need me to. Yet, for those people who are capable, who don't reciprocate, or for complete strangers, I will no longer accept their burden. They need to respect my boundaries and the natural consequence for their behavior if they don't. It is similar to when a man asks a woman to transport something for him in her purse because she is already carrying things. She has the capacity, so why not? Until the woman's purse ends up so heavy with the man's stuff, she finally snaps, telling him to schlep his own crap. I have done this, and I have witnessed it being done many times. It's the people who take advantage of you carrying their "water" who get the most irritated when you say you are no longer willing to do it. It is complicated to tell people, to set this boundary, as it can end relationships. At 65, it is beyond enough for me to say my time is short, and I have enough of my own to bear.

My rumination brings me back to the whole subject of dating as an older woman. I am divorced, but I have no feelings for my ex. I don't think about him except in passing. If a thought arises, I remind myself, *Yes, he was a passive-aggressive bastard,* and the thought is over. I don't have any need to forgive him. He is undeserving of my grace, and I have moved on. While this may sound harsh, I have, instead, forgiven myself for allowing things to happen that were not the best for me and for not having a stronger voice. Do I have regrets? Of course, I wouldn't be human if I didn't. I have chosen to examine them, painful as they may be, and attempt to learn and grow from them. Some regrets are rectifiable, but many are not. In that case, it is wise to reframe them. My marriage dissolved, but at least I had some grand adventures along the way, and it allowed me to conceive the light of my life, my wonderful child.

This is why, when I go on a first date with someone, and all they can talk about is their ex and how psycho they were, I think how they are SO not ready to be dating. They are ready to see a therapist. While I am one, I only work for free for strangers who I choose. For example, last week at the bookstore, an older man was looking for information on how to cope with Alzheimer's as his wife had been recently diagnosed. For someone like that, yes, wholeheartedly, I will give them brief therapy, empathy, and validation, but not on a first date with a grown man fixated on all the problems of his failed marriage.

As I rejoin the trail, I am amazed to see a stand of massive oaks. This section of the Northwest Trail is where the elders live—big and spreading and old, supporting innumerable other beings on their sturdy frames. The trail becomes covered by a soft blanket of needles. In this quiet part of the forest, the giant white and red pines create a remarkable silence. It is breathtaking, and a park I would not have considered if I wasn't on my Quest.

I return to the Brown Trail and start heading south to connect to the Blue Trail. I should have my mileage by the time I finish the Blue and return to my car. There are copious amounts of sizeable spiderwebs in the trees. They remind me of hiking in Northern India and seeing numerous webs over six feet wide. I was inquisitive about the size of the spider spinning such a home, and when I saw one, I was not disappointed! There is a particular term for the panicky feeling people experience when they accidentally walk through a web: an arachnoleptic fit. I would have surely had one had I walked through those monstrous spiderwebs!

The trails at this park are not well-marked. There are no "You Are Here" signs, no directions when a trail comes to a Y or a T. I can't stress enough the importance of having a paper map because cell service is spotty in the wilds of Wisconsin, and phone batteries can die. On the upside, though, the trails are wide and neatly mowed, dotted with those splendid benches. Therefore, I can't complain too much.

I hike the Blue Trail around to the shelter house for a view of the Wisconsin River. There is a charming beach on this slow-moving section, empty today because of the chill in the air. It's a genuinely tranquil place, and I take a moment to sit on one of the large metal swings and simply enjoy this splendid day. I head back along the road to where I parked, planning to drive the long way out of Council Grounds to see what else it holds.

A car starts slowly following me. The man pulls up beside me and starts trying to "Hey baby" talk to me through his open window. It is difficult not to notice his penis in his hand. I immediately turn and go in the opposite direction. The quickest defense from a dick in a car, literally and figuratively, is to reverse course because it makes it difficult for him to follow. I take a photo of his license plate as he drives away so I can report him to the ranger when I leave. As I have said before, if you're a man and you see a woman out by herself in the forest, don't be a fucking creep! A woman hiking alone is never inviting you to harass her.

After the annoyance of that ridiculous display, I regroup, trying not to let such an ugly encounter steal the joy from my day. I proceed north on the Brown Trail again for two reasons: to finish the last bit of my mileage and because I am curious about a trail leading out of the park. It is called the River Bend Trail, and I saw a sign for it earlier today when I went this way. It takes me to the top of a hill with a view of the river, but soon, the trail heads toward an extensive housing development. I turn back around in the direction of my vehicle.

On the drive out of the park, I stop to check out the hydroelectric dam. I take a rickety metal stairway down to the river's edge for a better view. A high-pitched squeak greets me as I walk up to the shoreline, a startled green frog quickly jumping from the rocks into the water. It is a delightful sight on this beautiful day. I look downstream from the dam and listen to the slow ripple of the shallow water over the river's countless stones. It is a holy sound and a superb way to end my time at this state park.

I wander back to the metal stairs to return to my car. A man is standing at the top of them, arms akimbo, blocking my ascent, and asks, "Is there anything interesting down there?"

I state, "Yes," and nothing else, walking with confidence up the rest of the stairs to escape his intimidating stance.

He responds belligerently, "Nice talking to you, bitch!"

I tell myself; *I don't care what you think of me, and fuck you! How dare you try to ruin my time at this park!* I have to be true to myself and trust my gut. I don't owe "nice" to random dudes blocking my path. I am not carrying the "water" of their ignorance and anger. To the "not all men" crowd I ask, why don't you hang out with lions? Why don't you give them the benefit of the doubt? The reason you would not trust lions is the same reason women should not be expected to give quarter to men who think we owe them a smile. To those who consider it an offense to their existence if we don't give them deference like this man obviously did.

I hurry to my car and drive off, thinking I will have to investigate Tasers. I rarely am harassed when hiking, but twice in one day makes me feel unsafe to return to this place. With all the wonderful forests to choose from, which I do want to return to, this park is a one-and-done!

Council Grounds State Park

The Questions

1. What about this chapter resonated with you?
2. How have you "carried the water" for others in your life?
3. In what ways has the ignorance of others negatively affected your life? What were you able to do to persevere?

The Particulars

Sticker Required: Yes

Map on the State Park's Website: Yes, and nicely detailed

Bathrooms for Day Hikers: Yes, in the office

Office or Kiosk: Office which can be closed depending on the day or season

Trail Markings: Not well-marked

Seasonal Closures: None

Flooding Concerns: None

Five Miles: Easy to get with no circles

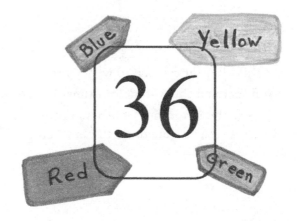

Rib Mountain State Park
Wausau

5.17 miles
Highest Point: 2,028 ft
Lowest Point: 1,759 ft

September 9, 2022
Color and Mottos

My mind is dancing all over the place while driving to this park. I am thinking about the dryer repair man who came four hours early. I am considering the woman I talked to yesterday at work whose mother suffered from severe depression. I need to stop letting my mind be tangential when I get out on this hike and start organizing my thoughts. It makes me wonder if my mind wandering off on its own adventures contributes to my geographical challenges.

I stop at the Rib Mountain office. It is a wonderful spot, full of friendly rangers and fun merch. I have not encountered any unfriendly rangers on this Quest. They are a hardworking bunch and should be paid much better! The rangers provide me with excellent maps and direct me to where to access the trailheads. They advise me to park by the upper picnic area. On the way there, I stop at the Vista Overlook for a view of the grand surroundings. Rib Mountain, the sign here says, is the third-highest mountain in Wisconsin. The highest one is Timm's Hill, followed by Lookout Mountain, but they are for another summer.

As it has been with several hikes on this Quest, this is not the hike I had anticipated. I had planned to go hiking here in early August with my friend Britt and her two teenage kids. It would've been a fabulous time. I was genuinely looking forward to it, but then COVID hit me hard, putting an end to that ambition. Today, hiking here on this mountain is about reclaiming the depth of my breath I lost for the entire month of August due to the virus.

The weird catch is back in my right hip. I pull out my trusty first aid kit and take some Tylenol as I begin. I won't let a few aches and pains prevent me from having an adventure. Nor am I going to allow internalized ageism to stop me. How sad my life would be if that were the case.

I challenge myself with a walk to the top of the 60-foot Observation Tower. Reaching the pinnacle, I am feeling strong and confident. The view of this unique geographical feature, one of the oldest on the planet, is definitely worth the climb!

The giant monoliths at the tower's base seem purposefully placed by the Gods. I weave around them, awestruck, as I head off for the start of the Red Trail. The Blue, Green, and Red Trails start together and then branch off in all directions into this picturesque forest. I am smiling wide and looking forward to the rest of my day!

In talking to other hikers about my Quest, I have had some scoff at my goal of getting at least five miles in each park. They sarcastically wish me "Good luck" in getting it at the state parks like Tower Hill and Rocky Arbor. However, only hiking the length of the available trails at the smaller parks is not the idea of the Quest. A vital element is having a minimum mileage, no matter the park size, not just setting foot in each one. Whether at Rib Mountain, with its 14 miles of trails,

Rib Mountain State Park

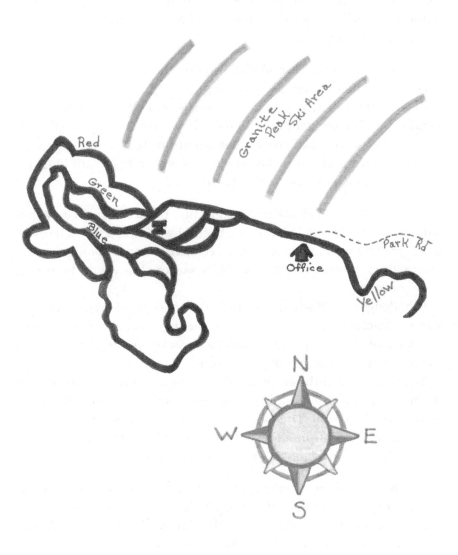

or at Belmont Mound, with only 2.5, a necessary component of this endeavor requires me to wind in circles and backtrack and try to find where to go. It is a powerful analogy and a mindful meditation of the journey of growing older.

The trails here are well-marked with bright metal panels designating the colors of each one. In considering the whole trail marking thing, it really is about equity and inclusion. What if I was an elder with some dementia issues who still wanted to be out hiking? Even the best of us, out here with family or friends, can get separated from each other. The anxiety of being turned around or lost from hiking companions would be much more intense with cognitive concerns. I believe having well-marked trails is invariably an issue of disability accessibility.

The Red Trail is filled with spectacular, little microclimates thoroughly shaded by enormous boulders. As a result of this lack of sunshine, the rocks are covered with vast cushions of mosses, lycophytes, and delicate little ferns dazzling in the shadows. Numerous crevices among the rocks appear to be snuggly burrows and tiny caves, making for cozy hibernating spots for bears, bobcats, and foxes. What a distinctive and surprising place!

I stop to take a moment to sit on a bench at the edge of a drop-off. Small trees surround it, filtering the intense daylight. I love the color behind my closed eyelids when I face the sun: the color of red and fire, and heat and blood. I must remember these days! In the coming winter, when I'm cold and the sky is gray, I can hold fast to these exquisite, golden days of my Quest as I plan for a new adventure next year, next summer. Warm memories and hopes for the future are the best gifts we can give to ourselves as we age.

I finish the Red Trail and arrive back at the Observation Tower. The Red Trail kicked my ass! I would describe it as difficult, but it could be the lingering impacts of COVID. My next trek is on the Blue Trail and then the Green Trail, which are both easy to moderate with many asphalted sections.

One thing especially inspiring about my time here is coming across three other women who are solo hiking. I stop to chat with each one about what a beautiful day it is, what great trails they are, and the whole idea of being out here alone. These are vastly different encounters from my experiences earlier this week at Council

Grounds State Park, where two different men harassed me. The very real concern of being threatened when we are out hiking is all too common for women. Today is a much better day in that regard.

Almost done with my five from the Red, Blue, and Green, I head off on the Yellow Trail. It is a gently rolling saunter through an open and drier forest, accentuated intermittently by large rock outcroppings. I only go as far as I need to get my Quest mileage, but I will definitely return to this park to do more of the Yellow. It is my favorite trail here.

Returning to my car, I set my hiking poles and backpack down. As I reach to open the door, an immense garter snake shows herself. She is phenomenal with her marvelous coloring and red tongue! She spots me, too, and when I take a step toward her, she slithers into an unseen hole in the rocks. I find animals' camouflage striking as well as their ability to disappear when they feel threatened and blend in so as not to be seen.

As someone who has recently turned 65, I think the idea of blending in comes all too easily. It's the whole idea of how people of a certain age become invisible in society. It is one of the reasons I have dyed my hair vivid blue and have multi-colored fingernails. One of my favorite quotes is by the outstanding artist Wassily Kandinsky: "Color is a power that directly influences the soul." I don't want to blend in! I don't want to give others an easy stereotype of an old person, one they don't need to acknowledge, one they can expect to move out of their way, one they can dismiss as less than. Soon enough, I will wink out of existence. Why would I want to fade into the background while I'm alive?

Driving home, I am thinking about when I was training for my hikes in England, Ireland, and India. I would go to Devil's Lake State Park and hike up and down both bluffs. Rib Mountain is a fine place to train, even though it is farther from my house. It would be even better to have a hiking buddy to talk with along the way. It makes me miss having my friend Britt here as we had arranged, but that's how life is. The wisdom of best-laid plans going astray is especially relevant as we age. Best to adapt, improvise, and always carry a well-stocked first aid kit.

As I leave Marathon County, I see a billboard emblazoned with their motto: "Where Time Is on Your Side." It is an idiom, meaning you will have time to waste. You don't have to use time so quickly. There's no need to make final decisions right away because they will come running back. I am not sure their motto works for 65-year-old me. Time on your side is a luxury not afforded as readily to us as we get older. Time on your side means believing the false premise you will never die. You believe you have control over how to spend it, to be able to wait for things to change, and possess the personal autonomy to influence it. One thing these languid summer days have taught me is time is of the essence. It is a precious commodity deserving of far-reaching appreciation. I need to do now rather than later. I don't have the time to wait. Time is a bane as well as a boon when you get to be sixty-five.

Rib Mountain State Park

The Questions

1. What about this chapter resonated with you?
2. As you get older, how are you able to avoid "blending in" with the stereotypes of how we should be as we age?
3. In thinking about the idiom, "Time is on your side," how do you feel it is and isn't?

The Particulars

Sticker Required: Yes

Map on the State Park's Website: Yes, and it is detailed in color

Bathrooms for Day Hikers: Yes, in the office and picnic area

Office or Kiosk: Office which can be closed depending on the day or season

Trail Markings: Intermittently well-marked

Seasonal Closures: None

Flooding Concerns: None

Five Miles: Easy to get with no circles

Merrick State Park
Fountain City

5.12 miles
Highest Point: 676 ft
Lowest Point: 632 ft

September 13, 2022
Isolation and Mirrors

Perusing this morning's newspaper, I decide to take rare note of my horoscope. It reads: "Today is an 8. Explore uncharted territory and take notes. Follow your intuition." I find this prescient because I plan to hike at a place I've never been, and, of course, I take notes! What does my intuition say? It tells me I need to keep embracing my creative self and keep hiking as I move through these next years of my life—these last years of my life. I need to keep storing warm memories, allowing me to recall them in winter's darkness. My hope for today is I will end up with a golden early autumn memory as I go to Merrick. It overlooks the Mississippi, one of the world's great rivers. How lucky I am to live in a state next to its mighty countenance.

On the drive to Merrick, the roadsides are full of cattails and towering yellow prairie flowers. As I reach the shores of the Mississippi and the commanding bluffs on either side, I find my eyes swelling with tears at the sheer beauty of this location along the Great River Road. It is an exquisite place, radiant with soaring turkey vultures and the shine of the sun on the wide, open water.

I reach the park after a circuitous drive, finding it to be a peculiar place. There is a one-room cabin for the check-in station. It's not open, but I peek in the windows. There is no merch or information. I'm glad I printed out a copy of the map from the DNR's website after reading about the history of this locale. John A. Latsch, a nature-loving man of wealth, used his fortunes to buy swaths of land and donate it to the state. It turns out the park is named for a steamboat captain of the 1850s whom John admired: George Byron Merrick. What a good setting for a time machine!

A road sign reading "Park Office" is marked on my map. I drive to it, but it's an office for employees only. I drive around to where the Nature Center is, but it is locked. I peek in those windows as well to see what's inside. It looks nice enough but appears to only be open for specific events.

Everything is closed, and I am one of a mere handful of people in this small park today. These circumstances are leading me to think about aloneness and its many challenges. Coping with aloneness is a huge part of this coming-of-age time. If we live long enough, we will all be alone. Even if we have a partner, it is a rare occurrence to die together in some bizarre accident. More likely, one will be left by themselves after the other passes away.

There are several downsides to living alone. It is simply more expensive. Food costs more as buying things in bulk makes little sense. Cooking for one is difficult as most recipes are written for two or more. I end up with tons of leftovers in my freezer, which can be a good thing and a bad thing. I do have people who check on me regularly and have a key to my house, just in case. I have a support network to help when I am sick, bringing soup and mowing my lawn.

Merrick State Park

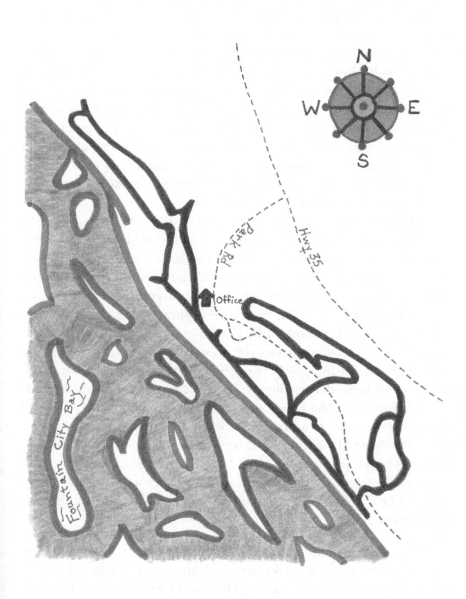

However, I have to make all the decisions by myself. I have to assume all the risks. After getting out of a toxic relationship and now living by myself for this long, I don't know if I could ever live with anyone else. I don't know if it would be a hindrance to having a long-term relationship at this point in my life. Is there even such a thing as a long-term relationship for a 65-year-old?

The isolation can get tough. In fact, it has been described by mental health researchers as "learned loneliness." It is the idea we learn to live with an unfulfilled need. I think of it more as a void we have to be mindful to fill, lest despair overtake us. We need to give ourselves the twin gifts of wonderful memories and hopes for the future. It is vital to have activities to define us as we age, like we did in our younger days. I have art and hiking, gardening and writing, and time spent with loved ones. We all have to decide for ourselves how to greet the void of time spent alone.

Enough with all the disadvantages. After all, there are many perks to living alone. Because I am responsible for all the decisions and consequences, I get to reap all the rewards. I am able to decorate in my style: black orbs with moon cutouts, ceramic crows, and claw-footed candlesticks. No one says the tree branches adorning the archways in my living room are inappropriate. I can bedeck them with colorful metal birds, sparkling paper stars, and a heart-shaped vial of sawdust from my now-deceased 60-foot-tall noble fir. I have my routine and my agenda. My space and my time are my own. Unbeholden to anyone, there is no need to hammer out a compromise on the new paint color for the bathroom. As for all the household chores and yard work, I did them before anyway, and now, it is decidedly easier. Most importantly, I am able to take care of myself first and better than I have at any time in my life. In a nutshell, just as we need to purge and downsize as we age, we must plan for being alone. We have to figure out how to hike on, how to continue the journey.

I sit to have a snack at one of the tables near the Nature Center. This is a strange little park, beautiful but weird. There are only a couple miles of trails, meaning I'll have to get inventive to reach my five. Nothing makes this park stand out to me. Maybe, if I had a boat. Its campground looks to be a convenient spot to stay close to Fountain City, a happening river town boasting of the oldest bar in Wisconsin and home to a local winery as well as several nice restaurants.

Behind the Nature Center, I connect to a trail and head off to the north. There are no names for any of the trails, and I find it offends my writer's mind. For heaven's sake, there are so many words, including the multiple languages of the Native people and settlers! Why are trails in the state parks frequently left unnamed? It reminds me of the street names in the small town in New Mexico where I used to live, many of which lacked basic imagination.

In Carrizozo, numerous streets are named with the letters of the alphabet. I lived on "B" Street in a small adobe house. My neighbor was an elderly Hispanic woman, the granddaughter of a Spanish land grant family. She had remarkable tales of her life growing up in the tall grass on a thriving ranch.

One day, over a cup of chamomile tea, I asked Carmela if she remembered the time when the bomb was dropped in the Jornada del Muerto Desert. The day prior, I had driven to Albuquerque and back, the road taking me past the entrance to the Trinity Site, and it was on my mind. She related a story, both commonplace and exceptional.

She was days away from the birth of her third child. Heavy with pregnancy, she found sleep elusive, a normal thing when approaching a due date. That night, she got out of bed, checked on her two other little ones, and walked to her kitchen sink for a glass of water. Again, a common everyday action done by a mom-to-be. I could sense the trauma in her voice all those years later as she shared what happened next. She stood, drinking cool water and gently caressing her swollen belly, staring out the window at the open range behind her house. The dark sky was suddenly as bright as a noonday sun. She placed the glass on the counter and leaned toward the window, wondering what in the world could make such an exceptional thing happen. In a few seconds, the night's darkness returned. The only thing her mind could find to make sense of what had occurred was to think she was overly tired, maybe hallucinating from lack of sleep.

The next day, her husband, Hector, called her, worried. He was working on the railroad outside of Tularosa, over 40 miles away. He had to take a horse cart for several hours from his remote location to even find a phone. However, his concern for his family was paramount. Carmela told me of their conversation. He entreated her to go to the doctor immediately to ensure she and the baby were alright. He told her something terrible had happened in the desert the night before. Hector and all the rail workers had seen it—the flash. No one knew what it was, but they all felt in their hearts it was an evil thing, she remembered with a shudder.

She did go to the doctor. Hector came home to be with her, and the baby arrived a few days later, right as rain on a dry New Mexico summer day. Weeks later, they listened to the radio news about the war in Japan, and they knew, she said. They knew then what had happened on the night of the nefarious flash. I remember sitting there in rapt silence, in awe of her incredible story. She and all of Carrizozo, and her husband and all of Tularosa, could have been obliterated when the Trinity bomb was dropped, an intensely sobering thought.

Carmela and I became good friends over the years I lived there. I held her hand as she grieved for Hector, who died of cancer soon after I moved to my little adobe. She delighted in my bright and happy child, treating them like a surrogate grandchild, as hers all now lived distances away. I drove her to doctor's appointments in far-off Alamogordo, and she provided me with sound mothering advice. I was in my 40s then, and having lost my own beloved grandmother, I truly appreciated her wise surrogate counsel. I will continue on my hike today, joyful in my memories of her, my sweet adopted abuela.

Onward, I go on this tragically unnamed trail. It takes me to the north campground. I wander around its circle until I find another trail branching in three directions. My map shows only two in this area. I decide on the furthest left-hand one to see where it takes me. It comes to a T, and I take a right, thinking at least I'm moving away from where I parked. The trail is nicely maintained, even though it doesn't match my map. I am the geographically challenged living the dream!

After walking around and enjoying this amazing sunny day, I discover the left and middle trails are the loop on my map. The right trail is actually a short spur out to a railroad track. I stand beside it, my face to the sun, and say a heartfelt thank you in memory of Carmela and Hector.

Walking back through the campground, I see a sign reading, "Water Access." This spur and its short stairway end up at a slough of the river, wide and surprising. I am glad I am here in mid-September. Significant parts of the park would be inaccessible in the spring or during times of flooding.

I take the trail back toward the Nature Center. It runs along the river and is studded with beautiful white pines. The path is full of their soft needles and the enchanting aromas of sap and late summer. In this direction, the trail leads to a boat landing and a fine picnic spot. I follow it as it crosses the road, bringing me into a dense, mixed forest away from the river. I make the two loops pictured on my map, coming across rangers out with their ATVs. They are knowledgeable and friendly as I stop to chat with them about the park. It is exciting to see young women kicking ass with chainsaws!

I do one more loop around, ending back at the Nature Center with my mileage complete. Reflecting on my Quest, I genuinely have a sense of pride about it. I have a sense of loss, too, because as I get closer to number 45, I know the summer is getting closer to ending. Therefore, I know this odd purpose for my days will end as well. I will have to develop something new to keep my heart happy and my soul at peace, something new to fill the void. I think it will be to return to my art, which I haven't worked on substantially this summer, and perhaps to go back through and write up my experiences on this Quest to share with others as many have said I should.

After all, there are not enough stories of older adults doing interesting things out there in the world. There are not enough coming-of-age stories, ones taking into consideration all the things we must process and go through. One thing I've been doing this summer is trying to find books with a main protagonist who is at least sixty-five. There aren't many of them, but the ones I have read are interesting and insightful. The coming-of-age stories about elders are decidedly different than the multiple ones available about young adults. Maybe the story of my Quest can add to the genre, at least in some small part.

Overall, Merrick is an unremarkable spot, but the drive here was extraordinary. My GPS took me on a labyrinthine route, across to the other side of the river and then back again to the Wisconsin side via a bridge at Winona, Minnesota. It was a bizarre way to get to the park's entrance, but sometimes that's what happens. The journey is what it's all about, after all. I would not have been moved to tears by the beauty if I had not followed those directions. I would not have found a golden memory to keep of this day.

Tonight, I am going through my art elements and formulating ideas for future projects. I am giving myself the gift of hope for after the Quest. My art uses mirrors and found objects to create 2-D pieces for outside display. When placed in a garden, they become like magical portals to another realm.

As I am moving boxes and thinking of creative endeavors, I accidentally break one of the mirrors waiting to be worked on. I don't give credence to the myths about mirrors; if I did, my entire life would have been unlucky. Considering the cracks in it, I decide to smash it further, committing to its destruction. All the different aspects of my life are reflected in the shards lying before me on my studio floor: mother, orphan, sister, friend, lover, therapist, gardener, artist, writer, hiker. The same ruggedly beautiful face, the same blue hair, and the same wrinkles appear within each fractured piece. Each is a portrait of my reflected life, each of a different geometric composition. What an interesting analogy of aging. Triangles one day, squares the next, and even a rhombus appears on occasion. I find, studying my broken mirror, I have become more at ease with the existential angst of turning sixty-five. I gather the best shards and label them with the various facets of myself. I place them on my work table as a reminder of the fragile and beautiful, liminal and gone-in-a-flash nature of life.

Merrick State Park

The Questions

1. What about this chapter resonated with you?
2. If you live alone, what do you find to be the most difficult part to deal with? What is the most positive part? If you don't live alone, how are you actively making plans to exist in that situation?
3. Make a list of all the different aspects of yourself. How have they changed as you have gotten older?

The Particulars

Sticker Required: Yes

Map on the State Park's Website: Yes, and nicely detailed

Bathrooms for Day Hikers: Only in the campground

Office or Kiosk: Small office which can be closed depending on the day or season

Trail Markings: Not well-marked, unnamed trails

Seasonal Closures: None

Flooding Concerns: Frequent flooding concerns

Five Miles: Circles required

Perrot State Park
Trempealeau

5.06 miles
Highest Point: 1,129 ft
Lowest Point: 603 ft

September 16, 2022
Art and War

One of the overarching themes of my Quest has been reclaiming. Reclaiming my heart, my future, my artistic self.

About six years ago, I started having my fingernails done in sparkly, often multiple colors. When I was hiking in Ireland in 2019, one of the women on our tour asked me why each of my hands had different colored nails. I declared, ostentatiously, "It is because I want people to know I am a member of the creative class." It blurted out, and once I had said it, I felt a bit embarrassed, but I realized it was true. It is, out of anything, how I identify myself. She loved the idea and said she was going to start doing the same. I was flattered and happy I gave her the impetus to express more of her own creative self to the world, as I was attempting to do.

I have lived my life as a creative person and a devoted art lover. One of my quintessential memories is of being in the Uffizi Gallery in Florence, Italy. My child and I had spent almost 10 hours viewing the art. As we walked to the exit, we both looked at each other and said simultaneously, "Let's go through again!" We couldn't, of course, as it was near closing time, but we both laughed as we embraced, thinking of our artistic selves.

Earlier this year, I shocked my tai chi class with my love of art. Folks were stretching, preparing to begin while commiserating about the horrible weather and how spring might never come. I told them the story of how Edvard Munch created his famous work, *The Scream*, and how he was inspired to paint the sky in strange, swirling colors because of the eruption of Krakatoa. The volcano changed the weather across the entire planet. I looked up, and everyone in the class was aghast in horror. It made me smile, all of them resembling the face in the painting. Art geek making trouble!

I firmly believe art saves lives. As a school social worker, I used art therapy with hundreds of children over the years. At one of the high schools I worked at, a student came into my office in the midst of a scary panic attack. I had her take a seat and she immediately asked about an item of my clothing, "Are those Keith Haring socks?"

I responded, "Why, yes! You are the first person to notice them." We proceeded to talk about how the majority of people don't notice things around them, how fabulous Keith's art is, and voilà, no more panic attack! The healing power of art doing its magic.

During the pandemic shutdown, the isolation prompted me to begin creating mixed-media garden art using old mirrors and found things. I invariably feel great comfort in making something discarded beautiful again. I have had my works in several Madison exhibitions and am hoping an art show will be in my future. However, my motto remains the words of Andy Warhol: "Don't think about making art, just get it done. Let everyone else decide if it's good or bad, whether they love it or hate it. While they are deciding, make even more art." After all, art is about the joy of creating, just like hiking is about the joy of being.

Perrot State Park

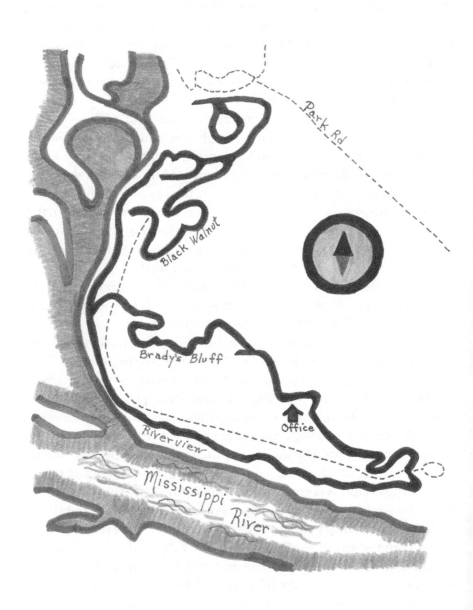

On the drive to Perrot, the colors are breathtaking! The subtle yellows in the soybean fields. The bursting reds of maple trees lighting the forests ablaze. The ruffled white and cream tassels of tall grasses. The coming of autumn can no longer be denied.

The park office is open. It has fun merch, maps, and information. Right inside the doorway is an exquisite thing, one of the most exquisite and rare things you might ever see. It is a colossal burl, at least three feet in diameter, taken from a green ash. That tree must have been a majestic giant! Knowing all the ash are dying and will soon be gone, I am flooded with a wave of melancholy. It is something never to be created again. The astounding and twisting grains of the wood and bark are a once-in-a-lifetime sight! When I tell the ranger about my Quest, she applauds my efforts. I tell her how, earlier this week, I went to Merrick State Park and thought it was pleasant but nondescript. She agreed, saying the main reason people use it is to get on the river with their boats, as I had thought when I was there.

I decide to start my five miles from the Nature Center, which is close to Trempealeau Bay. The rustic stone building is open, and even though no one is working in it, there are many displays about the history of the Native people who called this area home. I find out this park is studded with several unique effigy mounds.

The Riverview Trail begins behind the Nature Center and continues along the bay and the Mississippi River. For a time, it follows a ledge by a road past scarred and eroded cliffs festooned with ferns. At the fork in the trail, I take the left-hand side and start heading uphill. I'm unsure where it goes, as the trails aren't well-marked, but it seems well-worn. I feel confident it will lead me where I want to go, to the East Brady's Bluff Trail. This left-hand fork takes me to a parking area where I find the trailheads of the bluffs.

Set back off the road is a post with trail markings: one for Brady's Bluff to the left and one for Perrot Ridge to the right. A sign reads that Perrot Ridge has been badly eroded from recent heavy rains, advising against hiking it. I'm glad I had already decided to do Brady's!

Reaching the top of Brady's Bluff is challenging but extraordinary. The trail winds up to the summit with a mix of stone steps and narrow washes. There are times I stop for a view, and times I stop for a breath. I am remarkably happy! The vast expanse of the Mississippi spreads out before me on this glorious day.

At the apex of the bluff, approximately 500 feet above the river, the East, West, and North trails meet. I am in awe of the spectacular stone CCC shelter gracing this peak. A sign near the building speaks in praise of the young men who carried these innumerable rocks and planted thousands of pine trees across Trempealeau County before they headed off to fight in World War II.

I take the time to sit in the shelter, cozy and comfortable. I think about those who built it and silently thank them for their service. My mind drifts to a memory of a client of mine, James, and the story of war he told me. He was 87 years old when I knew him. Depression had taken him, hard and unrelenting. He sat with me and told me about his time as a marine in WWII, about the battles of Midway and Guadalcanal. He recounted his white t-shirt covered in the blood of his fellow soldiers, covered in the blood of death. After all the horror, he was granted leave, a brief respite on Guam. He was walking the beach, enjoying the rare day of tranquility, when crying and screaming broke his reverie. He went toward the sounds and found a woman giving birth alone in the jungle. He helped deliver the baby and, after its birth, escorted them both back to her village. James had removed his new, white marine-issue t-shirt and wrapped the newborn in it. When the woman returned it to him, it was covered in blood, the blood of new life. While he told me this story, we sat together, holding hands and weeping. He had been 18 years old when this happened. All I could be was a witness to his story, a witness to his healing in the telling of it. All I could say to him was, "Thank you for your sacrifice."

I descend the bluff via the West Brady's Trail. This way down is accentuated by numerous and precarious stone steps, a wooden stairway, and even more stone steps. I would hate to have been up here if it had started raining. I would've just stayed overnight in the CCC shelter rather than trying to come down all these stairs when they were wet and slippery.

Reaching the bottom and feeling proud of myself for doing so, I head back toward my car on the Riverview Trail. It is enchanting to walk this close to the edge of the green waters of the bay, with glimmering green frogs startling at almost every step. I could do without the mosquitoes, but they are few and far between this late in the year.

I stop for a snack and realize I have a bit more to go to get my mileage. I wander up the road to take the Black Walnut Nature Trail. The loop takes me through otherworldly rock outcroppings eroded by eons of wind and water. Once again, I am glad to need more distance, as it allows me to experience this novel and varied place. True to its name, the trail has magnificent black walnut behemoths and what can best be described as vertical potholes in the sandstone embankments.

On my way back to the Nature Center parking lot, I take a short spur trail leading to four conical mounds, a deer mound, and a wolf mound. I have never seen a wolf before! I picture in my mind's eye what the lives of the original people would have been like in such a lush and verdant place, living with the gift of the time to create unique earth art.

Driving home, I am once again awestruck by the setting sun's rays touching the abundant fields—the gold-illuminated tassels of corn and the acres of soybeans highlighted brilliantly on this late summer day. I know it may sound strange to be so enamored of the ubiquitous fields dotting the Wisconsin landscape. Maybe you have to have lived here for a long time to truly appreciate the beauty of the abundance at the end of the season. Or maybe you have to be a member of the creative class, someone who views the world from the shapes and the colors, the shadows and the highlights.

Tonight, I woke up from a dream about hiking at Perrot. It was about going down those intense CCC stone stairs. This has happened to me frequently on my Quest. I dream about the hikes the night after I finish them. My unconscious mind is working to permanently incorporate my adventures into my memory, and I am sincerely thankful for it.

Perrot State Park

The Questions

1. What about this chapter resonated with you?
2. In what ways do you express your creativity?
3. What are your memories of war: stories, news reports, personal service? How has the concept of war affected your life?

The Particulars

Sticker Required: Yes

Map on the State Park's Website: Yes, and nicely detailed

Bathrooms for Day Hikers: Yes, in the office and at the picnic areas

Office or Kiosk: Office which can be closed depending on the day or season

Trail Markings: Infrequently marked

Seasonal Closures: None

Flooding Concerns: Frequent flooding concerns on some trails

Five Miles: Easy to get with no circles

Pattison State Park
Superior

5.77 miles

Highest Point: 1,011 ft
Lowest Point: 786 ft

September 22, 2022
The Day Before

I am driving with Petra, heading toward Eau Claire on Hwy. 12. We pass the Volk Field Air National Guard Base at Camp Douglas. Flying low above the highway is a plane dear to my heart, a Douglas DC-3.

I grew up on a farm outside Oshkosh, close to the flight line of the Experimental Aircraft Association's (EAA) annual fly-in. When I was in my late teens and early 20s, I was constantly in pursuit of the perfect tan, one with no tan lines. This meant spending countless hours lying naked in the sun on the roof of a shed behind our barn. Even though I had an apartment in town by then, I would still go there to sunbathe.

Because of the farm's proximity to EAA, every late July, the skies above my home were filled with a multitude of aircraft of all descriptions. Over 10,000 planes continue to arrive every year for the event. During my tanning time, I would gaze up at them and delight in the roar of their engines and the intense summer sunshine reflecting off their shiny metal fuselages.

During one particular Hot Girl Summer, I dated a pilot who worked for a local aviation company. I have a marvelous photograph of the two of us in the cockpit of a DC-3. I will never forget their distinct shape and sound. In an effort to impress him and to entertain myself, I arranged an elaborate night out for the two of us. It involved a black dress, an airplane hangar, and a limousine.

I wore the black dress I had made for my high school reunion a couple of years prior. It fit me like a glove, and I must admit, I looked smoking hot in it. I had gone to the 10th reunion with my big love, and I hadn't had an occasion to wear the dress since that night.

One of my friend's parents owned a Piper Cub plane and kept it at the local airport. I convinced them to let me use their hangar as a place for an extravagant date. When you ask someone to do you a favor for a chance at love, they usually go along with it. Everyone likes a good love story. I had a limousine pick me up first and then the pilot, taking us to the open hangar overlooking the blue runway lights where I had a catered dinner waiting on a bistro table. His reaction to the situation was perfect, and we laughed and talked and enjoyed our fine meal. As the evening wound down, the limo took us back to his place, and well, the black dress didn't stay on very long.

Though our relationship fizzled out by the end of the summer, I still have wonderful memories of flying through the clouds with him. He was the only man I ever took to Kohler-Andrae State Park.

I miss the time in my life when I was a young woman, when I could turn heads and get almost any guy I wanted. Those days are gone now, but I am exceptionally glad I had those Hot Girl Summers, the ones that helped me heal from my broken heart. I'm decidedly happy I let myself be a sexy babe, even if it was just for a few brief years of my life. I think I need another similar summer, although now, it would be more of a Hot Old Girl one.

September 23, 2022
Hot Girls and Fly Boys

Petra and I arrived at Lake Nebagamon late yesterday afternoon. The cabin I arranged is situated somewhat equidistant between Pattison and Amnicon Falls State Parks, making it a good fit for a place to stay. After getting situated, we took glasses and a bottle of wine outside to sit on the dock and watch the sunset. I was, again, inspired by my idea of wanting a sunset-over-water view in my life on a regular basis. Maybe when I am in my 80s, and I can no longer do big hikes, I will still be able to amble down to the water's edge and bask in the emerging twilight.

The air by this lake was full of music—the mournful song of loons balanced by the cheerful creak of crickets. The warm wind of the day had settled into a light breeze. As we dreamily watched the dying sun, a sedge of cranes flew over our heads. With their dynamic wings, the seven sandhills made a glorious sound! The last of the dragonflies skimmed the lake's surface. By the time we finished the bottle, they were replaced by bats hunting the same prey. This lake is a bit south of Duluth, Minnesota, and autumn is taking hold—the air cooler, the sun lower, the days shorter. Yesterday was the Autumnal Equinox. Turning 65 is comparable to coming to this time of year in one's life. Now is about finding balance and harvesting memories.

The drive from the cabin to Pattison is thickly wooded, the roadsides adorned with ferns turned golden and cinnamon. The park office is open and has a friendly ranger there to help us on our way. The lobby is lavishly decorated with giant, stunning yellow, cranberry, and umber origami stars! Piles of green, lime, and emerald origami frogs are poised to leap from every surface. When I ask about the wonders of folded paper, the ranger relates they had gotten bored one day when there weren't a lot of campers coming in, deciding to decorate the office for fall. There is nice merch with an attractive park logo, which includes other up-north state parks: Amnicon Falls, Interstate, Copper Falls, and Big Bay. The names of the parks are arranged on a signpost similar to ones marking cabins down hidden lanes in a multitude of areas in Wisconsin.

I grab a blue pamphlet of the Big Manitou Geology Walk, which has vast information about the tremendous upheavals this land has gone through to form the falls. The only map the office has is the small one in the park's newspaper. I am glad I brought the one from the DNR's website because it is larger and shows the trails color-coded. I won't have to pull out my readers whenever I need to consult it. The newspaper does, however, have some fascinating history of the park. After being slightly disoriented, because what would a hike be for me without a bit of geo-challenge, Petra and I find our way to the Beaver Trail to start the five miles. This trail takes us along the edge of Interfalls Lake, lush with reeds, grasses, and tiny islands. When we reach the bridge over the Black River, we turn left to take the Little Manitou Falls Trail.

The falls here is remarkable, even though the water level is low this time of year. It splits in two, coming over an embankment of basalt. From the viewing place at the bottom, off to the left-hand side, is an odd, circular cave. I refer to my blue geology pamphlet and find out it is the remnant of a copper mine.

The trail leads up to a parking lot and picnic area. It is a more easily accessible approach to the Little Manitou Falls than the way we came. As we head back, we take a spur trail, bringing us up the basalt outcropping, along the side, and around the back of the falls. At the top, it makes sense why the falls splits in two. There are markers for the backpack camp area across the shallow river. What a great place to stay with the sounds of the running water as you snuggle down for the night, cozy in your tent.

Coming down the spur trail from the outcropping, there is a magical place. One spot, one small spot where, in the course of three strides, we go from hearing the rush at the top of the falls to the stillness of a quiet forest to the roar at the bottom. I walk it several times to revel in the curious, juxtaposing sounds. If I am ever in need of the wonderful feeling of being supremely awestruck, this is where I will come!

We head back on the Little Manitou Falls Trail to the bridge, not crossing it but instead taking a left to return to the Beaver Trail as it loops back on the other side of Interfalls Lake. We finish back where we parked and start toward the Big Manitou Falls Trail, taking

Pattison State Park

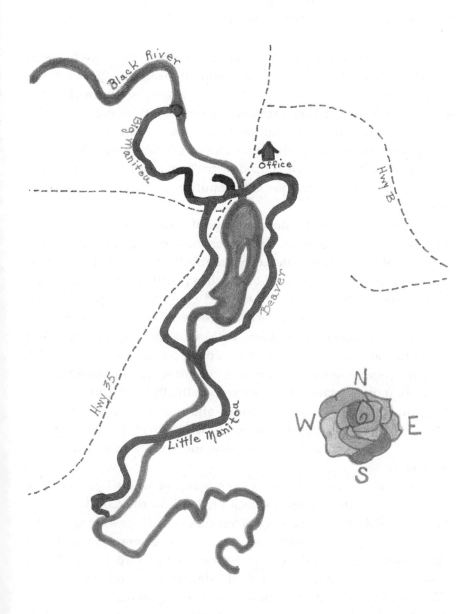

a tunnel underneath Hwy. 35 to get to the trailhead.

Hiking by the Big Manitou, there are numerous viewing spots to see this immense, spectacular falls, the highest in Wisconsin. Even with low water flows, the gorge it cascades through is extraordinary. The trail continues past the falls, warning of strenuous climbs on the way back up. We decide to take the dare!

The hike down to the shores of the Black River is definitely worth the hike back up. It is surreally quiet and intensely beautiful. It takes us close to the river at an area of transcendent wonder with steep walls of golden sandstone breaking off into shards along the banks. It is a location most likely covered in times of high water but not during this dry point in the year. There is a rock ring where fires have been built. Perhaps it is used by backpack campers or perhaps by teenagers looking for an isolated spot to rage against the liminal space of their lives.

I make my way on the peculiar mix of cobbles forming a bar in the river. I stand in awe of the phenomenal geology of this place— ancient volcanoes and paleo-oceans, the thrusts and fractures of centuries-old earthquakes, all of it subsequently covered by a mile-high glacier. I choose a small, spotted conglomerate pebble from the shores of the Black River to bring home as a talisman of this day.

As we head back to the trailhead to take the short spur on the other side of the falls, we encounter a bridal party posing for photographs. The bride resplendent in white, and her fair maids, dressed in vivid aqua, are radiant against the backdrop of the Big Manitou Falls area. We shout our hardy congratulations and receive waves and smiles in return. Later, as we cross the highly arched bridge to start on the spur trail, I find a small aqua rose from one of the women's silk floral bouquets.

I put it in my pocket and am reminded of when I passed by a small, 12th-century chapel in rural England on the Coast to Coast Walk. A wedding had recently taken place, and strewn among the venerable tombstones surrounding the church were paper hearts cut from romantic works of fiction. I picked one up and tucked it under my phone case for lack of a safer location to preserve it. It is where I keep it still. It reminds me of the existence of love in the world, however fragile, and the hope to find it, even at my age. When

I get home, I resolve to find a special place to preserve my newfound rose of aquamarine.

The five miles complete, we return for another evening of wine on the dock, the setting sun, loons, crickets, dragonflies, and bats. We follow it with a nice dinner on the broad deck of the cabin, listening to the hoots of faraway owls.

Pattison State Park

The Questions

1. What about this chapter resonated with you?
2. In what ways do you find balance in your life as you age?
3. As you enter the autumn of your life, what things will you be "harvesting"?

The Particulars

Sticker Required: Yes

Map on the State Park's Website: Yes, and it is detailed in color

Bathrooms for Day Hikers: Yes, in the office and near picnic areas

Office or Kiosk: Office which can be closed depending on the day or season

Trail Markings: Infrequently marked

Seasonal Closures: None

Flooding Concerns: Some trails during high water on the river

Five Miles: Easy to get with no circles

Amnicon Falls State Park
South Range

5.13 miles
Highest Point: 982 ft
Lowest Point: 732 ft

September 24, 2022
Beauty and Disgrace

I make coffee and take a cup with me out onto the deck, enjoying the hazy view of Lake Nebagamon. It rained heavily in the night. It's still lightly drizzling as I stand here on the uncovered part of the porch, listening to the raindrops on the wide maple leaves surrounding the cabin.

The morning my friend and I were supposed to leave for these parks, she called me to say a member of her extended family was positive for COVID while they were visiting. She was testing and would call me back with the results. I hoped she wasn't positive because it can be a difficult illness, and I wanted her to be safe above all else.

We ended our call, and I realized I might be going on this trip to do these two far-flung state parks alone, a journey reminiscent of one I did earlier on my Quest. I knew I would be fine if I had to go by myself to this cabin in the middle of nowhere. I'd done it before, and it was strangely all right, even though I had a bit of trepidation about that trip. Petra didn't test positive, thank goodness. It was brilliant to share Pattison State Park with her yesterday. It is a miraculous place!

Now, I find myself standing here on this quiet gray morning with the gently falling rain, the view of the lake, and the trees tinged with gold and red. I am thinking about the gift given to me by those friends who dumped me, for lack of a better term, on the trip in late June. The gift was knowing I could do this. I can go places alone, rent a cabin, hang out, and enjoy a beautiful location. Of course, it's nicer to have someone along, but I don't have to have them. With their breach of trust, those two people lost a kind and generous friend. Conversely, I gained the gift of knowing I can be a deeper friend to myself.

Petra and I linger over coffee on the deck while waiting for the light rain to end. We take our time packing up our belongings and bidding farewell to Lake Nebagamon and this nicely appointed place.

The drive to Amnicon Falls is overcast, the trees and roadside ferns heavy with the remaining raindrops. Coming into the park, we are surprised the office is a long way past the entry sign, but it is staffed by welcoming rangers. There is no merch, but there is information and literature. We grab one of everything and head out to find the start of the Snowshoe Trail as we begin to tackle these five miles.

With the rain last night and early this morning, hiking through this park has a primordial feeling. Everything is damp, dripping, and sparkling as the emerging sun filters through the clouds. The misty air lovingly embraces all around us and nurtures many fleeting surprises. The broad, cadmium-yellow leaves of aspen trees curled up in little cups fallen on the trail become miniature mirrors, their

Amnicon Falls State Park

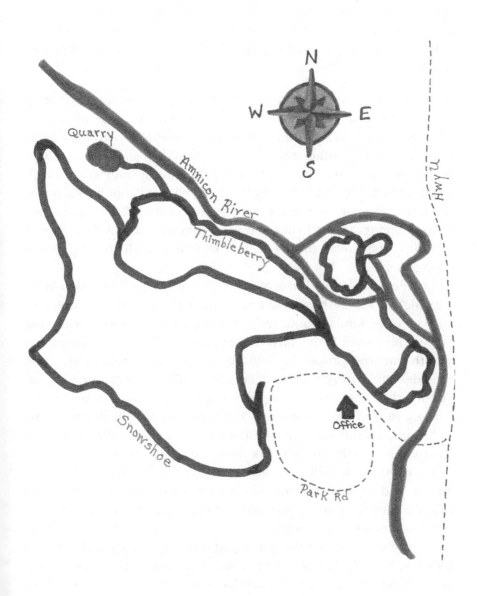

water reflecting the sky. The mandarin orange of minute fungal bowls, saving water for the tiniest of creatures to drink. They are evanescent pools for the woodland fairies. Vast swaths of lush moss blanket the sides of the trail, the primeval scene accented by the screeches of pileated woodpeckers as they dive and drill around us. I stop to take a photo of my hand, with its five different autumn-colored fingernails, touching the dark brown bark of a wet tree trunk.

It occurs to me how I miss the monthly rhythms of my body, miss those strange muscular sensations in my lower abdomen. The blood, each month, reaffirmed my aliveness. Sometimes, it was a welcome relief; other times, it was the sad realization of a lost potential. I miss the confirmation and the way my body synced with the women around me, the way it synced with the moon. Yes, it was often inconvenient and excruciatingly uncomfortable at times, but I miss it, nonetheless, living now in my old woman's body. I wonder if "aging gracefully" means to feel resigned to all those physical changes.

I ask Petra what she thinks of the term. She relates it brings to mind wearing suitable fashion, and having the right haircut for women of a certain age. I muse about the white-haired woman we saw driving a white Mercedes Benz convertible yesterday. Is that it? Having the wealth and the proper look to seem "ageless"? Is it minimizing wrinkles and worrying about crepey skin? Is it not moaning on about aches and pains? Is it deciding to spend money on plastic surgery rather than adventure? The term "aging gracefully" seems to be code for our value decreasing the older we get; it seems a box to be contained in lest we break the mold.

Fuck aging gracefully! It is high time to be comfortable in our own beauty and to be confident that it comes from within and always has. We need to continue to learn and to grow and to do. There is no need to spend enormous amounts of money on remaining youthful. It is reprehensible that the anti-aging industry makes profits in the billions and is on its way to even more as our population grows older. Why spend time chastising ourselves for wearing too short a skirt, having too long a hairstyle, or enjoying bright colors and clashing patterns?

So what if your nest is empty? Build a new one! Redefine what a nest is, reclaim it as a place of hope and creativity, not one of loss. Even though our bodies may have limitations, age DISgracefully! Live with purpose, find adventure, and embrace your friends. Stay curious, seek awe, and love fiercely. Stop focusing on yourself and pay it forward. Help the future be a better one. If you are lucky enough to get to be 65, hell yeah, enjoy it! Wear that dark red lipstick, laugh at your own jokes, and be kind even when others aren't. If you need help in the form of a cane, a hearing aid, or a grab bar, accept it wholeheartedly. It may be for the short term, but even if it isn't, it's better to use it and be able to keep doing what you love. You are at an age where the majority of the world never gets to be. Embrace the time too many are denied. Embrace the fact you get to be old!

Enough of my ramblings; it's back to the Snowshoe and the Thimbleberry. These trails run concurrently for a section. We finish the Snowshoe and then turn back on it to do the full Thimbleberry. The Thimbleberry Trail is perfectly named as they grow everywhere along it. We picked up a brochure about this trail at the office, and as we hike, we stop to read about the plants and trees. There is information on how the Ojibwe used them for their practical uses and healing powers. Petra reminisces about taking her children out thimbleberry picking when they were young, and we smile together, remembering their happy faces.

A spur trail off the Thimbleberry takes us to a long-ago Sandstone Quarry. While it was in operation, millions of cubic feet of the brownstone were removed and transported near and far to Minneapolis, Duluth, Chicago, and Omaha. Today, it is a welcoming pond for turtles, otters, and birds of all descriptions.

The trail to and from the quarry offers stunning views of the Amnicon River. It is low and slow here, flanked by brown sandstone cobbles and mysterious, dark forest. We take a moment to stand in awe under the immense white pines, their needles feet thick beneath us and fragrant with sap. I cherish this vision and store it, hoping to dream about it tonight.

Finishing this trail, we drive around to the trailheads for the four falls: Upper, Lower, Snake Pit, and Now and Then. This area of the river is tumultuous and strewn with boulders, gray and lichen covered. The trees are sparse, but the people are many, even on this cool autumn day.

Although the photographs on the park materials show the Amnicon Falls at their full force, we find them a fraction of their normal mighty nature due to the last few dry months. This allows us to see the folds, layers, and swirls of the underlying red, brown, and black rock, worn smooth by the endless flow. The photos of heavy water times beg us to return in the spring to see and hear these wonderful falls in all their glory.

We follow the trail across the river via the Horton Covered Bridge, dallying to take photos and enjoy the multitude of burbling, gurgling, and babbling from the falls. On the other side is a short trail to the Now and Then Falls. True to its moniker, it is but a seep today, but it is a fern and moss haven where fairies surely dwell!

The mileage complete, we are both reluctant to leave this enchanting place. We make plans to revisit and, perhaps, to camp in this park, spending more time exploring its unique landscape.

On the drive home, I am pondering an article I read regarding the remarkable 1,200-mile Ice Age Trail, which traverses the edge of the ancient glaciers of Wisconsin. It related the story of a man who recently became the fastest finisher of the trail. To do so, he hiked an average of 47 miles a day and was subsequently lauded for his accomplishment. I don't mean to diminish his phenomenal feat in any way, but I actually feel sorrow for him that he hiked the IAT so quickly. I know, having done many parts of it myself, there are places of beauty to weep over. I sincerely doubt he gave himself a chance to simply be in that beauty. Quite frankly, how could he, given he was hurrying to be the fastest one ever? I imagine if something was strikingly phenomenal, he told himself not to look at it too long—got to keep going. Whereas, when I come upon audaciously beautiful places on my hikes, I take a deep breath and stay in the moment. Petra and I did the same today at the glorious view of the Amnicon River under the pines like we have done countless times on our excursions together on the IAT.

For me, good hiking is about mindfully being in nature. It is about actively developing a habit of awareness, using all my senses to encounter the wild and the tame places I go. It's not about rushing to the end merely to say it is complete. It's about experiencing the colors and the textures, the smells and the sounds, and, sometimes, the taste of a rare, wild blueberry. It's about knowing inside myself I may never, ever be in this place again, and because of it, I am going to absorb everything I can. I will inhale all the wonderful fragrance and indulge in all the astonishment.

It takes time for the brain to move events in our lives from short-term into long-term memory. It takes the power of our dreaming mind. It takes the power of our body. The more ways we store memories in our fingertips, our knees, or our feet, the easier they are to find, especially in the event of Alzheimer's or dementia.

I like to store mine as a balm against the frigid parts of winter, when the days are short and the sun doesn't shine. As I go forward into the autumn and winter of my life, if I become fearful of my impending death, my memories of inspiring hikes are right there for me to recall, to close my eyes, and to see like they are my only true reality.

On the hikes yesterday at Pattison and today at Amnicon Falls, we kept a good pace, but we also stopped and soaked in the artistry of dark black basalt, of irregular holes left by pileated woodpeckers, of graceful pink leaves. We took the time to walk up to the river's edge, marveling at the tiny fish making their way, caught in the eddies and pools filled with jumping green frogs.

I don't regret taking a little more time to get the five miles at these two parks. It is not old age slowing me down. It is the desire to experience, to know, to see, to remember. It is to solidify the feeling that being alive in this beautiful world is enough.

As my favorite poet, Rabindranath Tagore, said: "I have suffered and despaired and known death, and I am glad that I am in this great world."

Amnicon Falls State Park

The Questions

1. What about this chapter resonated with you?

2. How has your relationship with your body changed as you have gotten older? What are the gains and losses of those changes?

3. In what ways do you practice mindfulness? What effect does it have on your well-being?

The Particulars

Sticker Required: Yes

Map on the State Park's Website: Yes, and nicely detailed

Bathrooms for Day Hikers: Yes, in the office and by the picnic areas

Office or Kiosk: Office which can be closed depending on the day or season

Trail Markings: Intermittently well-marked

Seasonal Closures: None

Flooding Concerns: Trails may be wet but no flooding issues

Five Miles: Circles required

Devil's Lake State Park
Baraboo

7.58 miles
Highest Point: 1,268 ft
Lowest Point: 706 ft

September 27, 2022
Body Memory and Lost Hikers

It's a cool day today with a high of only 54, but the sun is peeking through. I waited until late in the season to do the five miles at this park because it's invariably outstandingly busy in the summer. I didn't want to come on a day full of unprepared tourists trying to climb the Balanced Rock Trail, having no idea what they had gotten themselves into and needing my help and guidance. I merely wanted the solitude of a stair master hike on a crisp autumn day.

I am kind of discombobulated this morning. I forgot my maps, but I know this park has many available. I'm going to listen to the sounds of the forest today instead of my current audiobook. I am perfectly fine with doing so, as this is one of my favorite hikes!

I stop at the Contact Station on the South Shore to get a map. They have excellent Friends of Devil's Lake merch here. I head to the Visitor Center on the North Shore to see what's happening there as well. The concession stand in the center makes the whole place smell tainted by the cooking grease used over the summer months. There is an enormous amount of things for sale here, the most I have seen at any park. Seeing all the merchandise and books about Devil's Lake and the Devil's Doorway impresses upon me what an incredible uphill battle it would be to change the name of this place back to its Ho-Chunk name, Tewakącąk. Its original name means Spirit Lake or Sacred Lake, but for some reason, those who settled in this area decided to name it for their concept of evil. It's the worst designation to attach to this incredibly spectacular and unusual place, which stands witness to the astonishing power of the Ice Age glaciers.

I'm heading to the East Bluff on the South Shore because it's where I like to hike. When I was training for the C2C, I did this trail frequently, up to a couple of times a week as the date of my trip to England approached. One day, I came with a dear friend of mine, Bruce. We hiked up and down the East Bluff and then walked along the North Shore to do the same on the West Bluff.

In the height of summer, the North Shore is exceptionally crowded. We could barely see the lake's edge because of the crush of people! Sunshades and blankets—competing loud music was coming from everywhere. Frisbees and dogs and picnics; it was a continuous party as we walked along on the way to the West Bluff Trail. Bruce came up with a fantastic name for it, comparing it to a famous place in California. He termed it the "Venice Beach of Corn Hole." We both laughed over his cleverness. It was a perfect label for the substantial chaos of day trippers. On my hike today, the only crowds on the beach are flights of geese with their teenage goslings.

For me, the South Shore is the place to be. It does get hectic here in the summer, too, but still not to the level of the North Shore. It's not built up as much, and most people who come to the park for serious hiking start off on this side. It feels like centuries ago when I was here last, pre-pandemic. The last time I hiked it on a weekly

Devil's Lake State Park

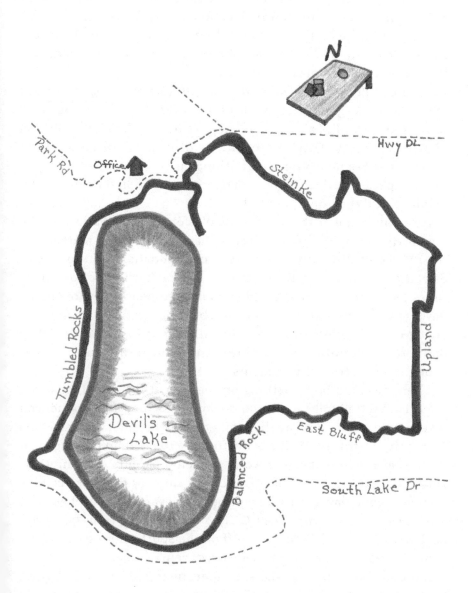

basis was when I was training to go hiking in Ireland with my friend Diana in 2019.

I've hiked this bluff and its trails countless times. I have stored them in my body memory, which is pretty amazing when you think about it. Body memory is a powerful thing, and out of all the places I've been in my life, I am glad She remembers how to maneuver through this sacred place.

Balanced Rock Trail is more than a half mile of stairs, comprised of uneven rocks going up the side of the 500-foot bluff. The negative thing about Devil's Lake trails is they are not marked for their level of strenuousness. There are mentions of it in the magazine I got today at the Friends' office, but nothing on-site or on the trail signs. In my experience, this creates a dangerous situation for elders, little children, and the unprepared.

It seems to me at this busiest of Wisconsin State Parks and the one with the most annual deaths, having the trails marked for the degree of difficulty is a basic accommodation for those with disabilities and, honestly, for everyone. I can't tell you how many times I've been here hiking and encountered people in dire straits: having trouble breathing, their hearts beating erratically, their limbs giving out. The bluff trails were too strenuous for them, and they didn't realize it until it was too late. They didn't bring water, proper shoes, or cover from the elements.

There needs to be something on the sign at the top of Balanced Rock Trail to tell folks not to go down unless they are experienced hikers. I did it once with all the right equipment, and I have no plans to do it in the future. My life is worth more to me than proving I can do that again! The absolute worst is seeing parents carrying their small children down it, oblivious to how slippery the rocks can be, even on a good day. The rock steps become especially treacherous if it is dewy, misty, or rainy. The CCC and the Potholes Trails bring you back to the bottom of the East Bluff on the South Shore and, though complicated, aren't nearly as hellish a decent.

Enough about the trail signs. I am at the top of the bluff, having finished the Balanced Rock Trail. On the way up, I encountered only three groups of people asking me, with desperate, frightened looks on their faces, "How much farther down is it?" On a busy day, there are remarkably more of these pleas.

I head out on the East Bluff Trail. It travels through a lovely, quiet forest, the trees arching over and the understory full of a plethora of plant varieties. It is one of my favorite parts of hiking here and leads to grand overlooks of the trees below the bluff. The views reveal predominately greens today, but vivid reds and oranges punctuate the scene. The trail winds along, and my thoughts turn to a particularly eventful hike at Devil's Lake about five years ago.

I had hiked up and down the East Bluff and back up again. I was almost done with my hike, heading toward the CCC Trail to go down the bluff. The temperature abruptly dropped, and a storm quickly rolled in. I grabbed my rain jacket out of my pack and continued on my way. I remember being a bit frustrated about the weather, as no storms had been predicted, but that's Wisconsin for you.

I was close to the start of the Pothole Trail when I was approached by two young women trying to figure out a way to get down. They were completely lost. They had climbed to the top of the bluff via the Balanced Rock Trail in flip-flops, bikini tops, and shorts and were shivering, cold, and wet.

Of course, I offered to help. Tessa and Wrenley accompanied me as we headed toward the CCC Trail. On the way down, both of them fell a couple of times. The trail's rain-covered steps were perilously slippery. We reached about halfway down the trail, where it tables out to a round open area with a minor bluff. There, we encountered four more young women, lost, not knowing where to go. They were dressed more appropriately, as they were there for a climbing class but had lost track of their instructor. We became a motley crew working our way down the trail.

A few more falls occurred, and I was not spared. I was relieved I had my hands inside the straps on my hiking poles because I think they saved my life. I slipped and started sliding down the rocks until one of my poles stuck in a crevice, halting my forward momentum. I ended up with a hell of a bruise on the back of my upper arm, but I didn't hit my head, and I didn't keep sliding off the edge. Thankful for small mercies, we persevered, providing each other with copious amounts of empathy and support, finally locating the rock climbing instructor farther down the trail.

She was a badass climber, carrying all the ropes and gear for the class she was there to teach before the rainstorm. She helped lead us the rest of the way down, ensuring everyone knew where and how to step on the wet rocks, limiting further accidents. With her wise instruction, we made it the rest of the way without incident.

At the base of the bluff, there were hugs all around, everyone laughing about what a grand day it had turned out to be. The rain was falling hard by then as we headed back to our cars. I was pleased to get into mine and drive home after my crazy foundling adventure.

I have come to the place on the East Bluff Trail I call the Tree Cathedral. You'll know it when you see it. It is at a triangular junction of trails continuing in three directions. There is a helpful "You Are Here" sign to guide you on your way, but it is best to stop for a moment to gaze up at the "cantilevered ceiling." It is a dome of magnificent trees greeting each other in their highest branches. I take the time to sit on Leonard and Arleen's memorial bench, simply enjoying the day and the delightful bends, arcs, and creaks of the trees overhead.

I am sitting here thinking about when I first came to do this trail. I was 59, soon to turn 60, and going to hike in England. I wish I could be hiking in some foreign land today, but the tiniest of creatures, a virus, has put those trips on hold for me. I feel damn proud of myself for getting to this place in my life, though. This is my 41st of 45 state parks this summer. I feel immense joy about my Quest!

I take the left fork of the trail away from the cathedral. It is the Upland Loop Trail, and it leads to the Steinke Basin Loop Trail. There is a lovely open meadow with a bench where they meet, and I take a right to proceed on to the Steinke. The prairie here is full of ripened milkweed pods and the last of the dragonflies. I pretend I am the embodiment of an autumn goddess as I sprinkle milkweed seeds in the air and watch their idyllic silk float along on the cool breeze. I stay on this trail surrounded by ruby red sumac until it meets the Upland Loop Trail again, and then head off to the left.

The last time I hiked here was before the pandemic. Now, there is a torn-down orange barrier in this area. My body memory tells me to finagle around it, as it appears countless others have done since it was initially placed. I'm going to try it. If it gets messed up, I'll turn around.

I know as a responsible hiker, I am not supposed to be doing this, but for auld lang syne, I am going to follow my body's map of this hike for one last time. After a while, I find out why they had attempted to close this area; a bridge is out due to a mammoth tree falling and crushing it. Because it has been dry for the last several weeks, the small creek it crosses is an easy jump, but I am wrong to have taken this way. I realize it will be a substantial amount of work to remove those vast limbs and repair the broken bridge. I make a mental note to donate a generous amount to the Friends of Devil's Lake for my indiscretion.

Reaching the end of the trail by the amphitheater, I take a small section of the IAT, bringing me around to the start of the East Bluff Trail back up to the top.

I stop for some reflection, a water break, and a snack. I am puzzling over the concept of time once again. This mental exercise seems to mollify the existential thoughts that come with aging. Why does time feel like it is speeding up as I get older? This is not the case when I am hiking or when I'm creating. When I am hiking, being in the moment, looking for beauty, filling my senses with experiences, time moves slowly. When I am creating, it seems only 15 minutes have passed, but it is four or five hours! The same thing occurs when I am consumed by gardening in my sanctuary. Time stops. But why, then, does it seem overall to be moving faster?

Perhaps it is because my days, as a retired person with no adult supervision, tend to encompass similar activities and tend to have a regular routine. When I was younger, my life was considerably more eventful; now, it seems steady and measured. Does this cause my days to all blend into each other, making time move more quickly? I know when I have a busy day full of work and friends, errands and appointments, it can feel like one day has been three days because many varied things have occurred. I think novel experiences cause time to stretch. My brain is absorbing new things, and when that happens, time moves slower. I resolve not to become complacent, not to allow routine to dictate my life. I will continue to seek out chaos and adventure and beauty. These three things definitely have power over time. This all reminds me of one of my favorite quotes by T. S. Eliot: "Time the destroyer is time the preserver."

My reverie ends as I realize the sky has taken a worrisome and ominous turn, bringing in black clouds of rain. I decide not to go back up and down the bluff, which I usually do on my hikes here, not wanting to be caught up there in the storm. I will go around the lake back to my car, thankful I always carry my rain jacket in my pack.

I have never hiked the Tumbled Rocks Trail before. I have only gone back up and down the bluff but learned my lesson the day of the foundlings. After all, I want to live to be able to finish my 45 rather than falling and sliding to my death. I choose, instead, to enjoy the peaceful quiet of the lake as I hike the gently rolling and asphalted trail. The views of the lake on the left side and of the monuments of talus on the right are stark and awe-inspiring. It is beyond my imagination to think of the powerful force of the glaciers pushing these rocks in front of them, creating the bluffs and the lake as they slowly melted away.

With all the trails I did, I am well over my mileage when I return to my car. I gingerly remove the maple leaf I had picked up and put in my pocket while on the trail. I want to take it home and seal it in wax paper. I saved many an autumn leaf in such a way when I was a little girl.

This leaf strikes me as a great metaphor. It has a hole in it; perhaps it hit a branch as it floated through the air to the ground. It is slightly beaten up but still exquisite with its swirling colors of red, orange, yellow, and green. It is perfectly wonderful, and I think about how it is similar to me. Yes, I have experienced obstacles and challenges since the last time I came here, but even with a dash of wear and tear, I remain my ruggedly beautiful self.

Devil's Lake State Park

The Questions

1. What about this chapter resonated with you?
2. How has your routine changed as you've gotten older? How has it influenced your concept of time?
3. What metaphors have you found to describe your life?

The Particulars

Sticker Required: Yes

Map on the State Park's Website: Yes, and nicely detailed

Bathrooms for Day Hikers: Yes, in the office and at picnic areas throughout the park

Office or Kiosk: Office which is rarely closed depending on the day or season

Trail Markings: Infrequently marked but with a few "You Are Here" signs

Seasonal Closures: None

Flooding Concerns: None

Five Miles: Easy to get with no circles

Potawatomi State Park
Sturgeon Bay

5.04 miles
Highest Point: 683 ft
Lowest Point: 559 ft

October 2, 2022
Motivation and Sheep

Yesterday, I was sitting in my garden on my blue Adirondack chair, catching up on my writing. It was a fantastic day, warm with a hint of autumn's coolness. The sky was cobalt, and the clicks and drills of crows and downy woodpeckers filled the quiet afternoon air.

I felt excited for my last trip on this Quest, an overnight to Sturgeon Bay. I booked a place outside the city, which bills itself as a "romantic country inn." There will be no romance for me there, but I decided to treat myself to an expensive location instead of a plain, nondescript motel.

The place looked to be bucolic and tranquil. I will be able to sit out on a little veranda, looking out at the grounds—a place to reflect upon how my Quest is coming to an end. I'm not going there to enjoy the two-person double tub or the soundproof rooms (darn it!) but as a cozy place to relax between hikes. It is too far of a drive not to stay overnight when hiking Potawatomi and Whitefish Dunes State Parks. When I arranged it, I was thinking back again to the lessons I've learned over this Quest, not the least of which is to truly be my own best friend.

On the way to Potawatomi, the sky is gray and cloudy, overcast with streaks of white and blue. The roadside farms are dotted with wagons full of pumpkins for sale. Yes, it is officially autumn.

The traffic to Door County today is not what I expected. After Appleton, Hwy. 41 North is busier than usual and painfully slow going. I neglected to consider that an at-home Packers game would bring traffic to a crawl around Green Bay.

Coming into this park is not a happy experience. There's no bathroom in the small office. It's my own damn fault. I should have stopped before I got to the park, as I usually do, having been confronted by a lack of bathroom facilities on numerous occasions. The office does offer some nice maps, though. I grab a few and hurry back to my car to head to the closest bathroom at the Nature Center.

I want to begin my five miles on the Hemlock Trail, which is supposed to be accessible at the Nature Center/Park Store. Sadly, it is not marked, and I end up wandering until I eventually see a rusty trail marker on a tree. One thing I have to say with this being park number 42, I am tired of trails not being well-marked. This is obviously a highly visited and wealthier park than most. I honestly can't understand why the money isn't there to update trail signage. I can't be the only geographically challenged person visiting Wisconsin's parks.

Finally, I start off on the Hemlock, locating it behind the woodshed near the Park Store. I follow the orange rectangles with the hemlock branch on them. I try to ground myself after that long, boring traffic situation to get here. One of the things I love about hiking is getting away from all the mess of civilization.

Potawatomi State Park

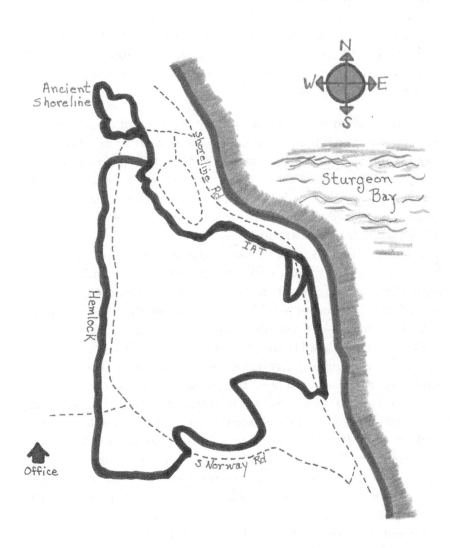

I am unsure how it happened, but I end up entirely off of the Hemlock Trail. Apparently, the trail markers are for the Hemlock and for snowmobile trails, branching apart at some point I must have missed. Thank goodness for the compass my friend gave me. I end up hiking along the park line where it meets county land, looking for a road that will take me toward the group campground, and hopefully, I can find the trail again.

Being turned around, I am reminded of the things I do to keep myself motivated to hike. As many times as I can, I ask a friend to accompany me. Having a friend along brings a higher level of fortitude, as well as a higher level of enjoyment. I set aside time for hikes, looking at my calendar and the weather, choosing a day to go, like I did for this trip. On the days when I have one planned but am just not feeling it, I give myself some grace and work on keeping my thoughts positive. For example, *You may be a bit tired today, but start at an easy pace and take the day as it comes, rather than giving in and saying you're going to cancel.* Once I am out on a trail, of course, I feel better about being there. I have noticed with my Quest, especially at the parks where it is a loop-de-loop, timber-go-round challenge to get in my mileage, it is essential to remember not to let myself down. I don't want to cheat because I would be cheating on myself! It has helped me keep going during those last few miles at several state parks.

If I get a bit lost, which happens frequently in the parks lacking well-marked trails, I feel safe knowing I have in my pack what I need to make it through the night if I ever go completely astray. Because I have those items, even though I have never had to use them, I feel confident I can figure my way out of any situation.

As I follow this wide trail, I see blue markers with skiers on them and green markers with bikes. At length, I come to a T, and there is a rare but very welcome "You Are Here" sign. I take a right, and I'm back on the Hemlock Trail! Thank the Gods, it is a fine day—a little cool with no bugs and ample sunshine filtering through the dense forest. I have been turned around on bad weather days, and it is absolutely no fun at all.

Coming to the picnic area, I realize it would've been a better place to park when I was desperately looking for a bathroom. I take a moment to wander onto the nearby handicap-accessible pier to enjoy the enchanting waters of Sturgeon Bay.

I continue on to hike a length of the IAT, the eastern terminus here in Potawatomi. It is a trail of uneven rocks, switchbacks, and slowly rising low cliffs. This must be part of the long-ago shore of Lake Michigan, when it was brimming with melted glacial water. The forest here is exceptionally dry and strangely uncommunicative, silent, and ready to find winter slumber. I continue up a steep hill and stop to rest, my heart hammering. I am feeling tired and ready to be done.

Soon, I come to a T, where the Ice Age Trail continues to the right, and the Hemlock intersects to the left. I follow it back to my car, but I am shy of my goal, so on to the Ancient Shorelines Nature Trail for the finish. It is a well-marked trail with informational signs about the geology of this area. I am glad I needed to hike it to finish this park, as it is remarkable. Now, to my romantic inn!

Ah! This is the life! I am sitting on the private veranda of my suite at the Chanticleer Guest House near Sturgeon Bay. What an incredibly beautiful spot! I can see sheep grazing in the meadow outside the garden area. It reminds me of the places I stayed while hiking on the C2C.

Happy to be here sharing my own fine company, like Agatha Christie's detective Hercule Poirot, I nibble one of the Guest House's excellent chocolate chip cookies as I enjoy a glass of wine. Yes, this place would be made even better if I had a beau to share it with, but this is where I am in life. I need to enjoy and embrace my aloneness, and be grateful for the gift of aging.

I go for a walk in their gardens, surrounded by the rhythmic sound of the gentle tearing of grass by the grazing sheep. A honking V of Canada geese fly over me, close enough to hear their wings beating in unison. The only other sound is the occasional Doppler of a car in the distance. A ram comes to check me out, but I charm him with my colorful fingernails, scratching his fantastic, horizontal ears. The sun glints off the yellowing trees in the early evening twilight. Bucolic bliss indeed! I almost want to ask them to sell me this place. The amount of work it must take to maintain, however, makes me appreciate my little 1960s ranch house and my own sanctuary.

This Quest, though coming to its inevitable conclusion, has brought me adventure and new experience! When I turned 60, I made a promise to myself to never stop trying new things and pushing myself outside my comfort zone. This trip to Sturgeon Bay, sheep and all, proves again how important that is, as do the cries of a great horned owl as I sit writing this and enjoying the views.

Potawatomi State Park

The Questions
1. What about this chapter resonated with you?
2. In what ways do you maintain a positive outlook on your life as you age?
3. How do you continue to push yourself outside your comfort zone?

The Particulars
Sticker Required: Yes

Map on the State Park's Website: Yes, and it is detailed in color

Bathrooms for Day Hikers: None in the office, but near the Nature Center and the picnic area

Office or Kiosk: Office which can be closed depending on the day or season

Trail Markings: Infrequently marked but with an occasional "You Are Here" sign

Seasonal Closures: None

Flooding Concerns: None

Five Miles: Easy to get with no circles

Whitefish Dunes State Park
Sturgeon Bay

5.12 miles
Highest Point: 655 ft
Lowest Point: 556 ft

October 3, 2022
Transition and Joy

I spend this morning on my veranda at the Chanticleer Guest House, drinking coffee and basking in the rising sun, watching the fog and frost burn off as the day begins. Sheep below, blue skies above, happy me. I am looking forward to my hike today, knowing I won't be a stranger to this picturesque retreat in the future. I will return to this idyllic place of romance every chance I get!

Driving to Whitefish Dunes, I'm enchanted by the fabulous browns and yellows of the drying corn in the fields waiting to be cut, by the intense greens of winter wheat sprouting, and by the dry rustle of soybeans still on the vine.

Entering the park, there's only a kiosk. No bathrooms anywhere close, making me exceptionally glad I found one before I arrived. It might sound weird to talk of bathroom access, but when one is older, sometimes there is urgency in these matters. Not only have I hiked in 43 parks so far, but I have peed in them as well!

I park my car, open the door, and am astonished by the sound of rushing water. It is as if there is a tremendous waterfall right beside me, but it's the surging waves on the shore of breathtaking Lake Michigan.

Off the parking area is the Nature Center and park office. The maps they have are the same as those on the DNR's website. There is no more information about the park, perhaps because it is late in the year, and they are done with printing for the season. After a few pictures on the Nature Center's viewing deck, I head off on the Red Trail to start my five miles at this state park. The trails are superbly well-marked, refreshing after yesterday, and making for an easier flow to my hike today.

I feel slightly sluggish as I start off. Perhaps because of the fabulous breakfast I had this morning at the Guest House. I rarely eat much in the morning, opting for fruit and coffee to begin my day. Maybe it was the confusing hike yesterday, but I am incredibly pleased to be back out on the trail. This park is sensational; the forest is healthy, the trail is wide, and it is a glorious day!

As I go along, I reflect again on the liminality of turning sixty-five. There is a great deal of work to be done at this transitional time in my life. I feel the need to revisit and redefine my identity, as I have over the years with earlier milestone birthdays. This is a solid practice to adopt, as it helps us to focus less on the losses of aging and more on the positives. It is part of a Life Review process and is beneficial for everyone to do as they grow older. After all, where we set our focus is a vital part of the battle against despair. Revisiting how we identify ourselves in pragmatic and optimistic ways creates key avenues to a sense of integrity.

I'm a Mother, but I no longer feel like I am a mom. When I think about being a mom, I think about being constantly on-call, always there to provide support and snacks, being consistently aware of where and what my child is doing, planning classes, events, sports,

Whitefish Dunes State Park

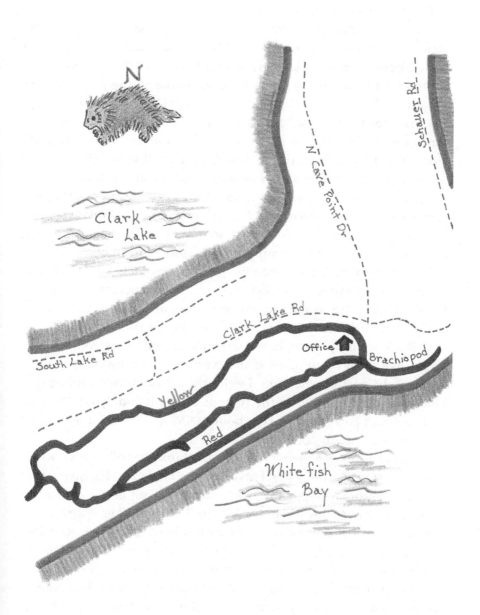

and playdates. It is the driving and cleaning, cooking and parenting. While I still do some of those things for my child, it's not like when I was a mom. My identity is now of Mother, and I also have the sincere honor of being their mother/friend.

Am I still a Social Worker if I'm not being paid to be one? My state licenses confirm it, and I feel like I am. I had a quality about myself before I went into mental health services. People would be behind me in lines at the grocery store, tap me on the shoulder, and say things like, "My husband died yesterday, and I'm here buying groceries for his funeral." I would be out shopping for clothes, and someone would walk up and say, "It's been a year since my child died. I don't know what to do." It was as if I had something written on my forehead, which said, *Please come talk to me if you are troubled and grieving.* These encounters have occurred all my life, starting way before I studied psychology. In fact, it's one of the reasons I decided on this profession. I will persist in my claim to Social Worker, continuing to validate and support strangers as need be.

I'm wanting Artist to become part of my identity. While I've always been creative, I want Artist. I want to be a person who makes art every day, who has art in galleries, and who sells art. I've been working toward this since I retired from my full-time job.

Will Writer be part of how I identify myself? It is something I would like to develop. Even if it never comes to anything, I want Writer to be part of who I am. I write thoughts, stories, and poetry. They all seem to center on the themes of death and dying. Perhaps my mom was correct to worry about me as a kid when I decorated my room with tombstone rubbings.

I want to continue having Hiker, and I think I've solidified it well. I reclaimed this identity when I hiked across England. I fell on my first hike at Governor Dodge State Park, sitting crying in the dirt, and I knew that's what I wanted to be. I wanted to be a Hiker again.

A large part of my identity has always been Gardener. As a kid, when I wasn't riding my bike to nearby cemeteries, I was planting and tending a half-acre garden at the farm. Everywhere I have lived, I've put down roots, planted seeds, and started gardens. The house I live in, the longest of any house I've ever lived in, has allowed me to witness a garden growing to fruition. It is one I've seen nurture not merely plants but hearts and souls. One blessed with parties and rituals, weddings and funerals. I have been able to plant trees and sit under their shade. Yes, I identify as a Gardener.

Between 65 and 70, I wonder what ways I will come to identify myself, what will change, and what will stay the same. My hope is I will still be able to claim all these facets and more. There was a time when I identified as a Warrior, fighting injustice in the world. While the Chinese proverb says, "It is better to be a Warrior in a garden than a Gardener in a war," I do not want to have to be a Warrior. I can be. I am able to be a bold and fierce one, but I no longer want it as part of my identity. I have put down my sword and shield. I want to be like Ferdinand the Bull, smelling flowers and enjoying the sunshine as I am today.

The Red Trail has frequent short spurs down to the beach, and the white noise of the waves fills my wanderings. There is also a cut-off from the Red to reach the observation platform on top of Old Baldy, the tallest stable dune in the park. It is a boardwalk with steps built over the sand. The views are stunning at the top, and I relax and enjoy a moment with them. Rather than backtrack to the Red, I take the boardwalk to the Yellow Trail. The Yellow soon forks, and I take the left one. I find I usually take the left at T's and Y's when I am hiking. I genuinely have no idea why I adopted this pattern.

I decide to turn around and head back the other way because I really want to hike the Brachiopod Trail. If I do this part of the Yellow, it will be well over five miles. It's not a bad thing, but with the long drive, I don't want to get home too late. I return to the fork, taking the right this time on the Yellow Spur Trail.

My desire to change directions rewards me with a splendid and unexpected treasure. This trail is narrow, and as I move quietly along, I see a porcupine! She seems like a first-year young one: small, lovely, and simply delightful. What a blessing it is to see such a beautiful creature! To witness her quietly munching on the sweet, green leaves growing among the reindeer moss about a foot from the side of the trail. It is almost like she was waiting for me to come by and admire her. I stand in amazement, watching her methodically choose the tastiest ones to eat. She gives me the side-eye once or twice but, obviously, knows I am not a threat.

After about 10 minutes, she wanders off into the forest. I watch, realizing how I would never have seen her had she not made herself known. She blends in perfectly with the brown underbrush and soon disappears completely.

I finish the Yellow Spur, catching the Yellow Trail back to the Nature Center. I have a snack in the amphitheater, reveling in the sun and the crash of the surf. I could sit here for the rest of eternity, but there are trails to be hiked. I head off to the Brachiopod to see the fossils!

This trail hugs the rocky shore north of the beach. I find I am constantly stopping to gaze out at the waves and marvel at the divinity of Lake Michigan. I am surrounded by venerable white cedars, their circumferences too massive for me to wrap my arms around. I only hike a short section of the Brachiopod to allow some time for walking near the water's edge. This park is definitely a place to recharge my chi, my life force, and my connection to the world.

Maybe next year, I will stay at the Guest House during the summer, come out here to play in the sand, and dangle my feet off the rocks into the eternally cold water. Perhaps, by then, I will have a beau with me. Even if I don't, I can come back to enjoy it for myself.

After I get home, I look up the spiritual meaning of having a porcupine enter one's life. I smile to discover their significance as a symbol of possibilities. My little porcupine came to remind me to celebrate and stand in awe of nature, to hold my heart open to new experiences, and to trust in the future. I go online and find an image of a porcupine I can tuck inside my phone case next to the paper heart I found in the old cemetery in England. Every day, it will be there to remind me to seek joy!

Whitefish Dunes State Park

The Questions

1. What about this chapter resonated with you?
2. How do you identify yourself? How has it changed as you've gotten older?
3. In what ways have animals been powerful in your life? As pets? As symbols?

The Particulars

Sticker Required: Yes

Map on the State Park's Website: Yes, and it is detailed in color

Bathrooms for Day Hikers: Yes, in the Nature Center

Office or Kiosk: Kiosk with no additional information, office farther in

Trail Markings: Extremely well-marked

Seasonal Closures: None

Flooding Concerns: None

Five Miles: Easy to get with no circles

Roche-A-Cri State Park
Friendship

5.14 miles
Highest Point: 1,199 ft
Lowest Point: 901 ft

October 8, 2022
Memories and Mementos

In the coming week, I will be attending two funerals: one for a work colleague and one for a friend's sibling. "The older you get, the more funerals you attend," my father used to declare. I remember it made me sad whenever he would make such a comment. I guess this solidifies the fact I am officially old. I think of all the funerals I have attended in my life for parents, friends, clients, and children. I think of all those who lived fast and died young. I am thankful I reached 65 years old. I've had fast times, sure, but through the grace of the Gods of Chaos, here I am still, driving today to Roche-A-Cri.

This unusual 300-foot-high sandstone bluff was once an island in the great Glacial Lake Wisconsin. On the way here, I see increasing signs of encroaching autumn. The fields are left with only the stubble of cornstalks. The ditches are burgundy red with sumac and burnished gold with the lacework of asparagus. The trees are in full glory with their changing leaves.

I'm glad I came today. Tomorrow is the last day the office is open and the last day the main gate entrance of the park can be used. When I arrive, I am greeted by a friendly ranger, an older woman like myself. She is very curious about my Quest. She relates her sister is visiting all the Minnesota State Parks, and she goes with her whenever she is able. What a fabulous idea! My Quest is an easily repeatable adventure for anyone in any state. Five miles at the 13 state parks in Rhode Island would be simple. Hiking five miles at each of the 85 state parks in California would be more of a lengthy challenge but still doable. Each of these examples has other designated state land areas, as does Wisconsin. It would be up to the Quester to define the parameters of their own endeavor as I did.

The ranger warms my heart by orienting me to where I should start the trails as she busily packs up merchandise in anticipation of closing day. I ask if there are any bandanas, and she hands me a wonderful, bright orange one decorated with a map of the park. I need some blaze orange with hunting season coming and accept it wholeheartedly.

I start my mileage on the Spring Peeper Trail at the ranger's recommendation, heading toward the petroglyphs on the side of the bluff. As I reach the creek, I take a right onto the Acorn Trail in pursuit of the rock art, of the drawings of the original people who occupied this sacred place. The petroglyph wall has faded from centuries of sun and rain and wind. Nevertheless, it remains possible to make out the fantastical shapes of animal tracks, human figures, thunderbirds, crescent moons, and canoes. They parade across the rock face, the artistry of the Ho-Chunk ancestors attesting to the need of all humans to create, to express their lives through art. My favorite is the mythical birdman, once a bold red-orange, now a subtle shade of ochre.

I continue around the eastern side of the "screaming rock," the literal translation of Roche-A-Cri. The sky today is azure blue, striking against the browns, tans, and reds of the layered sandstone.

Roche-A-Cri State Park

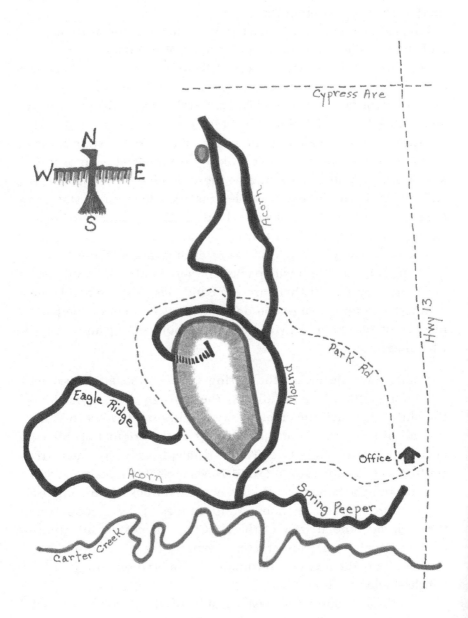

The shadows of the trees dancing on the curves of the bluff are mesmerizing!

The Acorn Trail connects with the Mound Trail, slightly past the campgrounds. I am on my way to reach the top of Roche-A-Cri, and I am excited to experience the surrounding vistas. After climbing 303 stairs, I'm at the summit. The views are breathtaking, especially on this bluest of blue sky days. There are not as many fall colors as I thought there would be. Perhaps it is because of the composition of the forest here, primarily oaks, white pines, and hickories. I am surprised to find groups of people on the observation platform. Throughout my Quest, I have been one of but a few at most parks, but this being a Saturday and the last day of the fully opened park must be the reason.

I am proud of myself for making it up these stairs, proud of all the towers I have conquered on my Quest. I was a little short of breath at times along the way but determined, nonetheless. It is the experiencing of adversity that makes reaching our goals all the more sublime. Encountering these types of climbs reminds me of the importance of resilience, especially as we age. We need examples of our own toughness, of our ability to push past discomfort, to withstand difficulties, and to endeavor to persevere.

I have spent a great deal of this Quest saving summer memories for winter's dark days. Now, with autumn in full swing, I am frequently reminded of my existential dilemma. I am in the autumn of my life, and it is, after all, the season of aging and decay.

With the intention of embracing the inevitable, several years ago, I bought a five-foot-tall plastic skeleton to use as a decoration for Halloween. I sat her in the backseat along with the other orange and black spooky things I had purchased that day. Driving home from the store, I glanced in the rearview mirror and did a double take to see a skeleton sitting there. It gave me the idea to pose her doing ordinary, mundane things around my house, taking photos of her activities to share. My skeleton mowed the grass, took a turn on my garden swing, vacuumed my living room, and sat across the table from me, all the while reminding me to be. Now, she sits outside every October 31 with her bony feet placed in old hiking boots. She wears a beat-up *National Geographic* hiking hat on her bare skull. She is not scary—purely an unavoidable fact. Knowing our skeletons exist reminds us to live fully while we are here. Acknowledging our mortality changes our relationship with time.

In my further efforts to reframe and reclaim autumn, I decided to think of it as a time to celebrate my resilience as a person. To acknowledge my inner skeleton, yes, but also my outward resolve. As part of this honoring practice, I dig up the herbs I use in cooking and plant them in pretty pots. Having their leaves gracing my house reminds my eyes of my favorite of all the colors. Green is my symbol for the power of resilience.

Spring is a time of possibilities, but autumn is as well. Rare colors of pumpkin, gold, and terracotta fill the landscape. There is a crisp chill in the morning air, letting me once again wear my coziest of sweaters. I get to burn things in my firepit, from fallen tree branches to emails from former toxic bosses, while drinking hot mulled wine with friends. I make a point to take stock of my life, to harvest, if you will, the many gifts I have been given over the summer: gifts of love, friendship, beauty, and purpose.

Autumn does bring with it, though, a sense of uncertainty. During this season of our aging lives, we must become comfortable when faced with chaos. It is a time when we might feel unsure of what is ahead and feel like we are losing control. Nevertheless, if we look for it, we will find our resilience there. It is in the part of ourselves seeking integrity, the part looking back in understanding at having successfully faced previous challenges instead of allowing them to become catastrophes. An intolerance for change, for hardship, for distress, is what leads to despair.

I credit the development of my resilience to my grandmother, Elizabeth. She had an amazing, terrifying, and incredible life. Growing up in Appalachia, she was taken out of school at age seven to care for her blind father and married at 13 to her 35-year-old coal mining husband. The mother of 10, she lived to see four of them die before her. She babysat the grandchildren of Devil Anse Hatfield and used a cast-iron frying pan to fight off a cougar stalking her toddlers. She was fierce and gentle, creative and steadfast. She was a fantastic gardener. Everything she touched sprang to life and burst into flower. "Look for beauty," she would tell me. "In it is where you can continue to live and continue to hope even when life is at its darkest." Searching for and finding beauty is how I honor her and where I discover my resolve and determination.

In her rural self, she had the wisdom of the ages. What she believed is strikingly similar to the early Zen Buddhist koan entitled "The Tiger and the Strawberry." The story relates the misfortune of a man faced with certain death in the jaws of a tiger. In his last moments, he savors the beauty of a ripe strawberry. Even in our most desperate circumstances, beauty can still be found.

In searching for beauty, I often peruse stores full of odd, old things. When I lived in Rocky Comfort, Missouri, I worked at a mental health center nearby. After particularly stressful days at the job, I would stop on my way home to browse at a local antique store. It was complete mayhem on three floors, giving me lots of time to wander and process the day's events. It was there I found my memento mori—an artistic token, its name taken from the Latin for "remember you must die." It is a Victorian-era coffin screw, ornate and filigreed, brass and triangular. I have given it pride of place in my home since it became mine. It has helped me, as my talisman, during times counseling dying and grieving clients. It is my reminder to live life, not just be alive. It helps me when faced with unimaginable pain in the world, to remember there is also immense joy. This may all sound morose, but as I said earlier in my writings, I have always been a Morticia looking for a Gomez to go with me on adventures.

I have become lost in my reverie about resilience and beauty and death, standing at the summit of Roche-A-Cri. It is high time I descend the stairs. On the way down, I marvel at the twisted tree roots fighting for purchase on the rock outcroppings. Reaching the bottom, I head back to where I cut off the Acorn Trail, heading north toward Chickadee Rock. The trail here begins to narrow, and the crowds begin to thin.

I am excited to visit Chickadee Rock. I have fond memories of hiking out to it with my child and their friend when they were preteens. All three of us climbed on the 25-foot rock outcropping, feeling bold and confident. I tried to make sure my child knew being an adventurer was one of life's important things. Never give up on finding new challenges, and never give up looking for beauty.

I pointed out to them the bloodroot plants growing in abundance near the rock. I dug up a root to show them how the plant got its name and told them the story of how my Appalachian grandmother, Elizabeth, knew this plant. She would use the roots to dye muslin flour sacks an interesting reddish-brown before using them to make clothes for her brood of children. On a whim, we took turns smearing our faces with the oozing "blood," laughing ourselves silly over how fierce we looked.

When I reach Chickadee Rock, I take a long moment to stand with my back against the sun-warmed surface, my face to the brilliance. I close my eyes in memory of that day of shared wonder and adventure. I think of the mythical birdman painted on the rockface of Roche-A-Cri. Although there are several theories as to what it represents, it reminds me of the Ba found in ancient Egyptian art. It had the head of a person and the body of a bird, and represented the soul. Perhaps the timeworn art here has a similar sense due to humans the world over seeking to gain insight into the afterlife. The powerful geographical features of this Ice Age island definitely cause my soul to take flight.

I circle back on the Acorn Trail toward the Eagle Ridge Trail. I want to be back among the changing trees and the caress of the forest. There is a grand historical marker describing the history of this area where Eagle Ridge meets the park road. It speaks of Indians and voyageurs and Cambrian sandstone. I breathe an earnest sigh for my ending Quest as I trace my steps back to my car, another five miles accomplished. With only one more park to go, I feel the shift of the seasons on a visceral level.

Autumn is a season of liminality. It is a season of revision, fluctuation, and volatility. It becomes even more vital to be in the moment. As a practice of being, hiking helps me to accept the gain and the loss, the dark and the light times of my life. In the beauty of nature, I find the resilience and the fortitude to move through this coming time, to enjoy all its colors, and to endure all its sufferings with integrity and grace.

Roche-A-Cri State Park

The Questions

1. What about this chapter resonated with you?
2. In what ways do you find pride in yourself? What accomplishments have you been able to achieve despite adversity?
3. Remembering we all must die, how have you begun to come to terms with your inevitable demise?

The Particulars

Sticker Required: Yes

Map on the State Park's Website: Yes, and nicely detailed

Bathrooms for Day Hikers: Yes, near the picnic area outside the office

Office or Kiosk: Office which can be closed depending on the day or season; kiosk for use during times the office is closed

Trail Markings: Well-marked

Seasonal Closures: Yes, the main gate closes in early October for the winter; steps to the summit open at sunrise and close at sunset

Flooding Concerns: Possibly along the creek during periods of high water

Five Miles: Easy to get with no circles

Governor Dodge State Park
Dodgeville

8.14 miles
Highest Point: 1,312 ft
Lowest Point: 1,014 ft

October 15, 2022
Prosecco and Bittersweet

I woke up from dreams of winter this morning on the day I will hike the last park of my Quest. My dreams were filled with wind and snow and cold. I am thankful I have saved countless memories of warm sun and brilliant green, of pine needle fragrance and the rhythm of waves to help me make it through the coming dark months.

I am thinking about all this Quest has given me: strong thighs and a strong back, a renewed sense of friendship with myself, and a trove of adventures. I have reclaimed, redefined, and discarded. I am feeling the most complex of all emotions, happy-sad, as I am set to finish. All good things come to an end, and I have to embrace the sorrow to feel the joy. I must stand bravely in this transitional, liminal space between the beginning and the end, between the hope and the loss.

I saved Governor Dodge as my last park because it was the first park I came to when attempting to reclaim my hiking spirit. When I started training to do the C2C for my 60th birthday, I decided to lace up my new Asolo hiking boots and boldly head out to this state park.

The bad things about my decision were many. The new boots and all the problems with not having them broken in were one thing. I didn't have appropriate hiking clothes anymore, only cotton ones. I didn't bring an extra water bottle, just my hydration pack. I did not have hiking poles, and there you have it.

I set off to do a nine-mile loop. I don't know what I was thinking. I had been walking five miles a day on city sidewalks, but it's very different to walk on smooth concrete than it is to hike through a forest. After about four miles, as I was coming down a fairly steep, gravelly portion of the trail, I fell and cut my knee badly, tearing my pants and injuring my hand in the process.

I sat on the trail with my leg freely bleeding, no first aid kit with me, either. I openly wept, thinking what I was trying to do was simply ridiculous for a 60-year-old woman. Feeling entirely defeated, I sat there in the dust and rocks for a long time sobbing, my body surrounded by ravenous mosquitoes and irksome midges.

I was crying because I had injured myself, but it was much more that kept me there, weeping. I was crying about my divorce a few years prior, about the burden of all the things I had to take care of because I was by myself. I was crying about my empty nest, about being old, about what the fuck to do with the rest of my life. I was absurdly ill-prepared. No one was going to come save me, so I made myself get up and keep going.

My water ran out about another mile in, it being a scorching, humid summer day. I thought I was never going to make it back to my car. I didn't have enough water, my knee hurt—I was tragic. It brought to mind a good opening sentence for a book. *The human remains discovered in Governor Dodge were mine.* It would be a great hook into a mystery, right?

Governor Dodge State Park

I hiked up a small hill and was greeted by the concession stand at the beach on Cox Hollow Lake. I hadn't realized it existed. Heaven for me, on that day, was a wonderful picnic area with the most welcome water pump I had ever seen. I filled my hydration pack and sat to have a snack.

My cotton pants were not only torn, bloody, and filthy but looked like I had peed in them because of all the sweat. I imagined anyone who saw me must have thought I was some crazy woman who had been lost in the park for weeks. It was a low point, but not as low as it had been when I was sitting, weeping in the dirt.

I gathered up my pride, my gumption, and my renewed cache of water, and headed out to finish the last miles of the hike. When I finally made it through the magnificent Lost Canyon leading to Stephens Falls, my heart was filled with joy, even though my legs were completely jelly. I walked up to the falls and stuck my head under it to cool myself—blessed relief on a sweltering day. I had made it back to my car. I had persevered and reclaimed my love for hiking! I had completed my first nine miles in over 20 years, and I would hike it 15 more times that summer before I left for England and my grand adventure on the Coast to Coast Walk.

As I have spoken about before, in other park essays, scars are powerful things. The scar on my leg from the fall on the Woodland Trail is now graced by the tattoo I got in commemoration of completing the C2C. This park taught me I might not know everything I'm going to do with the rest of my life, but when I set out to accomplish something, I need to have supports in place in ways I didn't when I was younger. I need to keep striving and doing even if I get hurt, whether it's physically or emotionally, and to remember I am tenacious and resilient.

While I am packing up for today's hike, I look back at what I had written about the first hike of my Quest at Governor Nelson State Park. I wrote about being prepared, about my fabulous Asolo boots, and about grief. It creates a wonderful full circle for today.

I decide to bring a tiny bottle of prosecco in my backpack to celebrate my final park. I am including a lovely, pink depression coupe glass, the same glass from which I drank the last of the elderberry port, described in my writings for Straight Lake. I plan to open the bottle as I sit on the rocks, admiring Stephens Falls.

The drive to Governor Dodge is filled with every shade of tan and brown imaginable. Hazel, bronze, and cinnamon. Amber, buff, and chestnut. Tawny, brick, and caramel. The last ruby red leaves of sumac accent the muted shades. There are still dry, uncut cornstalks in the fields, and they make for a fine backdrop to the thick road cuts of layered sandstone. Highway 18 West is newly paved, smooth, and open. My GPS tells me 37 miles straight on until the state park on this serene blue day.

The office is open, and it is one of the largest ones I've been in on my Quest. There's a taxidermy display, information about the original people living here, and those who homesteaded the area. I grab some maps and interesting pamphlets before jumping back in my car to drive to the trailhead near Stephens Falls to start my five.

After taking a quick peek in the Spring House to marvel at its surprising coolness, I hike north, heading to the Goldmine Trail. It turns out the trail lives up to its name. Filling the underbrush as I cross the road and head up the hill are the gold delights of autumn: the vibrant yellows and vivid oranges of cracking bittersweet seed pods. The trail seems in synchronicity with me regarding this last park. This section is the threshold, the place for the liminality between happy and sad, bitter and sweet. These complex and conflicting emotions teach us to be resilient in times of change, to have integrity, and to approach life with a sense of awe and wonder, no matter the cost. True happiness cannot be found on its own. It walks in companionship with sorrow.

The Goldmine Trail is wide as it turns into the forest. It is littered with acorns and black walnuts, diligently attempting to turn my ankles. It makes me pleased with my big old boots, my hiking poles, and my prepared backpack!

Governor Dodge has the best signage. There are "You Are Here" signs at every trailhead and every trail juncture. I come to the T of the Goldmine Trail and the Meadow Valley Trail. My body memory is strong here, just like at Devil's Lake. I keep going straight on Meadow Valley. Going to the right would take me to the Lost Canyon, and I'm not ready for it yet.

Today is a striking, sapphire sky day. The sun is weak, not sharing much heat, but it is 50 degrees, and the skies are open and cloudless—a perfect autumn day to hike.

At the next T, I head to the right to stay on the Meadow Valley Trail. In the past, I would've gone straight on the Woodland Trail to get the nine-mile hike in, but today, striving for my five, I will try to keep it around eight instead.

A mother and her 10-year-old stop me and ask for directions to the Cave Trail. I pull out my map to show them and smile in memory of all the adventures I have had over the years with my child.

The trail takes me through incredibly diverse scenery. There is a primal forest filled with the cries of pileated woodpeckers, their piano key wings extended. There are captivating views across the inspiring green-blue of Twin Valley Lake. There are open glades filled with goldfinches collecting the last seeds from the coneflowers and compass plants.

The hike on Meadow Valley Trail up from the parking lot by Cox Hollow Lake is strenuous. The first time I did it, on that leg-bleeding day, I didn't think I was ever going to reach the top. This summer, with 44 state parks under my belt, it is cake! Well, maybe not angel food, but cake, nonetheless.

Eight horseback riders come up beside me as I continue on the Meadow Valley Trail. What an exquisite day to be out riding. All the equestrian trails are one of the incredible things about this park. In the past, my child and I took advantage of them by renting horses and a guide for the day from a local stable. I stand watching them as they pass, breathing in the distinct and cherished smell of horse, transporting me back in time.

Throughout my Quest, I've done a lot of thinking and writing about time. Time is a commodity, after all. We spend it on the things, on the people we think are important. I learned an indispensable concept in my years as a hospice social worker. No one speaks, as they lay on their deathbed, of regretting they didn't fill every single moment of time with too busy-so busy-too busy. Instead, they speak of wishing they would have taken more time to share with loved ones, to visit gorgeous places, more time to just be.

Standing here watching the horses pass, I am thinking of the places on this Quest where time stood still for me because of an overwhelming sense of awe and wonder. I am reminded of when I was able to behold the grand geology of long, deep time on the cliffs of Lake Superior, of ancient shorelines, extinct volcanoes, and glacial islands. I am reflecting on a place where the human concept of time was revealed as mere folly when one zone was inches from another, in a lighthouse on an island in a great lake. I am aware that while I am hiking, while I am forest bathing, while I am wandering, I lose my sense of time. I don't think about the past or worry about the future, and it makes my soul lighter and my heart happier as a result. This, to me, is the most significant benefit of hiking. It stretches time.

I reach the junction where the Meadow Valley Trail meets the Lost Canyon Trail. I slow my pace, not wanting to pass through this enchanting area too quickly. The trail meanders back and forth over the cold, spring-fed stream flowing through this lovely place. Microclimates of ferns and mosses are abundant in the fiercely shaded canyon, resplendent with rock outcroppings and wizened pines.

I feel the nearness of the falls as the air rapidly turns cooler than any place in the park, the spring water crisp in the surrounding air. Walking up to the falls in my confidently waterproof boots, I put my head under it. It is tradition for me. I look for a somewhat comfortable place to sit and unpack my celebration. I perch on a nearby boulder, sipping prosecco, listening to the trickling waters of the end of the summer falls, and watching the antics of four young boys playing on the logs and stones at its base. Admonished by their father not to get their shoes wet, all four promptly do so with wild abandon. The youngest one in plastic boots shouts his feet are not as wet, but his father doesn't hear him, too busy with the older three, soaked up to their knees.

I watch the lazy trace of the falling leaves around me and smile, enjoying the heady scent of autumn. The leaves drift down and land in the stream's current, moving them on to their new, unknown destination. So, like life, carrying me along from one existence to another. I am proud of myself and the completion of my Quest. My backpack contains bittersweet. My face is damp from the water I blessed myself with as I finish the bubbly wine and pack everything away.

On the hike out of the canyon and back to my car, I remember being in Florence, Italy, with my child in 2017. We were walking near the church of Santa Maria Novella, and there, etched in the concrete of the sidewalk, were the words, "Every step I have taken in my life has led me here, now." True words then, true words now.

Governor Dodge State Park

The Questions

1. What about this chapter resonated with you?
2. What times in your life have you felt the emotion of bittersweet?
3. How do you choose to spend the precious commodity of time?

The Particulars

Sticker Required: Yes

Map on the State Park's Website: Yes, and it is detailed in color

Bathrooms for Day Hikers: Yes, but in the office

Office or Kiosk: Large, nice office with displays; can be closed depending on the day or the season

Trail Markings: Outstanding signage with frequent "You Are Here" maps posted

Seasonal Closures: None

Flooding Concerns: None

Five Miles: Easy to get with no circles

The Segue

Before I started my Quest, I created parameters to help me decide which parks to do. As a result, I chose the original ones because the Quester gets to choose. Plus, I liked the alliteration of the 5s—45 parks with five miles in each to celebrate turning 65 years old.

Over the course of the summer, I started thinking I would do the last five I had not initially included. They are the ones with an odd outlier status, the ones I call the weird five. They are the new one, the city one, the defunded one, the one with no sign, and the one you must pay to get into: Lizard Mound, Lakeshore, Lost Dauphin, Cross Plains, and Heritage Hill State Parks. I had planned to do them in the spring, giving me the bragging rights of having completed five miles in all of the 50 state parks, even those not meeting my original guidelines.

My thought was to have the essays about them be an addendum to the ones from the original Quest. My winter goal being to purge my house, make art, and spend time with friends. I was set to focus on recalling all the wonderful parks I had visited, especially on cold, gray-sky days. I would spend the coming season dwelling in memories of the warm sunshine and dazzling waters of miraculous places like Kohler-Andrae, Big Bay, and Pattison. It's what I planned to do, but chaos intervened.

I encountered many dogs on my Quest: small ones, large ones, gigantic ones. There was an enormous Harlequin Dane at Amnicon Falls! Most were on leash, as they are required to be on all state park trails. Some were off leash, resulting in buckled knees when they crashed into me from behind or clothes full of muddy paw prints when they jumped on me. A few were aggressive, but the majority were adorable, happy to be out hiking with their owner, and eager for a pat from me.

Somewhere along the line, I must've encountered a Hound of the Apocalypse, as you will come to understand as you read the rest of the story—the story of what happened before I could finally hike those last five weird parks.

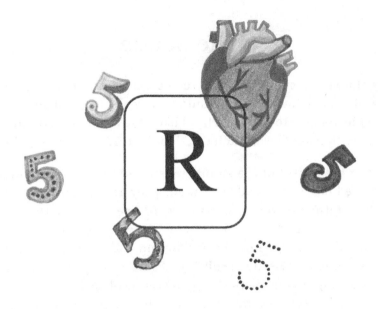

The Rest of the Story
Dane County

20 feet to 3.50 miles
Highest Point: First Hike After
Lowest Point: Told of Need for Surgery

December 1, 2022–April 16, 2023
Hearts and Wendigos

December 1, 2022

I had a heart attack yesterday and found out today I will need a bypass. This surgery could take away many things. My writing and art will be put on hold. I won't be able to winter hike to get some sun despite the cold. My despair-fighting tools have imploded. How will I battle it now?

All this aside, I am decidedly fortunate to have health care, supportive family, and friends. Despair, get thee behind me! I cannot dwell with you. I am alive, and I will embrace integrity.

December 2, 2022

My doctors asked me what I was doing the day before the heart attack. I hiked five miles at Pheasant Branch Conservancy and spent the afternoon straightening my garage. The next day, I had pain in the middle of my back between my shoulder blades. I thought it was from lifting heavy things in the garage and dismissed it, taking a couple of Tylenol and going about my day. The pain persisted, though, and finally, at around 8:00 p.m., I looked up "back pain" online, finding it can be a sign of a heart attack in women. I finished doing my dishes, drove to the ER, and was promptly admitted. It was analogous to being in labor all day and not realizing it!

December 3, 2022

I am in a state of uniquely bizarre liminality. I am certain Rod Serling will show up as one of my nurses! I am on hold for the heart surgery as arrangements are made for surgeons and space. I am confined to this hospital room, attached to an IV and monitor, waiting. I seek beauty by watching the snow fall outside my window, dreamy and ethereal, as it lands on the treetops and the roofs of houses.

I am allowed only two visitors due to COVID restrictions. My cherished friend Diana visits me daily. Today, she shows up with a trove of coloring books, markers, and colored pencils sent from the neighborhood women. These gifts will truly help keep me mindful and calm, as creating art always does. My favorites are the one with hygge designs and the one with "Fuck This" surrounded by pretty flowers.

My child visits daily, too, and I work to keep a positive outlook. I am, after all, modeling how to persevere in such a moment. How to hold on to hope, how to say what needs to be said, how to reassure, how to be vulnerable.

December 4, 2022

To provide myself with a bit of normalcy, I have been using my social work skills on the staff who come in to take my vitals, check my IV, etc. I genuinely ask them how they are, validate their experiences, and thank them wholeheartedly for their kindness and care. If they have tattoos, which many do, I ask about their ink and invariably receive a fascinating story in return. Being a good listener in this distracting chaos is the least I can do for this amazing medical staff.

I have to receive a shot in my stomach every day to keep me in this stasis. Because it leaves a bruise, I ask the nurses to make a beautiful design for me to see when I am able to look in a mirror again. I am pleased to watch them study and think about creating art on my belly; each shot, each bruise, adds to the composition.

December 5, 2022

During this existentially frightening time, I search for integrity and am confronted with the very basic idea of trust. According to Erikson, Trust versus Mistrust is the first stage of our development, the one we resolve between the ages of birth to three. It is our most primal need. Can we trust the world to take care of us, or will we perceive it as a harsh, unforgiving place? I find myself revisiting that first stage as I endeavor to relinquish control to my medical providers.

I have to trust someone will be there for me as I have been and will continue to be for others going through complicated journeys. All the lost hikers I helped point in the right direction. All the suicidal children I helped make it one more day, one more year. All the grieving souls I gave a tiny spark of hope. Mckenna, an exceptionally kind young woman, has taken me under her wing. She is a traveling nurse, and she is my someone.

December 6, 2022

Today will be a defining day. I have to continue to trust that as I approach the abyss, I will find the help I need. Mckenna the Traveler shares with me the sense of loss she feels, which comes from never knowing how people are after their surgery. As a gardener, I fully understand this complex emotion, the not knowing if the seeds planted ever grew, if the care given ever helped. We share phone numbers, and I promise her a text on the other side.

I have a tele-meeting with the heart surgeon from another hospital. It feels detached, impersonal, and empty. He seems all well and good, answering my questions and concerns, but the human factor is missing, and I find it disheartening. I am to be transferred there today for surgery first thing tomorrow morning.

I ask my child to work on my Christmas present, a new laptop. I need tech-native capabilities to ensure I have what I want. It will be something for them to work on when there is nothing else to be done but worry. Diana presents me with a spring green envelope, instructing me not to open it until she leaves. With powerful hugs and tearful smiles, they are both gone.

I am alone in my room, looking out the window over the snowy landscape. I write a goodbye letter to my child and tuck it in my overnight bag, just in case. I open the card from Diana to find an extraordinary, three-dimensional, bejeweled dragonfly. How completely fantastic! She has no idea of all the dragonfly experiences on my Quest, yet the synchronicity of the world had her choose this card for me. I sincerely wish I could experience change and time the way dragonflies do while I am in this liminal space. At three times faster than humans, this all would be behind me now.

The EMTs arrive to transfer me to the next hospital. They are kind and full of expressive tattoos. They tell me stories of theirs, and I tell them stories of mine as we make the drive. When we arrive, as they hand me off to the new staff, one says, "Be good to this one. She is really cool!" It makes my heart happy.

I am awake at 2:00 a.m., still being processed into this new hospital. The room here is nowhere near as pleasant—the view before of a quiet neighborhood, this one of a red brick wall and a small triangle of gray sky. I am thankful I have my summer hiking memories to bring beauty into this environment.

December 7, 2022

I meet my surgeon this morning, and he explains my surgery has to be rescheduled due to a heart coming for transplant. This change in plans allows me to meet him in person, which is significantly better than via video.

December 8, 2022

My sleep remains elusive, devoid of dreams and full of trepidation. I am awakened around 4:00 a.m. by the clandestine arrival of a phlebotomist. His manner is terse, and he huffs at my slowly awakening self. I bemoan the fact we don't have *Star Trek* medical facilities, and he pauses in his pursuit of my blood. "You like *Star Trek*?" he asks. "I haven't met anyone in ages who likes it. That hits me right behind my com badge!" I respond with questions about his favorite captain and episodes, and soon we are as old friends geeking about sci-fi. His irritation from his extreme schedule lifts ever so briefly. He thanks me for the respite as he leaves my room, running behind in his duties but happier now in his countenance.

My surgeon visits again. I am still on hold, but he hopes to do the procedure in a few days. Being here longer allows me to develop a relationship of sorts with him. I tell him when I was a hospital social worker, I dealt with two types of surgeons: the defiantly cocky ones and the humbly confident ones. He pauses to think for a bit, then relates he is more of the latter but cocky nonetheless, as he is exceptionally good at what he does. I take his hand and tell him he has a divine gift—the ability to repair hearts. He smiles, a humble smile, as he heads off to his next patient.

December 10, 2022

I am told my procedure will definitely be tomorrow. I feel decidedly more confident about it than I did the first time it was scheduled.

One of my nurses is a dark-haired bride-to-be. She tells me of her own heart surgery as a teenager. Ever since then, she has been a gardener planting seeds about hearts and how to take care of them, working with children having similar experiences to her own. I smile, knowing I am in safe hands.

Tonight, I take a last shower and bid a tearful farewell to my scarless chest. As I drift into a fitful sleep, I imagine I am holding an elk antler in my right hand. My heart will hear the loud bugle of an elk, as it did innumerable times on hikes in New Mexico. The bugle will remind Her to return to me, to beat again, to continue living.

December 11, 2022

They come to get me first thing, taking me to the operating floor. They leave me alone in a small room. It is probably all of a minute, but it feels like hours, days, in the bending of time happening right now.

As I am waiting, I pray my surgeon will open my heart with gentle reverence. I hope he remembers to put everything safely back in before he uses titanium plates to reconnect my sternum, before he connects the skin of my chest into a fiery scar, before I am wheeled back to the recovery room in an anesthetic slumber. The hugs from my mother, advice from my father, my big love and all the smaller ones, the awe of sunsets, the beauty of my baby's heartbeat inside me, the grace of a noble fir tree, every single solitary day of my life, tragic or sublime. I hope he makes certain all my joys and all my aches are where they should be, that they are planted carefully again in my gardener's heart, which holds the map of my existence.

Two anesthesiologists enter, the one who left me in this room and another older woman. As she speaks to me, her voice gentle, melodic, and soothing, I feel my apprehension ease. He says he is going to give me something for the anxiety. I entreat my kind heart to come back to me, to listen for the elk's bugle, and I am gone.

December 15, 2022

An ordeal of pain, hallucinations, and brain fog for the last several days, but my heart returned! She beats again, strong and solid, and for now, that is enough.

I remember strange occurrences. I kept seeing fives all around my room. Dancing and moving on every surface. I laughed about them as they were pretty and fascinating and freaky. My anesthesia brain must have been processing all the five miles I had done. I kept seeing human shadows moving, too, not scary but oddly comforting.

December 16, 2022

I woke up about 4:30 a.m. this morning after a restful and happy sleep. Today, I am increasing my strength and enjoying the soft waves of the oceans of love and kindness around me. I text Mckenna the Traveler and tell her I am on my way to recovery.

December 17, 2022

I don't remember a lot of this fever dream of C-ICU time. I do remember the tattoos. All the perfectly straight tribal lines, all the delicate flowers and insects, ships and fierce faces. All the stories of children and family, reclaiming and redemption, of earnest love and visceral grief. I am pleased I ask about the tattoos. The connections I make with the staff because of my curiosity are helping me find my way home.

My reputation with the nurses has come to be the kind woman who loves to hike and has cool tattoos. It helps that Petra has made a magnificent collage of photos of me hiking on my Quest and put it up in my room. I am finding more hope every day.

I continue to ask any nurse giving me the daily stasis shot to add creatively to the design. They each take my request to heart, scanning my belly thoughtfully before inflicting another small bruise. In that brief moment, it gives them a chance to see me as more than a patient, to see me as the artistic spirit I am. It gives them the opportunity to slow down on their busy schedule, to laugh with me, and take the time to care. We all need the human factor, the immeasurable tonic of healing that comes from social connections.

December 18, 2022

When this whole thing started, I talked with my child about helping me with new technology. Doing something for me, by the action of it, by the thought of my future, helped them believe their mother was going to be okay. If you can give those who love you something tangible to do, it helps them during the chaotic time when one's life is in the hands of the Gods.

My nurse today is here while her mother is dying. I have heard numerous stories of courage, grace, and perseverance during my stay in these hospitals. I share with her my hope that her work today provides her a brief respite from the weight of anticipated grief. She embraces me as we walk slowly together in the hallway, whispering stories of her mother.

My surgeon and his entourage come in to check on me. I am one of a few patients he has gotten to know personally before he performs his life-saving miracle. We chat and ask questions of each other. I tell him it feels like there is a railroad spike embedded under my skin above my heart. I ask him if it will ever go away, telling him I don't want to be a reverse Quasimodo. He reassures me it is merely my swollen sternum. I totally blame it on the opioid painkillers, as I blurt out, "A reverse Quasimodo sounds like a sexual position." He and I and the other staff in the room burst into laughter. It is an excellent way to end my days in the cardiac unit.

December 19, 2022

Yesterday was a long and brutal day. Discharged at 10:00 a.m. and finally allowed to leave at 6:00 p.m. When I reached my front door, I tripped slightly up the two small stairs, the arms of my child and the metal of a walker keeping me from falling.

It is as if we are finally back to our remote Viking village after a fierce battle where I suffered a potentially life-ending wound. This morning, I am by the fire, eating warm cinnamon-laden oatmeal, and it is the beginning of my healing journey.

December 20, 2022

I finally get to see the completed design made by the nurses who gave me a shot every day I was in the hospital. Some told me it already looked like a star, a heart, a face, or perhaps a constellation. The multitude of small bruises looks to me like an exploding star system with my belly button as the birthplace of the universe. I remain slightly trippy from the painkillers, but I find it beautiful!

December 21, 2022

I am having a better day and feel sparkling hope as I think of a tattoo to surround my new impressive scar. My resident tech native has added Studio Ghibli screensavers to my new laptop. We talk about *Howl's Moving Castle* and the boy who drew a lovely scene from it for me. He presented it to me as he told me I saved his life from suicide. His mom grasped my hands, similar to the way I did my heart surgeon's, with a sense of deep thanks and appreciation.

A quote from the film perfectly encapsulates my experience: "A heart is a heavy burden." I remember my trust in someone being there in the world for me, as I have been for countless others, and the idea for my new tattoo is born!

When I worked as a school social worker, if I saw a student with a visible injury, say a broken arm or a bandaged ankle, I would ask them how it happened. It was usually some banal reason, and I encouraged them to come up with a better story: shark encounter, ninja battle, or heroic rescue of a kitten. When such an injury occurred to me by way of tripping off my front patio, the kids inevitably asked me about it. I told them it was caused by a Chupacabra, a mythical fanged beast which kills by drinking blood. They were mightily impressed! But how to describe this recent situation? My child chooses the perfect crypto-creature—a Wendigo. They dwell in dense forests and are known to sneak up from behind to rip out an unsuspecting victim's heart. Yep, a Wendigo attack is what happened!

December 23, 2022

My child tells me the secret they have kept from me due to my surgery. My brother, whom I visited during my hiking adventures this summer, had a stroke about a week ago.

Even though it is difficult, we can never forget to allow our loved ones to have agency, especially as they get older. We all rage against the dying of the light in our own ways. Each of us will confront our own existential slaps as we age. We need the support and, ultimately, the freedom to decide for ourselves how we will emerge victorious.

December 24, 2022

Being off my sleep pattern and being in pain has become miserable. I know intellectually there are multitudes of people worse off than me. I have intense compassion for people who have appreciably more difficult lives than I do. I have a warm house, enough to eat, a child caring for me, friends loving me. That's a great deal more than many millions of human beings on this planet. Today, though, this understanding doesn't ease my suffering. As I used to tell my clients, "Everyone has trauma, and minimizing yours as you compare it with others is not healing."

I am thinking of the comments made by several of my doctors over the last month. "We've seen this after patients recover from COVID." This being a sudden change in heart health. My routine blood tests in early 2022 were all in the normal range. A life-long vegetarian, hiking over 250 miles, and then, bam! It is disconcerting to consider how the virus will continue to manifest in the future.

December 25, 2022

Convalescing. It is fundamentally an innocuous word, bringing to mind pictures of Alpine scenery, summer days, and lounge chairs. In many 1940s black and white films, the heroine was in the Alps convalescing, perhaps in the Poconos or Malta. It seems like it's a relaxing escape from the stress of everyday life you purposely take for yourself. Convalescing is entirely different than it sounds. It is a transition where time comes to a standstill, liminality to the 10th degree. The hours and days creep along, slogged down in the quicksand of healing. It makes me angry time changes tempo for sad things but is so fleeting for happy ones. *The time with my new baby flew by*; every mother will say it. Why couldn't such sweet time have had this slow cadence?

My sister is coming tomorrow to spend a few days with me. This will allow my child to return to their job and me to transition out of their constant care. It will be good to have some time with her. Perhaps we can decorate my house for Christmas, after the fact, simply for the beauty it will bring to my living room.

December 28, 2022

This is the first night I have spent alone since November 29 when I went to the ER. In a way, it is a return to normalcy, but too many questions remain unanswered, only to be reconciled through the passage of time. Will I regain the strength and stamina I had? Or will I succumb to despair, no longer able to hike, to do my art? I hope, as all true gardeners do, for the coming spring, for the resurgence of life, for the promise of new growth.

December 30, 2022

I walk the same path inside my small ranch house over and over again. It's too cold to be outside these last weeks. Today, the snow has melted, and the sun is warm on my face as I stand on my deck overlooking my sleeping garden. I say a prayer to the trees and the slumbering plants that when the first day of spring arrives, I will be returned almost to my former self. I am thinking about the many times on my Quest I would save a view or a hot summer day as a strong memory to help me through the darkness of winter. I am thankful I have them to sustain me now—those memories of hiking on 95-degree days, dousing my head under waterfalls, the hum of cicadas, and the brilliant sunshine filtering through the forests.

January 1, 2023

I wish I could be doing a First Day Hike. It is 38 degrees and sunny. I'm trying to look forward to doing what I had planned before all this happened: to hike the last five state parks I had not originally included. I don't know if I will be able to do five miles, but at least a hike in each one. They seemed an easy undertaking before this considerable setback. Now, they have become a Quest of their own.

January 3, 2023

I have my final appointment with my surgeon. The last stitches are removed, and my scar is healing nicely. I tell him how blessed I am to have had him heal my heart, about the hearts I have healed as a social worker, and about my plans for a tattoo. I thank him, again, for his divine gift, which has allowed me to continue to live. He gives me a big hug and leaves the exam room. His PA comments, "He never hugs a patient!"

I text Mckenna the Traveler, to let her know my surgeon has given me a clean bill of health, and he expects I will live 10 years or more. She responds with genuine happiness for the good news, asking me to keep in touch.

January 4, 2023

When I started my Quest, I had in mind it was a coming-of-age story, one about reclaiming and acknowledging my life now at sixty-five. Never in my wildest dreams did I think I would be facing open-heart surgery and the disability of a sibling shortly after my birthday. I thought I had considerably more time and space before those things started to occur, but such is the chaos of life.

My neighborhood friends have begun bringing dinners. My friend Britt brings over a fabulous vegan stew. Her quick wit makes me laugh, pointing out how now, I have a vertical scar to go along with my horizontal scar from the C-section. It must have some significance, she relates, as I am quartered. I will have to give this some thought.

January 9, 2023

I hardly recognize the person in the mirror, the one with pale skin and mousy gray-brown hair. Where has the tanned, smiling, blue-haired woman gone? She was the one who was expanding her world and going on Quests. How do I get back to her? I am having trouble believing any of what happened to me in the hospital was real, the trauma preventing me from experiencing it as reality.

January 18, 2023

It is in the high 30s today. I put on my boots and cleats and go for a walk outside. I have been doing this regularly on any somewhat decent weather day. Today, I make it eight blocks!

January 28, 2023

There is a polar hush over my garden. The arctic sleep of winter is here. The world is buried under days of powdery snow and headed for minus-zero temperatures tonight. The frozen stillness is healing and peaceful. One of my neighbors brings over two ice lanterns, placing them on my front patio where I can see them glowing. Their light and her care on this frigid night give me great comfort.

January 30, 2023

When I was discharged after the surgery, I was assigned a cardiologist. I rank her as one of the three worst doctors I have ever had the misfortune to meet. She didn't wash her hands, wouldn't answer my questions, took multiple phone calls during my appointment, and left the room several times. She made me feel shamed, belittled, and dismissed, all of which do not support health. I don't need a "touchy-feely" doctor, but as a mental health provider myself, I expect a physician to have a minimal idea of the emotional needs of their patients. It is about my heart, after all!

Don't ever put up with a physician who discounts you, minimizes you, or deflects your questions, especially one who shames you about your body. None of those things are healing, and none of them create a therapeutic bond between yourself and your doctor. That bond and your ability to trust the person to address your health needs is the most essential part of wellness.

February 2, 2023

I am sincerely grateful for the friends in my life. They have brought me fabulous meals: Greek, Italian, Indian, Moroccan, and everything in between. They have lit lanterns in my darkness, literally and figuratively. They have given me rides and provided me with support, conversation, and news from the outside world.

I wrote this poem a couple of years ago while spending a weekend at a cabin with my neighborhood women. I have known most of them for almost 20 years, and they are true blessings in my life:

Weekend with the Ladies

We talk about men and penises
fire and stars
we dance and drink wine
and talk about how much we love each other,
this tribe of women I have in my life.
We have raised children together; we still raise children together.
All the drama and realities of our children together,
of ourselves together.
All the bloody naked truths of each other.
All the tampons and pads and births of each other.
All the walks in the forest picking ticks off each other.
Bloody love of women friends, the thick and thin of each other.
The true nakedness and the raw truths of each other.
The deep smiles on our faces as we acknowledge
the inner selves of each other.
In the moonlight,
In the firelight,

In the starlight,
dancing.

February 5, 2023

Studying my face in the bathroom mirror this morning, I look decidedly older to myself than I did before the Wendigo attack. I count myself fortunate, though. There are too many who never get to see their face, as an old face reflecting back to them.

Depression is a common side effect of surgery, especially on the heart. The trauma of the experience opens up long-ago chapters of dark books, chapters I had resolved and put away. It makes me wonder if the wounds of trauma ever fully heal, as they can be easily broken open by life's difficult circumstances. As I continue my journey, I need to remember to treat myself as I would a dear friend, with patience and loving kindness.

February 8, 2023

I can't wait until the sore, burning feeling on my chest is from a new tattoo rather than from a healing scar. The tattoo will be a source of pride instead of the insecurity of the wound marking my surgery.

In an effort to accept my new reality, I go online and look for Wendigo merch. I buy some fun stickers, cute Chibi versions of the horrible monster, to put on my new laptop. I also purchase a t-shirt with a fantastically wicked design of the crypto-creature holding an anatomical heart. I will own this beast!

February 11, 2023

I think back to the Chupacabra attack when both my feet were injured so extensively I had to use, first crutches, and then a cane for several weeks. I recall how my ex told me he was embarrassed to be seen with me because I needed walking aids.

I remember how the principal at the school where I worked, refused to issue me a key to the elevator. It was commonplace for students or staff who had mobility issues or injury to get access to them. Even with a doctor's note describing the deep tissue damage in both my feet and the severe ankle sprain, she refused. Looking back, I see it as the harsh, inhumane action it was. At the time, I viewed it simply as yet another example of the near daily retaliation. The seven other teachers who reported the concerns along with me had all since left the school or the profession, leaving me the sole remaining target.

To be able to continue performing my job, I had to maneuver the three flights of stairs multiple times a day, slowly and painfully, one at a time. As I ambled along, the loving concern of the students offering to carry my planner and helping to make way for me in the crowded hallways between classes, was my saving grace. When you are in the midst of something like that, it is interesting how much trauma can be, for lack of a better word, normalized. The experience gave me profound insight into the lives of the children I worked with who were dealing with complex and on-going trauma of their own.

That crypto-creature's assault helped me realize being alone is easier than staying with someone who would never be truly loving. I also learned, when you blow the whistle, you have to be brave. Those involved in the injustice will be crueler than you can ever imagine, especially to someone with a kind heart.

I finally get around to unpacking my hospital overnight bag. I find a coloring page of an elk with flowers festooned among its antlers. I had worked on the page the day I was waiting to be transferred for surgery. I found the soft scratching of colored pencils on the paper incredibly calming and centering. It makes me happy to see it again after all this time, and helps me put those dark books of trauma back on the shelf where they belong.

February 14, 2023

On this Valentine's Day, I am sending cards to the cardiac units of the two hospitals where I stayed. The cards read: "The birds are singing. The sun is shining. My heart still beats, thanks to your care and healing. My sternal precautions are at nine weeks, and I am up to walking two miles a day, from only a few sidewalk squares when I first got home. Your compassion is deeply valued. Your kindness is sincerely remembered. Thanks to you all." I signed my name followed by the words: hiking woman with the cool tattoos.

February 25, 2023

I have been reading about the distress of a sports injury, the common feelings related to it, and the ways to cope. I don't know if this qualifies as such, but it has taken away my sport: hiking. It will be at least for the next few months until the weather is warmer and the trails are less icy.

I'm definitely feeling grief about the changes in my ability to hike, but I keep track of my recovery and walk a little farther every day. I'm giving myself beautiful stickers on my calendar as a reward for my efforts. I'm looking for community because it is a big part of recovering from a sports injury, even though I usually hike alone. Such an injury can create some angst. I turned 65 and was attacked by a Wendigo—definitely a major angsty time!

February 26, 2023

It is traumatic for me to remember how severe it was when I first got home from the hospital. How I tripped up my small front steps for lack of strength, how I was utterly spent walking the length of my own sidewalk. Some days, like today, are more difficult than others.

March 1, 2023

I need to find a new cardiologist who genuinely understands how hearts function, not just physically but holistically. The ancient Egyptians took all the organs out of the body except the heart because it was the "house of the soul." The ancient Romans believed there was a *vena amoris*, a vein of love from our left ring finger directly to our heart, which explains the placement of wedding rings. It wasn't a line to our spleens! When we hear poignant stories, we don't reach to put our hands on our kidneys! We put our hands on our hearts.

March 4, 2023

My child and I start watching videos of how to camouflage heart surgery scars. We go shopping to pick out products needed for such an endeavor: full-coverage makeup, primer, setting spray, green concealer, and more. When we get home, we try several different ways of using it and are able to make the scar almost disappear. It helps increase my confidence exponentially. Maybe, a low-cut neckline is not entirely off the table.

March 8, 2023

As I sit on my deck, feeling the soft warmth of this late winter day, I close my eyes and see the color fire red behind my lids as I turn my face to the sun. I remember hiking at Rib Mountain State Park and the overlook with the small trees. I smile to think of the interesting motto of Marathon County: "Where Time is On Your Side." After this heart surgery, perhaps this idiom now works for me. I was lucky enough to get extra time on this earth. Many in a similar situation do not. I am feeling somewhat guilty as I convalesce because I'm not accomplishing more or living larger as a result.

In an effort to prevent despair from taking too firm a hold, I go online and order a new 2023 Wisconsin State Park sticker. Because I am 65, the cost goes from $28 to $13. Money well spent!

March 10, 2023

My chest is hurting off and on today. With an abundance of caution, I have my child drive me to the ER. I am to be admitted for an overnight evaluation. As we wait for all the cogs to be in order, we have fun on a website full of goofy tests.

We are working on one when the hospitalist comes to finish the admissions process. He asks how I am doing, and I respond I am in a quandary about whether a dingo yips like a coyote, barks like a dog, or howls like a wolf. He stands there, dumbfounded, gears rapidly turning in his brain. "That's the dog from Australia, right?" he laughs. "I have no idea." It is a funny, lighthearted exchange, which makes him relax and take more time with me. It helps when people are feeling stressed to chuckle at silly things.

March 11, 2023

The overnight hospital stay brings lots of tests but no conclusions. Yet, I do meet an outstanding cardiologist! I tell her I am searching for a new one, wanting someone who knows the truth about hearts and all they contain. I speak of idioms while she examines me. There are multiple ones: to follow your heart, to wear your heart on your sleeve, to have a heart of gold, to die of a broken heart. She tells me the last one is true; people do die. It is called "Takotsubo cardiomyopathy" or "broken heart syndrome." I tell her I wrote my master's thesis about this very subject, and she says I should be her patient!

March 15, 2023

Today, I am trying to get my act together, starting to work on cleaning my house and organizing my stuff. I decide to throw out my hospital-issued, heart-shaped pillow. The pillow was a much-needed accessory when I first came home. I hugged it, ensuring I didn't move my arms to protect my healing sternum. I used it to prop up my swollen legs, where they took veins out to fix my heart. For a couple of months, this rough cotton, red pillow with an image of an anatomical heart was my constant companion. It feels remarkably healing to throw it in the trash.

As I do, it reminds me of my belief about people when they are under stress. We behave according to our true, core selves. When I was in the hospital, fundamentally anxious and overwhelmed, I resorted to my social work skills of being a listener, offering validation to others, and finding solace in that giving.

I had an experience at a local theater a couple of years ago, which cemented this belief. Coming in, I noticed an elderly man struggling to walk. I stopped and held the door for him and his companions. They made it into the building, and he promptly collapsed on the floor. Some folks in the crowd immediately dialed 911. Some stood still in shock, and many ignored the situation. I took his wife by the arm as several medical providers pushed through the crowd. As I held her hand, I whispered, "Growing old is not for the faint of heart."

She whispered back, "It gives you many gifts but exacts a terrible price." Her wise words are on my mind today.

The ambulance came moments later, gathering him up. As quickly as it happened, it was over. Sometimes, when death comes, all we can do is be a witness, but sometimes we can be a gardener, planting seeds of human kindness.

March 17, 2023

There is a person at the cardiac rehab clinic who comes with his wife and walks with her around and around the indoor track. I see them walking in the neighborhood on fair-weather days. It makes me downhearted to know my erstwhile spouse would not have done this for me—not when I was pregnant, when I had the Cesarean, or when the Chupacabra attacked me. He didn't want the burden of caring for anyone. In my mind, being able to care for someone you love is a gift.

My emergency C-section was markedly traumatic. I remember being numb in the recovery room, clutching a Polaroid photograph of my newborn to my heart. What helped me reconcile the harrowing birth was surreal. After my maternity leave, I returned to my job as a hospice social worker. I was assisting a family with the impending death of their eight-month-old, the same age my baby was at the time. Inexplicably, being present when he died helped heal me from not being fully present when my child was born.

This all has me thinking I am a human compass now that I am quartered. I have a scar going north and south and a scar going east and west. I wonder if I put my arms out at precisely the right angles, on exactly the right sunny summer day, if I could become a sundial. I could be a teller of time, a harbinger of days, a foreshadower of moments.

March 20, 2023

On this, the Spring Equinox, I am working on reframing the painful trauma of coming into my house, the memory of it greeting me every day at my doorstep. Two small steps, only seven inches high, which I could not maneuver when I arrived home after the surgery.

I buy pink, red, and yellow roses, lavender stock, and white carnations. I stand by my front door, scattering the petals all over the steps until they are lavish with color and fragrance. I walk in beauty up and down them several times, strong and certain, as I remember my prayer from December. The first day of spring is here, and while I have not completely returned to my old self, I am considerably more like her.

March 24, 2023

My first hike since the Wendigo attack is three miles at Lake Kegonsa State Park. The forest is muddy and sleepy, but the prairie yields numerous owl pellets to investigate and even a delightful singing bluebird. It feels spectacular to be back out on the trail! My new friend Luna is with me, and since she is an avid hiker, I am sure we will venture to more places together soon.

I send a selfie of me reclaiming my hiker identity to Mckenna the Traveler. She texts back, "You have made my heart incredibly happy." She says I have no idea how much, but I do. After all, I am a gardener. I know how it feels to see the seeds of care and support grow and flower. We wish each other a summer full of adventure!

March 27, 2023

A fairy princess accosts me on my walk through the neighborhood. She is wearing a sparkling silver tiara, a rainbow unicorn t-shirt, and a hot pink tutu over her jeans. She comes running at me with a stick in her hand. I stop and say, "How very fierce you look, brandishing your stick."

She adamantly replies, "It's not a stick. It's a wand!"

"Pardon my mistake, your majesty," I humbly apologize.

She pronounces, "My wand can give you healing," and I tell her the magic of healing would be wonderful. She warns me, "It can also give you poison!"

She put healing on me and poison on me, a drop of both. It is like the world: a little bit of good, a little bit of bad. The tiny fairy princess understands this even in her six-year-old self. With the ends of her stick, she understands what life is—a two-sided coin, a double-edged sword. There are always trade-offs and exchanges, gifts of light and gifts of darkness. What a funny day.

April 1, 2023

Sadly, something new has to be incorporated into my identity. It is of a Heart Surgery Survivor. I'm not sure what this identity means. I am still figuring it out and working to minimize the scarring. I am endeavoring to come to terms with the trauma, and kick that damn Wendigo's ass!

April 5, 2023

I have several new scars. Of course, there's the big one, the one cutting open my chest, the one which has turned me into a human sundial. There is a scar on each of my legs from the Frankensteinian vein harvesting. I credit my surgeon's loving sensibilities for ensuring neither of those new leg scars interfered with my hiking tattoos. I have new scars on my lip, my neck, and my thigh. There are also ones I can't see, the internal and the metaphysical scars left on my heart.

I imagine it is rare for anyone to reach 65 without having scars. If I had not jumped on a sandy beach, my knee finding broken glass, fell on sharp farm machinery, or skipped through barbed wire, how would I be able to cope with these new scars? All those wounds brought their own gifts. All these new wounds make me more ruggedly beautiful.

April 6, 2023

I am finally sitting in my stylist's chair to get my hair cut for the first time since the Wendigo attack. There is an older woman here complaining the nail colors they sell are all too bright and too vibrant. She wants something nude, neutral, and muted. The horror! It is the complete opposite of me. I want to become more colorful as I age, not less. I am here to get my hair cut, with sections bleached, in anticipation of re-bluing it soon.

April 8, 2023

I feel my convalescing is officially over! For at least three weeks, I have been walking 3.5 miles daily, except on rainy ones. The sun is shining, and the ducks are back on my pond. Hellebores are blooming and tulips are bursting.

Now, to arrange a day to start working again. I'm excited it will be later this month. I have missed the people I work with, not in the way I miss someone I love, but in the way I miss something comfortable and familiar. I will be glad to, once again, have the social connections and easy banter about a shared experience as well as the fine company of books.

April 10, 2023

I am visiting my brother today. He is recovering yet still in an existentially liminal space. A few weeks ago, I sent him a black t-shirt. It had a white design of a hand giving the middle finger and the word *stroke*. He tells me he wore it to his first meeting at a stroke support group. When he walked in, the facilitator questioned if he was in the right place, as he appeared very able; everyone else in the room was sitting in wheelchairs. He flashed the shirt from under his black leather jacket, and now he's the rockstar of the group!

This winter, I didn't think it was possible to be here on the farm with him again. We smile in joy at the songs of redwing blackbirds in the fields and the croaks of leopard frogs in his pond.

We commiserate about medical providers becoming more patronizing as we've grown older. They have recently begun to talk with both of us in the high-pitched, sing-song voices usually reserved for babies and dogs. They use excessively basic vocabulary and often speak too loudly. This condescending cadence is referred to as *Elderspeak*. As two intelligent and learned people, we both find it offensive. Even if it may come from a place of caring, it makes us feel less than. If anyone ever calls us "sweetie" or "honey," we will not be pleased. We both agree—respect us or fear our wrath!

April 11, 2023

One more step back to my previous existence. I am getting my nails done. I choose two flashy colors: one hand in blue and one in green. It feels marvelous to go from mousy and non-descript back to colorful. With my hair and hands vibrant, I see myself again when I look in the mirror.

April 16, 2023

As I'm working on getting these writings together, I am reminded of an elder who was a hospice patient of mine with the standard diagnosis of six months or less to live. He had had a near-death experience with an exceptional effect. He wanted to write down every single detail of what he saw and connect it with his entire reality. It was a Life Review on a grand scale—his manifesto about dying and returning. Though in his late 70s, he bought himself a computer, learned how to use it, and taught himself to type. He purchased a printer and studied all about how it functioned.

Six months passed, and he stayed in hospice because he had a terminal diagnosis. He was on the highest level of oxygen any of the hospice staff had ever seen a patient survive on. It took him 18 months to finish his writings. He printed it out, finally having it done exactly the way he wanted it. He straightened the pages and laid them out on his desk, and he died. I wasn't there with him on his final day, but his family was, and they related the story to us. Our brains have an astonishing power to keep our bodies here even when they may not want to be. Our mind's sense of the infinite is there when we least and most expect it.

The Addendum of the Five
Triumphs and Norms

After returning home from dinner at my friend Petra's house, I'm relaxing on my deck this early spring evening. She and I spoke about the quality of grief processing taking place as we confront this time in our lives and work to recover from what we survived this past year. She spoke about the idea of "compared to the norm."

"It is not our norms being referred to; it is the general norms of people our age. We are laboring to get back to our individual normative functioning," she stated.

As she described how this felt, she forced me to think about the unusualness of my Quest—walking five miles in 45 state parks and then, after a significant life-threatening event, pursuing the last five locations. It's not a general norm for people who are turning sixty-five. However, as she pointed out, it is normal for me. Her reframing was a surprising realization. Old women, who are slightly overweight, and trying to figure out what the fuck to do with the rest of their lives, would more than likely not decide to embark on such an adventure, especially doing the majority of it alone. Perhaps by sending my account of the parks out into the universe, I will plant the seeds of possibility for others celebrating this milestone birthday. Hopefully, it will become the norm!

I have heard about a woman who has completed hiking all 11 national scenic trails. I feel rightly humbled and insignificant in light of her stunning accomplishment. Yet, I must remind myself what I am doing is, nonetheless, a worthy endeavor. Just as we can't compare our traumas to others, we can't compare our triumphs to others, either. Everyone does what is within their reach. Everyone fights the battles they encounter. Everyone takes their own journey.

With that, I begin the last five state parks and update my Quest equation to read: (45 x 5) + (5 x 5) = 65.

Lizard Mound State Park
West Bend

5.10 miles
Highest Point: 938 ft
Lowest Point: 912 ft

April 18, 2023
Healing and Panthers

Lizard Mound is a place of ancestors and old things, a perfect place for me to start these last five parks, the ones I had chosen not to include previously. They were outside my original parameters. Mine are not the same as somebody else's might be, but a Quest is in the eye of the adventurer. I decided to include an addendum to my initial goal by completing these remaining few.

Little did I know after finishing my 45 x 5 = 65 Quest, I would embark on another one. One with its boundaries encompassing life and death, healing and uncertainty. I was forced to reestablish a connection to my body and to experience a level of weakness I had never felt before. My legs could not lift me, could not walk me. They were swollen and sore, bloody and scarred, unable to bend due to the grizzly need for the extraction of veins to repair my heart. When I looked at them, I was dismayed by how their appearance seemed distant and alien. On an especially defeating day, I brought to mind a man who was a hospice patient of mine. Remembering his strength and grace helped me through those dark times. At the end of this park essay, I include the poem I wrote for him as I held his hand as he drifted off to sleep.

I remain on my healing journey, building strength and battling self-doubt. Today, it feels spectacular to finally get back to the point where I can start hiking these final parks. This is park number one of the Addendum Five Quest, or the Quest AF for short. These are the five I had laughingly thought would be easy additions to the originals. They have since taken on a spirit of their own, helping me overcome my Wendigo attack. I find it oddly comforting to describe the open heart surgery and all it entailed as this crypto-creature. Personifying the trauma as a forest beast who attempts to steal the hearts of the unsuspecting gives me an enemy to thwart, an adversary to overcome. Part of the recovery from the events of any major surgery involves coming to terms with such a beast's companions: fatigue, indecision, and body grief.

We experience body grief when we have to incorporate complex changes related to our internalized self-image. It occurs under various circumstances: extreme weight gain/loss, amputation, pregnancy, intense scarring, and even the inevitable shifts in our aging bodies. For myself, I grieve the loss of my stamina and strength. I mourn the loss of my scarless décolletage and the injury to my self-esteem as a result. Like any form of grief, actively processing it and acknowledging the accompanying emotions helps us find our way to a point where the loss has a settled and restorative place to reside.

As I ready my backpack to leave my house, I feel trepidation. This is the first time hiking by myself since the surgery. I've had some short hikes with friends at Lake Kegonsa State Park, and at Pheasant Branch and Pope Farm Conservancies. However, this is the first time I'm out by myself and driving 180 miles round trip to a park with the objective of completing at least five miles. I sincerely don't

Lizard Mound State Park

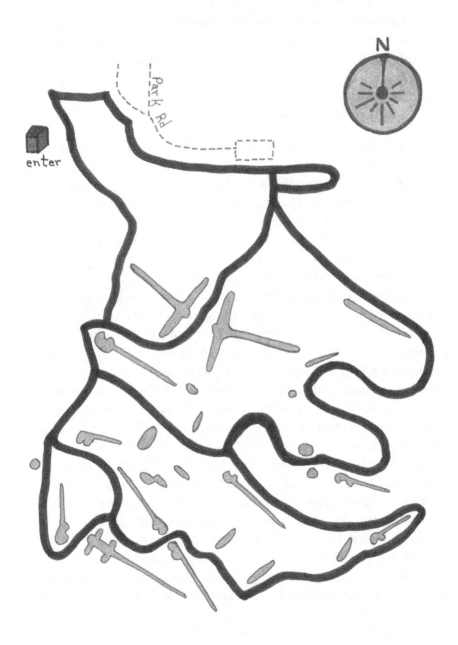

want to stay at home and be fearful, though. It's not how I want to spend these days I worked immensely hard to have. My sternum was broken, my heart was stopped for these days. I want to enjoy my life and be a role model for my child. I want them to have a trail map about how to navigate this strange, liminal year of turning sixty-five.

I make it to Lizard Mound, the newest of the Wisconsin State Parks. It has an unimpressive, brown rectangular sign by the side of the road—nothing more, no grand entrance. This is the first time I have ever had to stand in the ditch on the side of a country highway to take my park entry selfie photo. Nevertheless, I'm excited to be here and thankful for this rare day. On a spring day like today, sunny, warm, and beautiful, I think to myself, *I made it! I made it through all those brutal winter months.*

A wonderful gazebo structure is located along the road as I drive into the park. It has a center section, which apparently speaks when you touch the available buttons surrounding it. Unfortunately, it is out of order today, but it looks to verbally explain the why, when, and how of the mounds. It is an innovative approach to address the disabilities of park visitors. Fanciful metal sculptures in the shape of lizard mounds surround it. Each has a large circle at the top, containing information about the site and its history.

Not too far from the gazebo is a small lot where the trail begins. The sadly unnamed trail is made of limestone gravel, consisting of several loops around the effigy mounds. May apples are starting to peek out everywhere I walk, their little party umbrellas getting ready for warm summer evenings. I stop close to the tail of a panther mound. I close my eyes to the genial spring sun, feeling the breeze on my face. My mind imagines hundreds of years ago, a person might be standing here, closing their eyes, enjoying the soft caress of air as I do—the world different and yet the same. Nature is its own time machine, and I am deeply humbled to be in the presence of these ancient works of art.

There is a location farther along the trail winding between two more panthers, their heads together in rapport and concentration. I take a moment to stand in reverence between them. The energy of their beauty and power is palpable. They rise from the earth not far from the grand namesake of the park, the lizard mound.

A group of people is out here today hiking around with a friendly ranger. I eventually cross paths with them as I circle to and fro to get my mileage. I ask them what brings them to the park. The ranger tells me they are the stewards working on future planning. They appear to be a fascinating group trying to ensure the surrounding forest is cared for, and the mounds respected and preserved.

An older man with wild curly hair asks me if I know about the significance of this park. I respond by saying, "Why, yes, it's a magical and sacred place!" They all nod their heads and smile.

His face lights up as he responds, "It definitely is!" He tells me this is the most extensive collection of Native effigy mounds in an area of this size. Now, I am even more impressed with this lovely little park. The ranger, a supervisor for a large swath of state lands, invites me to return when the forest is alight with trilliums in late spring and in autumn when the trees are colorful and fabulous. I can visualize how remarkable this park would be in the fall with its incredible variety of trees. One of the people in the protectors' group is a Native woman with striking blue hair. Of course, we hit it off! We talk about embracing our aging selves as we walk along for a spell together. She confides, "We have blue hair, but not as we witnessed old women have back in the salons, back when we were children. Then, they would dye their hair blue-gray and have it in short, tiny curls." We laugh about our long hair in bright and sparkling shades of indigo and sky as we wholeheartedly seize these years of our lives, refusing to be invisible!

As I continue on the trail, I think about the art museums I have visited: the Uffizi, the Galleria dell'Accademia, and the Met, to name a few. I think about the places of ancient architectural wonder I have seen: neolithic stone circles, Acoma Sky City, Cahokia, and numerous others. Lizard Mound State Park is a place belonging to both categories.

Hiking around among this sensational collection of venerable art reminds me how every place I go, every park I've been to, has its own charm and its own remarkableness. It evokes in me once again the Quest I made for myself, and now its addendum, is always more about the journey than it is about anything else.

For Bobby: Double Leg Amputee

In your dreams, do you walk?
*   Are the strides of your long, strong legs*
*   filled with power and grace?*

In your dreams, do you run?
*   Does your heart beat hard and loud*
*   as your swift legs take you toward the horizon?*

In your dreams, do you dance?
*   Do you press your virile thighs against a*
*   beautiful woman and glide her across the room?*

In your dreams, you are not an old man,
*   skeletal and emaciated, struggling in vain to*
*   scratch the itch on your legs, long since gone.*

In your dreams,
*   Do you walk?*
*   Do you run?*
*   Do you dance?*
Tell me, Bobby, do you fly?

Lizard Mound State Park

The Questions

1. What about this chapter resonated with you?
2. In what ways have you experienced body grief in your life?
3. Nature is its own time machine. What are the places you have visited where you encountered such a connection to the ancient world?

The Particulars

Sticker Required: No

Map on the State Park's Website: Yes, and it is detailed in color

Bathrooms for Day Hikers: Portable restroom available

Office or Kiosk: Kiosk with additional information available

Trail Markings: Not named, marker only at the start

Seasonal Closures: None

Flooding Concerns: None

Five Miles: Circles required

Cross Plains State Park
Cross Plains

5.05 miles
Highest Point: 1,142 ft
Lowest Point: 967 ft

April 27, 2023
Melancholy and Bluebirds

It is a beautiful day projected to reach 70 degrees. The fields are starting to green, and the road to this park is full of wonderfully rolling hills. Cross Plains has a parking lot, but no office, just a nearby kiosk primarily for the Ice Age Trail. The sign for the park is even smaller than the one for Lizard Mound. It is a four-by-six-inch yellow state park boundary marker mounted on a green metal pole.

There is no consistency in what constitutes a state park. Take, for example, Mauthe Lake in the Kettle Moraine. It has a picnic area, swimming beach, bathrooms, marked and named trails, and a campground replete with teepees. Yet, it is not a state park; rather, it is a state recreation area. It makes sense to me, being here, why I didn't include this one in my original Quest. Even the most basic parks like Natural Bridge, with its sorrowful kiosk and graffitied bathrooms, have more infrastructure than this place.

As I lace up my hiking boots, I see an older woman leaving the park. I start a conversation with her about available trails, as there are no maps on the DNR's website. She tells me there are two well-maintained loop trails once you're inside. Crossing the road to get my ubiquitous entry photo, I'm going to enter into the unknown and try to find them. Beyond the wall of trees, I find a T intersection. I take the left fork to do the first of the loops the woman recommended. It starts with a series of limestone steps, going down and then up, following the terrain. It is inspiring to see bloodroot growing and black raspberry canes beginning to leaf out. Hiking up the trail to another T marked by a stump painted the yellow of the trailblazes of the IAT, I continue on the right fork. I am happy I have my trusty GPS and my sweet little compass so I don't get lost.

The deeper I get into this forest, the more strikingly cacophonous the birdsong. I turn on my Merlin Bird ID app, and it hears scarlet tanagers, Baltimore orioles, and rose-breasted grosbeaks, along with all the usual suspects. I read an article earlier this week about how birds and their songs are good for our mental health. I knew this; it is part of why older people like birds, after all. We take time to marvel at their beauty, to let their delightful music fill us with joy. We know being too busy/so busy is not worth the existential price, and it is best to slow down and pay attention. Apparently, bird interactions positively affect our brains for hours after an encounter. The scientists called it a "time-lasting link." I like the sound of that! It makes me wonder how birds experience us and how they experience time.

At the next Y intersection, I take the left-hand side leading out onto a meadow. I am thinking about how this Quest of mine has been done in such a strange and eclectic order, not arranged by region or size or even alphabetically. I am reminded, in this chaotic world, that's how life often plays out.

Reaching the top of the hill, I am in awe of the stands of exquisite white birch surrounding me. I think I'll walk on this for a while. There's no rhyme or reason out here today. It's an improvisational

Cross Plains State Park

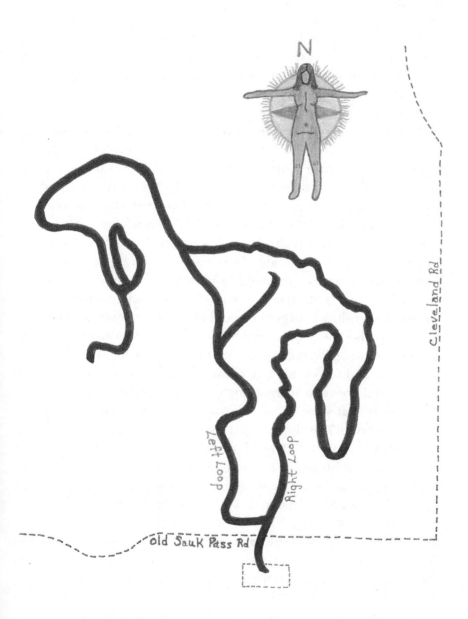

jazz hike made up of the Quest AF, the five miles, and the beautiful day, which has me doing what I love. It is a day reminding me how lucky I am to have made it through, my heart healing and pumping hard again. Soon, another branch of the trail leads sharply downward into the forest, but I'll stay in the meadow for now. This is a moderately strenuous trail, or maybe it is because of my rebuilt heart. I'm getting a good workout today. I could see using this as a training trail because it is close to my house and fairly rugged. It is a surprisingly marvelous place!

Finding another T, I decide to take the left-hand side because I am curious about something I thought I saw at the top of a ridge. As I follow this short spur loop, out here in the middle of nowhere, is an incongruent picnic table. I continue on the trail until I hit another T, deciding to go to the right by a downed and massive oak tree. I am ready to wander into the forest again. We'll see where it goes.

A few minutes in, I realize it's quickly descending the steep bluff. Since I don't have a map and don't want to wander in here too far from where I started, I'm going to head back out again. I'm taking it slower on this trail, trying to remind myself I'm only four months out from open-heart surgery. I would be jamming along if I had been hiking on this trail last summer before the Wendigo attack. It makes me melancholy, grieving for the energy lost. I am genuinely thankful to be here and for everything going perfectly for me to be able to be alive. Yet, I have to acknowledge there is grief as well: the grief of lost time, of lost stamina, and of something else I don't know quite how to describe. The closest I can come up with is the grief of losing a sense of complete independence. This morning, I found myself questioning my decision to come out to a park I've never been to before, not something I did at all last summer. Even though I remain fiercely independent, the grief is in the second-guessing.

Buoyed by birdsong, I retrace my steps back to the beginning, back to where I entered the park. I plan to do the loop starting from the right-hand side this time. It's a strong hike upward, but this trail is alive with wildflowers: Dutchman's breeches, hepatica, wild ginger, and bloodroot in bloom.

The lack of maps for these trails is disconcerting. There may be some on one of the trail apps that can be purchased or that require watching advertisements. I think a state park needs to have a map posted and available in some capacity. I am working to stay oriented, though, and am thoroughly enjoying this lovely forest and the views of the ridge. I will come here again.

I finish the right-hand loop as it meets the meadow trail I previously hiked. It is a steep grade coming up out of this small canyon. I have to stop several times because my heart is beating fiercely. The medicine I'm taking keeps her from working too hard, and I try to give her grace and kindness, although I am slightly irritated with my slower-moving self. As someone with a respiratory disability, I don't take the freedom of health for granted, but now I must slowly work to regain it. The top of this trail is the deeply angled cutback I saw earlier. I think I am getting the gist of this place! I decide to return to the small loop with the oddly placed picnic table. I think if I do and then head to my car, I'll have my mileage.

Hiking last week at Lizard Mound State Park felt triumphant, like a return to normalcy. Today, in this park, I'm feeling the grief of this return hampered by the lack of a full recovery I am impatient to have. I think about the long road back. How many more miles will I have to hike to get anywhere close to last summer when I pounded up the Balanced Rock Trail at Devil's Lake? Everything is a process. It is an important thing to remember. The victory over a life-changing injury is certainly not all fun and games. It is not all celebration, but equally as much tribulation and effort.

As I stand here with a glorious open meadow rising above me to the right and a dark, boisterous woodland below to my left, I turn my face to the sun and close my eyes. I thank the Divine for this incredible day, even if it is bittersweet with achievement and frustration. It is life, and I still have it, and I am extremely grateful.

Leaving the meadow, hiking again toward the forest, a magnificent red-tailed hawk flies low enough over my head for me to feel the wind of its wings. It reminds me to look at the bigger picture and see with eyes not mired in minute details. I must be and enjoy the journey.

Back at my car, as I'm changing out of my hiking boots, I hear a unique birdsong. I pull out my phone, checking my app to identify it. It is an eastern bluebird, and I find they are singing all around me.

As I glance over into the forest of the park across the street, I see one sitting on a branch—a blue flash of light, celestial and miraculous. Life is glorious, and I have a time-lasting link!

Cross Plains State Park

The Questions
1. What about this chapter resonated with you?
2. What things provide you with a "lasting link"?
3. In what ways do you process and return from setbacks in your life?

The Particulars

Sticker Required: No

Map on the State Park's Website: No map of park trails, only of the Ice Age Complex as a whole

Bathrooms for Day Hikers: None

Office or Kiosk: Kiosk with no additional information available

Trail Markings: Not marked

Seasonal Closures: None

Flooding Concerns: None

Five Miles: Circles required

Lost Dauphin State Park
De Pere

5.16 miles
Highest Point: 598 ft
Lowest Point: 458 ft

April 28, 2023–May 4, 2023
The Days Before

April 28, 2023

Today is my first appointment with the new cardiologist. She fills my heart with comfort and trust. I leave her office smiling instead of weeping as I did after the former doctor, the one who thought it was therapeutic for a heart to shame and marginalize it.

This evening, Diana is having a bonfire party with our outstanding tribe of loving neighborhood friends, the first of the coming summer—another heart-happy experience ahead!

May 2, 2023

Because I understand trauma is a wound to the body, I am having a massage today. Trauma is not only the event itself; it is the processing of the event that goes along with it. Healing the wound of an incident starts with bodywork and moves on from there. I leave the appointment relaxed and connected to myself in a way I haven't been since the Wendigo tried and failed to steal my heart.

May 4, 2023

There is an ebb and flow of energy in our bodies, and it becomes disrupted as a result of injury. Reiki is a way of realigning our energy and addressing trauma. Our understanding of this is held in the right brain, where we process our sense of creativity and story. In the story is where trauma is healed.

When I lived in Carrizozo, I worked at five, rural New Mexico school districts, simultaneously. Today, sitting here in the waiting room of my Reiki provider, I am reminded of a second grader from one of them. He had experienced deeply traumatic events at too young an age. One day, during our art therapy session, he told me a story of healing. He wanted my help building a castle out of Play-Doh, and he placed within it two sculpted books he called "the books of love and madness." He envisioned himself as a knight on a quest to find the books, which were protected by a never-defeated dragon, one that no spear could kill. With his play, he was able to conquer the dragon with a potion of "frog's legs and goodness." In his clever mind, he had realized anger was not a healing force, but with magic and a true heart, he could emerge victorious.

As I give myself over to the energy work, I feel immense tension leaving my body. I knew I had significant trauma in my heart and legs. I didn't understand how much I had in my right arm and ear. I discover it had developed there due to holding fast to the imaginary elk antler and listening for the bugle to call my heart back to me. It was in the story!

When I return home, I immediately bring my elk antler out of my basement storage area. It has been there on a shelf since I moved from New Mexico to Wisconsin. I found it on a hike in the Manzano

Mountains, southeast of Albuquerque. I had forgotten how massive it is! It is over 40 inches long and 15 inches high with five grand spikes. I give it respectful pride of place on my living room coffee table, and it takes up the entire space.

May 6, 2023
Chainsaws and Trolls

The DNR's website has no maps for Lost Dauphin. I found one obscure reference to it on a trail app, finding a map to download. I don't want to be completely blind going out today. This is why it wasn't on my original Quest—the lack of information. It is questionable whether it remains a state park. When the original house of the supposed dauphin was torn down back in the 1970s, it is rumored to have lost its state park status.

To get to this park, I take Highway 41 north between Oshkosh and Appleton. It's full of billboards hawking cheese and cannabis, sex toys and Jesus, and several kinds of beef jerky. The traffic flows incredibly fast through this corridor. It is Wisconsin's autobahn.

I find it decidedly ironic, given my geographically challenged brain, that the spellcheck on my phone keeps correcting the name of this park to "lost often." Ha, that's me all over! The park is named for one of the dozens of blond men who pretended to be the youngest child of Marie Antoinette and Louis XVI. It consists of land settled by one such man. Apparently, the real dauphin had been imprisoned during the Reign of Terror and died while in confinement. Reports of his continued existence permeated the news in the late 1800s, so much so Mark Twain referred to him as the "lost dauphin" in *Huckleberry Finn*. The story of the inconvenient prince became a popular conspiracy theory. One of the curious and macabre parts of this tale involved the cutting out of his eight-year-old heart upon his demise. It was preserved over the centuries in a crystal jar, eventually becoming mummified. It remains located in a crypt beneath the Basilica of Saint-Denis, north of Paris. I am saddened to think of his small withered heart, of his young life taken too soon merely because of an accident of birth. It reminds me of the preciousness of my own heart and my desire to keep it beating in my chest for as long as possible.

Across the street from the nondescript parking area, there is an outstanding view of the Fox River. Its waters are luminous with flocks of white pelicans. I take my required selfie by the entry sign reading only, "Lost Dauphin Park." The word *state* is conspicuously absent, but it remains listed as one on the DNR's website. Oh well, I am on my Quest AF, and this is one I have to accomplish.

As I begin my mileage, the forest reveals a flush of spring blooms: a troika of trillium, a sanguine of bloodroot, and a hover of trout lilies. A great horned owl flies over my head and lands in the black walnut tree above me, surprising and breathtaking! It's a little squishy out here on the trails due to the considerable rain recently. Yet, it's not raining today, and I have my big, comfy, bog-worthy boots, keeping my feet happy and dry. I'm glad I came here on a cool, early spring day. It is decidedly marshy throughout most of the park. In the height of summer, I imagine it becomes a mosquito hellmouth.

The miles here are a slog—a hard-fought battle. It is not because of internal stamina or continuing heart issues but because it is a dispiriting sort of spot. The people who live in the mega houses surrounding it on all but the riverside probably enjoy it. But, for me, it's a sad reminder of how this place, once so wild and beautiful, is now surrounded by excessive grandeur and exceptional waste, reminiscent of the reign of Louis and Marie.

In every park I have hiked on this Quest, I try to appreciate the journey and to find beauty. Here, the pelicans and owls are the thing, as are the small creeks, abundant wildflowers, and the delightful signs installed by neighbors, warning of trolls hiding under the frequent bridges. I need several circles to achieve my five miles. Each time I return to the overlook at the park's entrance, I take a moment to revel in the marvelous views of the mighty Fox.

On the way home, I stop to visit my brother on the farm outside of Oshkosh. We have an everything under the sun conversation. This time, it centers on lost things, chainsaws, and children.

He is grieving, as I am, the loss of our previous selves. An existential

Lost Dauphin State Park

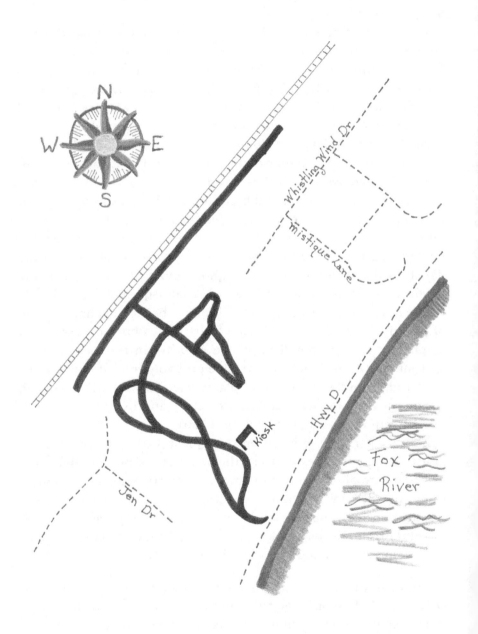

slap still burns on both our cheeks. We have had great ordeals these last few months. We both have lost many things: skills, stamina, and the innocence of not having to confront impending doom.

He bought a new kickass rechargeable chainsaw. Afterall, destruction is the divine twin of creation. Unable to create for the time being, his new chainsaw is a perfect present to give himself. He bought it and promptly spent the day felling dead ash trees. He tells me of watching cranes and egrets marching through the farm fields like volunteers in search of evidence. Only they are predators in search of their prey; the recently emerged frogs and toads seeking the nearby pond.

For our children, there are many facets to consider. We share our hearts as we drink dark and bitter black coffee in the kitchen full of a lifetime of memories, its windows reflecting the blue glass bottles on the sills. Money; how best to set them up for the future? We talk of trusts and wills and transfers upon death. Love; will they be cared for as time winds on? We know they are and will continue to be which is of great comfort.

Driving home from the farm, I am thinking of a time when, as a hospice social worker, I helped a man say a last goodbye to his mother. I include the poem I wrote on that emotional day:

Doug to Nannette, Dying

The final goodbye.
"What do I say? What can I say?"

A fifteen-minute goodbye.
Would this be enough time
to say a whole lifetime of words from child to parent?

She touches my face like when I was her baby.
Fifteen-minute goodbye forever.

"You are dying. I have to go home."
"My life goes on without you."
Clear my throat, start again.

"I've come to say goodbye."
"I live far away, and now, I have to go home."

Fifteen minutes.
A lifetime.
Plenty of time.
Never enough.

Lost Dauphin State Park

The Questions

1. What about this chapter resonated with you?
2. In what ways do you find beauty in life even when it is difficult to see?
3. How will you provide for your family after you die?

The Particulars

Sticker Required: No

Map on the State Park's Website: None

Bathrooms for Day Hikers: Portable bathroom available

Office or Kiosk: A kiosk with bird species and a large sign with the park's history

Trail Markings: Not marked

Seasonal Closures: None, but the park is closed from sundown to sunrise

Flooding Concerns: Trails may be wet, and could have flooding issues

Five Miles: Circles required

Lakeshore State Park
Milwaukee

5.06 miles
Highest Point: 531 ft
Lowest Point: 310 ft

May 13, 2023
Love and Coolness

Last summer, I had an Alfred Hitchcock scene by my back door. Robins had built a nest there and attacked me whenever I went into my yard. They have returned! They are dead set on building in the same place, even though I have covered it with a ball of rabbit hutch wire. I feel slightly guilty when I come home from work and see the piles of dried grass on the steps, but I pick them up and wait for the birds to do it again the next day. My heart goes out to them as they labor under their instinctual mandates, but I don't want to be repeatedly divebombed as I was last summer. I am hoping they move on to a more pleasant nesting spot soon.

I am having difficulty deciding what to bring to Lakeshore. I won't need my backpack with its helpful collection of hiking gear or my boots or poles. I won't need to spray myself for ticks. It's just walking five miles on a paved sidewalk, similar to what I do almost daily in my neighborhood. What should I bring? Maybe a small bottle of water and some snacks?

Because tomorrow is Mother's Day, my child and their partner accompany me. I am remarkably fortunate to still be here for this holiday, and having them with me makes this park extra special. They are the beauty in this place! After, we can stop for lunch at some lively spot in the Third Ward, this being a decidedly urban state park.

Arriving at Lakeshore, the challenge is finding free parking due to there being none at the actual location. As a result, I am including some distance outside the park's boundaries in my mileage. This is the first time I have ever done that. Yet, if I have to walk .03 miles from the closest free place, I am counting it!

We follow the Hank Aaron State Trail from our parking spot to the boundary of Lakeshore. A surprisingly beautiful bridge accents its entrance. It looks to be made of aluminum, all lustrous and shiny silver. It is a bridge how every bridge should be—not just function but form and embellished with *ars gratia artis*. Adorning the spans of the bridge are sunrises commemorating the eastern view over the lake, diamond kites with ribbon tails, and single-hulled sailboats. It is a fitting threshold to this liminal space between a metropolis and an inland sea.

My original Quest parameters make sense to me here. It has the designation but is so unlike the majority of my original 45 state parks. There is a wonderful sign by which I take my prerequisite selfie. However, there are no bathrooms, no office, and, as I said, no parking. There is a stately kiosk for handouts, but only one brochure is left, and it isn't even for Lakeshore.

It really is a city park, of which Milwaukee has many great ones. Lakeshore is on an island, with multiple city parks to the north: Veterans, McKinley, Back Bay, and Lake. Again, I wish I understood why state park status and funding are given to some areas and not others. I wish there were a minimum standard, like at least a porta potty within the boundaries.

Lakeshore State Park

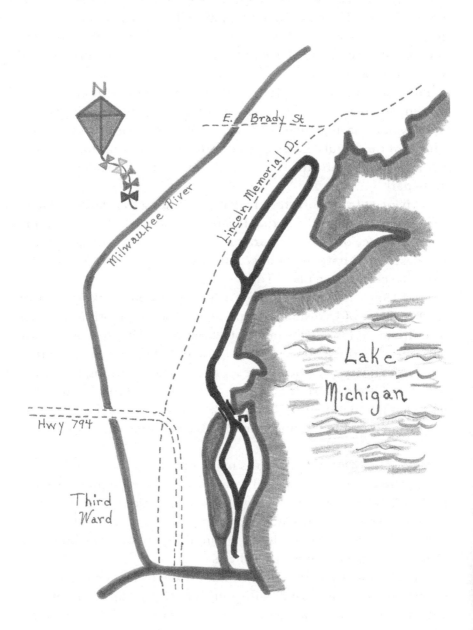

As we walk the path, we see awakening prairie areas full of red-winged blackbirds establishing territories, their sharp trills filling the air. The sky is dotted with gulls of all descriptions, and the pebble beach is home to Canada geese and their tender, newly hatched goslings. Flashes of yellow catch my eye as goldfinches circle among the burgeoning spring plants.

The city's skyline is remarkable from this green space as the Summerfest grounds come into view. We talk of concerts and late nights spent dancing in the rain, of standing endlessly in line to use the overcrowded restrooms, of watching fireworks over the lake on music-filled evenings.

I feel happy-sad because I can't revisit those summer days of flirting with boys, and the carefree beauty of thick hair, no wrinkles, and no tan lines. I think about how cool I thought I was then, back in my frequent concert-going days: all tight skirts, high heels, and sexy bras.

Can someone still be cool at 65 years old? How cool can we be with compression socks, sensible shoes, and readers? With canes and walkers and minds contemplating our fast-approaching mortality? If we can be, how are we cool after a certain age? Is it in the same ways or totally different ones?

For myself, I think about how the young people I work with at the bookstore say I am cool. Perhaps it is because I make them feel at ease. I am interested in what they are doing and what they have to say. Many of them struggle to define themselves, as I did in my 20s, and I try to be supportive and nonjudgmental of all their different styles. Being cool is about being comfortable in your own skin. Cool is not being afraid to be silly, to make mistakes, to be humble, and to not take yourself too seriously.

Back in December, the EMTs who transported me from the first hospital to the second one filled my heart with joy when they said, "She's really cool." We only had about 30 minutes together. I was dressed in a medical gown, and I don't think my hair was even brushed. During that brief time, though, I asked them sincerely about themselves and their tattoos and shared quick stories of mine. Is being cool as an older person about finding meaning in all types of situations? Maybe it is about being authentic with others, not hiding from our emotional selves, being sensitive and respectful. This subject of "coolness" is something I will continue to ponder.

The clockwise and counterclockwise turns around the park yield almost five miles. By the time we get back to my car, we will be right on the money. Walking back along the Hank Aaron State Trail through Veterans Park, we spot an unbelievable schnitzel of marvelous miniature dachshunds, at least 30 of them! The dog owners are all aglow with pride in their tiny sausages. We ask why and find out it is the Milwaukee area wiener dog meetup. What a fun and purely happy event! There are dogs of every color and coat: brown and brindle, smooth and wired. Several are in costume. Our faces hurt from smiling; it is too much joy and goofiness. Maybe cool is being able to take your long, little dog, dressed up like the Pope, to spend time playing in a park, simply because it is a fresh spring day and it feels fabulous.

Before the drive back home, we stop for a cozy lunch at the Comet Café on Farwell Avenue, not far from Lakeshore. The journey to my house is a pleasant one, full of memories of the day. As part of our long Wisconsin goodbye, my child and their partner come inside with me for more conversation. They are shocked to see the enormous elk antler taking up the surface of my coffee table. "What in the heck is that?" asks my child. I remind them of telling how I envisioned holding an elk antler in my hand before the heart surgery. "I remember, but I didn't know you actually had one! That's so cool!"

Lakeshore State Park

The Questions

1. What about this chapter resonated with you?

2. How do you define what it is to be "cool"? In what ways can you still be "cool" as an aging person?

3. What do you like to do that is purely silly fun? What brings out your inner geek?

The Particulars

Sticker Required: No

Map on the State Park's Website: Yes

Bathrooms for Day Hikers: None in park, but a porta potty bathroom is available near the Summerfest grounds

Office or Kiosk: Kiosk with no additional information available

Trail Markings: Not marked

Seasonal Closures: None, but the park is closed from 10:00 p.m. to 6:00 a.m.

Flooding Concerns: None

Five Miles: Circles required

Heritage Hill State Park
Green Bay

5.10 miles
Highest Point: 697 ft
Lowest Point: 273 ft

May 26, 2023
The Day Before

Thinking about going to this state park is anti-climactic. It's like a hoop needing to be jumped through rather than the feeling of my original Quest, where each park was an adventure and a new step toward finishing something vitally important to me. This seems more of a *let's just be done now,* not the joy I felt in completing Governor Dodge State Park.

These Quest AF parks have been strange. Out of the five, even though I haven't been to Heritage Hill yet, the only one I think should have been on my original Quest was Lizard Mound, but it wasn't on the 2022 *Rand McNally* state map at the time because it is so new.

I genuinely like Cross Plains State Park and have been back several times with friends. I enjoy the rugged trails, and I'll continue to do those. They're a challenging hike close to my house. Yet, I don't consider it on the level of other state parks. There is much infrastructure development to be accomplished, including bathroom facilities, trail markers, and an actual sign.

Lost Dauphin was discouraging, surrounded by a development of extravagantly huge houses. It was a pretty spot, but why doesn't it say *state* on its sign? Lakeshore State Park was not significantly different from the other city parks running along the corridor where Milwaukee fronts Lake Michigan.

Tomorrow, I will be doing Heritage Hill, one I have to pay to get into, even with a state park sticker. It has 1.5 miles of sidewalk. I will have to traverse it several times to get my five miles. Nevertheless, I have done circles before, and it is forecast to be a lovely day. I will enjoy the drive, the sunshine in the cloudless sky, and doing something different and new as I finish this last addendum park. I am confident I will find beauty there, as I have at every place.

I complete my Quest AF with the firm belief I am able to go for five-mile hikes whenever I feel like it, my stamina continuing to improve, my second-guessing diminishing. Persisting with these final five has been life-affirming yet somewhat mundane. It is not the same energy and wonder of my original Quest. Rather, it is something I'm doing to make sure all my t's are crossed in doing the Wisconsin State Parks. All in all, though, these addendum hikes have helped me reclaim my identity as a Hiker after the Wendigo attack, and that is a wonderful thing!

May 27, 2023
Haymows and Time Machines

With this park, the last of the Addendum Five, there is no delicate coupe glass and mini bottle of prosecco in my backpack to celebrate. For this one, there is merely the feeling of fulfilling a self-imposed requirement. Today, instead of being under soaring trees and seeing boulders, cliffs, and lakes, I will be walking on a sidewalk around buildings. I was looking at the DNR's website last night, and it says this park is run by a company renting the land from the state.

What really is the definition of a state park?

I adore all the green along the roadways as I drive to Heritage Hill: the citron gleam of golden locust trees in all their spring glory, the dusty aqua greens of hayfields in want of mowing. It's the time in Wisconsin of expanding green, every shade you can possibly imagine.

I make it to the park without much trouble. There is no friendly ranger in the cavernous entry building, only a retail desk clerk selling tickets. Tickets for a state park seem wrong! At least I pay $10 instead of $12 as a 65-year-old. (I found out after the fact the ticket price is 50 percent off with a state park sticker. I could have paid only $5 had I known beforehand.) The entry building has maps, a coffee bar, fun t-shirts, and historical reproductions for sale. It's a pretty location, and despite the cost of getting in, I'm going to try to have a good attitude about whatever the day brings.

First things first, I look for a picnic table in the shade to have my lunch. It is a splendid late spring day, sunny and warm. On my first turn around the park, I set off counterclockwise. I find it well-marked with bathrooms everywhere, so I can't fault it.

As I wander, I decide to take the tunnel under the highway to cross over to the other side of the park. Every building has an information sign, and many of them have friendly reenactors in period dress. This section has a replica of an Iroquois longhouse, which is incredible. My map shows a couple of loops to walk, and after I return under the tunnel, I follow them along, enjoying the day.

Drifting into the 1894 cheese factory, I am flooded with memories of being in my dad's cheese factory when I was growing up. Many of the tools on the walls are ones my father had, which my brothers and sister still possess: hand-carved wooden shovels, cheese harps, and curd rakes. I take the time to play dress-up in the cheesemaker outfit hanging on the wall. I think about how my dad used to wear a white cheesemaker's hat to work every day. Waves of grief fill my eyes with tears, remembering his beautiful face and the sound of milk cans clanging together. I think about all the times I rode with him in his colossal bulk trucks, going out to visit dairy farmers. I genuinely enjoyed the feel of a Holstein's rough tongue on my hand when I gave them grass to eat as I waited for my dad to finish his

Heritage Hill State Park

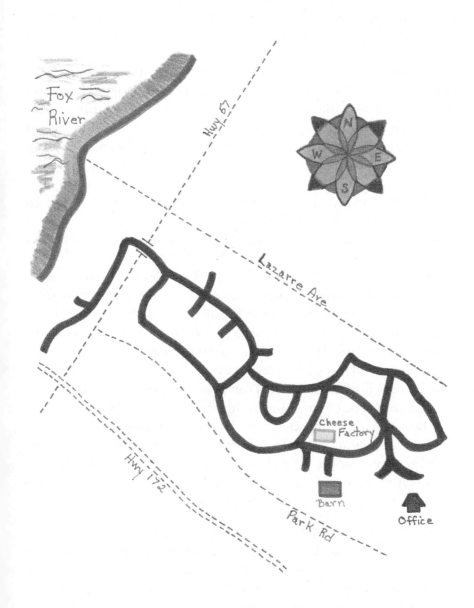

conversations. The displays in this building share information about the interesting chemistry involved in making cheese. It reminds me of my dad and my grandma Anna testing milk and centrifuging for butter fat. My father would have really loved this place! I still have a small, wooden rennet barrel from him, and it is one of my dear possessions.

The agricultural section of the park, with its buildings from 1845 to 1900, draws me near. I step into the old Belgian barn and immediately feel the surprising level of coolness its thick walls contain. It's like stepping into a cave on a hot day. Displays are filled with all manner of interesting equipment, things like we found in the buildings on the farm our family moved to after living above the cheese factory for many years. There's a six-foot scythe. I still have the one I found on our farm. One year for Halloween, I dressed up like a bat, and my big love dressed up as the Grim Reaper. He carried that scythe with him to complete the effect. It is a talisman of many grand adventures.

Walking into the haymow of the barn, I am pleasantly charmed by the aroma. Smells have tremendous power to bring back memories— memories of halcyon days spent in our rustic red barn. My big love and I would sneak out and hide in the hay bales to be alone. It was blissfully romantic. With the smell of this place, I can almost sense his arms around me, all but feel the saddle on my russet brown horse as I rode out through the field. I can practically hear my sister's voice as we talked about everything in the whole world while we groomed our horses, Titania and Oberon. I have the sensation of the sun on my back as I painted the entire barn and listened to the new album by Fleetwood Mac, *Rumours*. I made sure to trim all the windows in white for protection except for the Devil's window so as to allow any negative energy a path of escape outward.

As I finish my first loop back to the entry, there is a wedding taking place on the open plaza area outside the main building. In all deference to the proceedings, I stop off to the side, not wanting to be rude by walking through. I watch as the bride floats up the aisle in her sparkling white dress. Standing in the shade, hit once again by waves of grief, I tear up. I quickly sneak around the back to continue my walk as all eyes turn to the bride and groom.

Here I am at this, the last of the 50 state parks, the last one of the Quest AF, walking around crying. I never could have foreseen this was how my day would play out! To paraphrase the Tin Man in *The Wizard of Oz*, at least I know I have a heart as it is overflowing with memory and emotion on this fabulous spring day. After everything it has been through—ripped from my chest by a crypto-creature, stopped, cut open, restarted—my tender and sensitive, sentimental heart is definitely still beating. I am thankful beyond words.

Almost to the other side of the park, making another loop, I hear a large cheer rise up from behind me and a wave of applause. The "I do's" are complete. I'm sincerely happy for them, having such a picturesque day to start their lives together. I hope they return to this park for a walk on their 50th wedding anniversary.

Done with my five miles, I circle back around to sit inside the barn. I want to linger on the bench in the haymow, my eyes closed, remembering being in my own barn when I was younger. I often muse about wishing I had a time machine and about the days I would revisit in my life if I actually acquired one. I would go back to a time in my wonderful big red barn when a kiss from my big love, the neighing of the horses, and the warmth of the sunlight were my entire existence. As I sit quietly, a small tuxedo cat with bright green eyes approaches me, ever so much like all the cats we raised on the farm. My barn is gone now, dismantled and sold to people who make fancy new things from its century-old wood. It is an illustration of the poignant haiku by Mizuta Masahide: "Barn's burnt down, now I can see the moon." Even when places are lost, beauty still remains.

I'm sitting here in a barn thinking about a time machine, certainly not something I thought I was going to be doing today. The closest we, as human beings, are able to come to that ultimately coveted piece of machinery is in our brains. It is in our memories and our sense of smell where many forgotten thoughts silently remain. I will have to tell my child if I am ever in a battle with Alzheimer's or dementia, they should bring me here and let me dwell in this barn. I know I would remember the stories of my time growing up on the farm, my big love, and my Quest to hike all the state parks.

Back home after, I feel the need to celebrate even though it's not the same as celebrating the end of my original Quest. It is a significant milestone for me to have done these last five and to have my heart beating and rhythmic again. I grab my Dancing Dragonfly Winery glass, the one I bought on the way home from Interstate. I fill it with the wonderful Island Orchard apple lavender I purchased in Ellison Bay after hiking in Newport.

I sit on the old porch swing by my pond, listening to the waterfall, sipping enchanting cider out of my unique glass. I'm astonished by how emotional it was today. I should have known well enough. All endings, no matter how anticipated, no matter how wanted, are times of loss and need to be acknowledged. I'm honestly excited to have finished my addendum hikes. Now, I'll be able to say, *yes*, I've hiked five miles in all 50 Wisconsin State Parks! It wasn't exactly in a year. It was over the course of 13 months, 45 within seven months, and five within two, with a slap of existential chaos in between.

I still need to research what constitutes a state park. I'm actually curious after all these hikes. But for now, I'm content watching my fish swim, listening to the bubbling water as it reflects the sky, and purely enjoying being.

Heritage Hill State Park

The Questions

1. What about this chapter resonated with you?
2. What experiences act as time machines for you? Where in your life would you return to if you had such a device?
3. At what times in your life has the loss of something still allowed you to discover beauty?

The Particulars

Sticker Required: No

Map on the State Park's Website: Yes, and it is detailed in color

Bathrooms for Day Hikers: All over the place!

Office or Kiosk: There is no park office, only a retail desk

Trail Markings: Well-marked, and there are two "You Are Here" maps in the park

Seasonal Closures: Hours and days of operation vary depending on the time of year.

May–October: closed Monday; Tuesday–Saturday, 9–4; Sunday, 12–4

November–April: closed Saturday–Monday; Tuesday–Friday, 10–4

Flooding Concerns: None

Five Miles: Circles required

The Ending
Celebration and Goodbye

I have finished the 50 Wisconsin State Parks, hiking at least five miles in each, and now my story is done. When I finished Governor Dodge, the 45th one of my original Quest, the ending was happy-sad, bitter-sweet. In fact, bittersweet vines were bursting with their cadmium orange and yellow fruits as I hiked through the park. The last hike of the Addendum, of the Quest AF, is not bittersweet. It is happy and joyful. I am gifted another summer, and I am positively anticipating it—humidity, mosquitoes, and all!

Looking back at my introduction when I first started writing this book, I smile to remember my wonderful tree companion, Baldar, the noble fir. I lovingly placed a few of his needles in a jar and added a handful of his sawdust. I use a thick slice of his trunk as the bistro table on my front patio. Remarkably, five infant firs are growing like gangbusters; now they are out from under their father's formidable shade. They give me shining hope! Someday, like mine was, they will be grand 60-foot-tall trees. I won't be around to see them, but someone will, and I am positive they will cherish them as I did their parent tree.

Will I keep hiking? Of course I will! Being a Hiker is part of my identity. Will I keep writing? Yes, it has become part of my identity, too, in this whole process of the Quest. Will I keep planting seeds and making art? Absolutely! In this ending, I am feeling a clear sense of purpose for the future. And, low and behold, I finally found a list of all the state parks at http://dnr.wisconsin.gov/topic/parks/findapark. It needs to be searched as it includes state trails and recreation areas, but it has all 50 state parks listed in one place. Also, a new DNR *Wisconsin State Park System Visitor Guide* is out with a welcome message by Governor Tony Evers. It even includes Lizard Mound! It can be downloaded from https://www.travelwisconsin.com/order-guides.

What am I going to do next? I'm not sure, but there are 20 or so Wisconsin State Forests and Recreation Areas to explore. The Ice Age Trail, Iceland, Cornwall, and Scotland are on my bucket list. However, those won't be a quest. They'll be the way my life is as the years roll on. I'm going to hike and play with my friends and nurture my garden. I will spend as much time as possible with my loving child. I'm going to save memories and live in the moment, wear bright red lipstick and have colorful fingernails. I will move forward confidently and be aging disgracefully until my next big milestone birthday, if I'm lucky enough to get there. When I am 70, I want to be in love, lounging in bed with a breakfast-worthy man having recently returned home from a grand adventure. I will be thinking of a new tattoo, and my hair will be champagne blonde. Hey, a girl can dream, can't she?

If you gleaned something from all my trail information, crazy musings, and poignant memories, I hope it is similar to what I learned from this journey. Be your own best friend. Treat yourself like someone you love unconditionally. Don't be afraid to let go of people and things no longer serving you. Never stop having adventures, no matter how large or how small. Fuck the aging stereotypes. Seek beauty and focus on the positives. Embrace a colorful, creative life. Put yourself in places where you will experience awe and birdsong and dragonflies. Most importantly, spend more time just being. It definitely slows life down, and at 65, having time move even a little bit slower is an exceptional thing.

As you probably know after reading this hiking journal, I value the importance of a good ending. Therefore, I am sharing the Ending Ritual I wrote while on the Coast to Coast Walk across England. I performed it with my 18-person *National Geographic* hiking group on the beach of the North Sea near Robin Hood's Bay, North Yorkshire. There was not a dry eye after.

Circle all together.
(*We create a ritual space through our collective statements.*)

I would like you to all repeat after me.
We began. We walked. We have arrived.

This walk has been a time out of time,
a time set apart for a journey.
It's been a time of struggle and of triumph.

A time of pain and of healing.

And now it is ending, and so it deserves a time
out of time for us

to create the space to say goodbye.

What we have done has changed our lives.

What has happened, we will always remember.

We take this time to celebrate and give thanks for the
time we have spent together.

As we go around the circle, I would like you to answer
these two questions:

What are you grateful for from this experience?

What will you take forward into your life as a result of
this journey?

For me, I am grateful for and deeply honored by the kindness of
strangers. I will take with me a renewed sense of being able to do
anything I set my mind to.

(*Everyone gets a chance to say their answers to the two questions when
they feel ready.*)

As we wish each other well, at the end of our journey, at the end
of our time out of time, goodbye is our celebration.

This ending was always a part of our plan; it was part of our goal,
and here we are!

This quote by Jimi Hendrix is a good fit for us.

"The story of life is quicker than the blink of an eye; the story of
love is hello and goodbye."

Please repeat after me.
We begin. We walk. We continue.

Thank you, everyone.

The Photo Log
Blue Hats and Bandanas

The Recommended Reading
Scientists and Protagonists

Following is a list of articles and books referred to in various park chapters. Also included is a list of some of the books I listened to while I was hiking in which the main protagonist is over 60 years old.

The Basics

Aksa, Candan. 2020. "The Waste Problem of Antimicrobial Finishing." In *Waste in Textile and Leather Sectors*, edited by Ayşegül Körlü. Intech Open, March 2020, https://www.intechopen.com/chapters/71611.

Cann, Helen. 2018. *How to Make Hand-Drawn Maps: A Creative Guide with Tips, Tricks, and Projects*. San Francisco: Chronicle Books.

Sanderfoot, Olivia. 2017. "Air Pollution Impacts on Avian Species via Inhalation Exposure and Associated Outcomes." Environmental Research Letters, August 11, 2017, https://iopscience.iop.org/article/10.1088/1748-9326/aa8051.

The Introduction

Erikson, Erik H. 1986. *Childhood and Society*. New York: W. W. Norton & Co., Anniversary edition, 1986. First published 1950.

#1 Governor Nelson State Park

Serle, Rebecca. 2023. *One Italian Summer*. New York: Atria Books.

#6 Blue Mound State Park

Lang, Ruth Emmie. 2018. *Beasts of Extraordinary Circumstance*. New York: St. Martin's Press.

#8 Buckhorn State Park

Tekiela, Stan. 2021. *Wildflowers of Wisconsin*. Cambridge, WI: Adventure Publications.

#9 Hartman Creek State Park

Kidd, Sue Monk. 2003. *The Secret Life of Bees*. New York: Penguin Books.

#13 Kinnickinnic State Park
Li, Qing. 2010. "Effect of Forest Bathing Trips on Human Immune Function." *Environmental Health and Preventive Medicine*. January 2010. www.ncbi.nlm.nih.gov/pmc/articles/PMC2793341/.

#14 Willow River State Park
Penner, Sarah. 2021. *The Lost Apothecary*. New York: Park Row.

#18 Straight Lake State Park
Lesy, Michael. 2000. *Wisconsin Death Trip*. New Mexico: University of New Mexico Press.

Press Office. 2022. "Research Reveals Which Animals Perceive Time the Fastest." *British Ecological Society*. December 20, 2022, www.britishecologicalsociety.org/research-reveals-which-animals-perceive-time-the-fastest.

#19 Interstate State Park
Moreton, J., Kelly, C. S., & Sandstrom, G. M. "Social support from weak ties: Insight from the literature on minimal social interactions." *Social and Personality Psychology Compass*, e12729. 2023.

#22 Yellowstone State Park
Frankl, Viktor. 2006. *Man's Search for Meaning*. New York: Beacon Press. First published 1946.

#26 Lake Wissota State Park
Feil, Naomi and Klerk-Rubin, Vicki de. 2022. *The Validation Breakthrough: Simple Techniques for Communicating with People with Alzheimer's and Other Dementias*. Maryland: Health Professions Press. First published 1993.

#30 Peninsula State Park
"Age-Friendly Healthcare," Changing the Narrative-Ending Ageism Together, accessed August 13, 2022, https://changingthenarrativeco.org/age-friendly-healthcare.

Levy, Becca. 2022. *Breaking the Age Code: How Your Beliefs About Aging Determine How Long & Well You Live*. New York: William Morrow.

#35 Council Grounds State Park

Pink, Daniel. 2022. *The Power of Regret: How Looking Backward Moves Us Forward.* New York: Riverhead Books.

#37 Merrick State Park

Franco, Marisa. 2022. *Platonic: How the Science of Attachment Can Help You Make and Keep Friends.* New York: G. P. Putnam's Sons.

A2 Cross Plains State Park

Sima, Richard. 2022. "Why Birds and Their Songs are Good for Our Mental Health." *The Washington Post*, May 18, 2022, www.washingtonpost.com/wellness/interactive/2023/birds-song-nature-mental-health-benefits/.

Fiction with Older Protagonists

Lyons, Annie. 2020. *The Brilliant Life of Eudora Honeysett.* New York: HarperCollins.

Osman, Richard. 2020. *The Thursday Murder Club.* New York: Penguin.

Raybourn, Deanna. 2022. *Killers of a Certain Age.* New York: Berkley.

Rooney, Kathleen. 2017. *Lillian Boxfish Takes a Walk.* New York: St. Martin's Press.

Van Pelt, Shelby. 2022. *Remarkably Bright Creatures.* New York: Ecco Press.

The Index
Order and Alphabet

Made in the USA
Monee, IL
24 September 2024

65802427R00256